FOR ORGANS, PIANOS & ELECTRONIC KEYBOARDS

E-Z PLAY® TODAY

452

70 YEARS OF POPULAR MUSIC

The Fifties

PART TWO

215-2-735

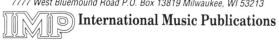

HL® Hal Leonard Publishing Corporation

7777 West Bluemound Road P.O. Box 13819 Milwaukee, WI 53213

IMP International Music Publications

FOR ORGANS, PIANOS & ELECTRONIC KEYBOARDS

E-Z PLAY® TODAY

Regi-Sound Programs

- Match the Regi-Sound Program number on the song to the corresponding numbered category below. Select and activate an instrumental sound available on your instrument.
- Choose an automatic rhythm appropriate to the mood and style of the song. (Consult your Owner's Guide for proper operation of automatic rhythm features.)
- Adjust the tempo and volume controls to comfortable settings.

Regi-Sound Program	
1	Flute, Pan Flute, Jazz Flute
2	Clarinet, Organ
3	Violin, Strings
4	Brass, Trumpet
5	Synth Ensemble, Accordion, Brass
6	Pipe Organ, Harpsichord
7	Jazz Organ, Vibraphone, Vibes, Electric Piano, Jazz Guitar
8	Piano, Electric Piano
9	Trumpet, Trombone, Clarinet, Saxophone, Oboe
10	Violin, Cello, Strings

70 YEARS OF POPULAR MUSIC

The Fifties

PART TWO

CONTENTS

All The Way

Regi-Sound Program: 6
Rhythm: Fox Trot or Ballad

Music by Sammy Cahn
Words by James Van Heusen

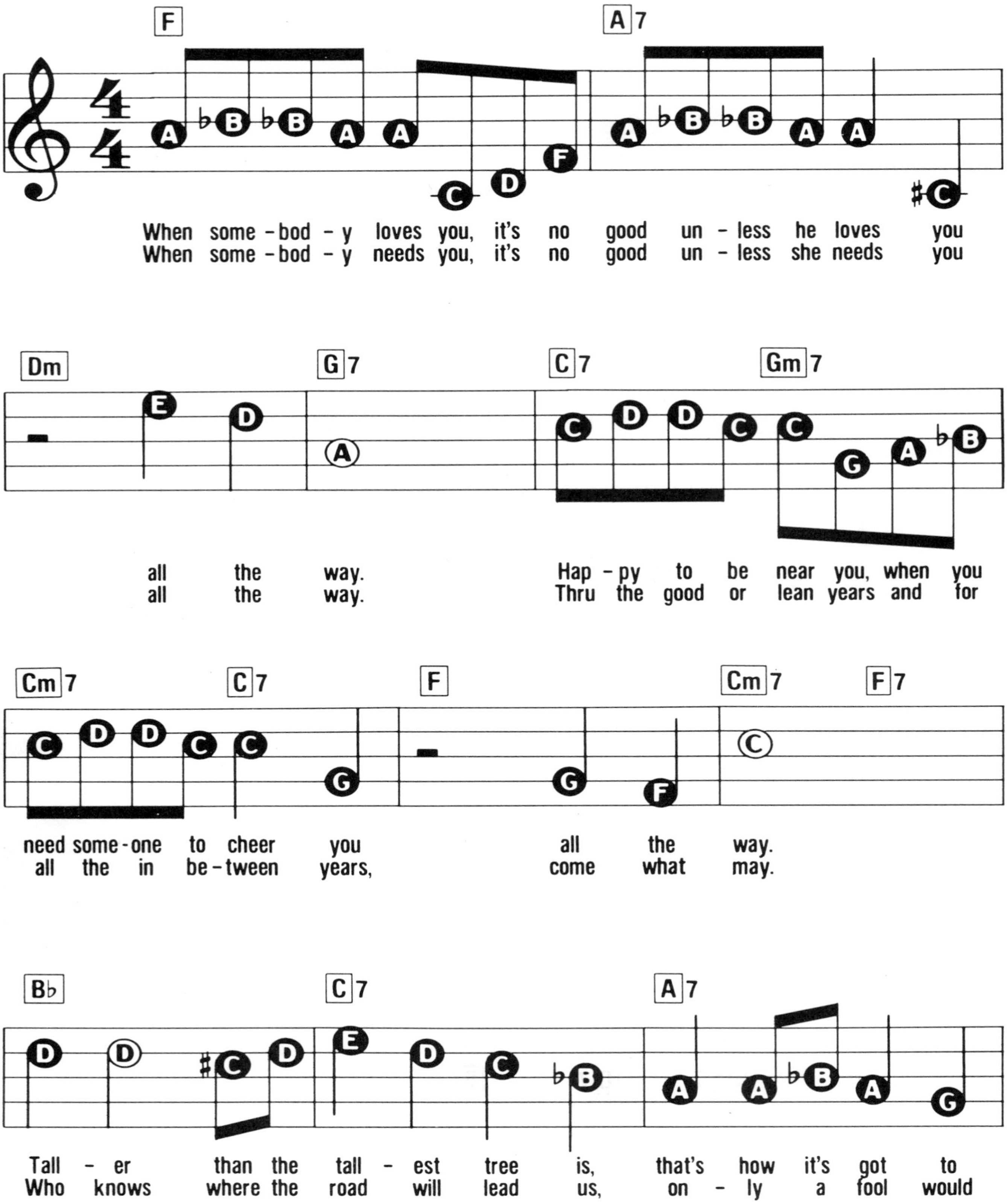
F
A7
When some-bod-y loves you, it's no good un-less he loves you
When some-bod-y needs you, it's no good un-less she needs you
Dm
G7
C7
Gm7
all the way. Hap-py to be near you, when you
all the way. Thru the good or lean years and for
Cm7
C7
F
Cm7
F7
need some-one to cheer you all the way.
all the in be-tween years, come what may.
B♭
C7
A7
Tall-er than the tall-est tree is, that's how it's got to
Who knows where the road will lead us, on-ly a fool would

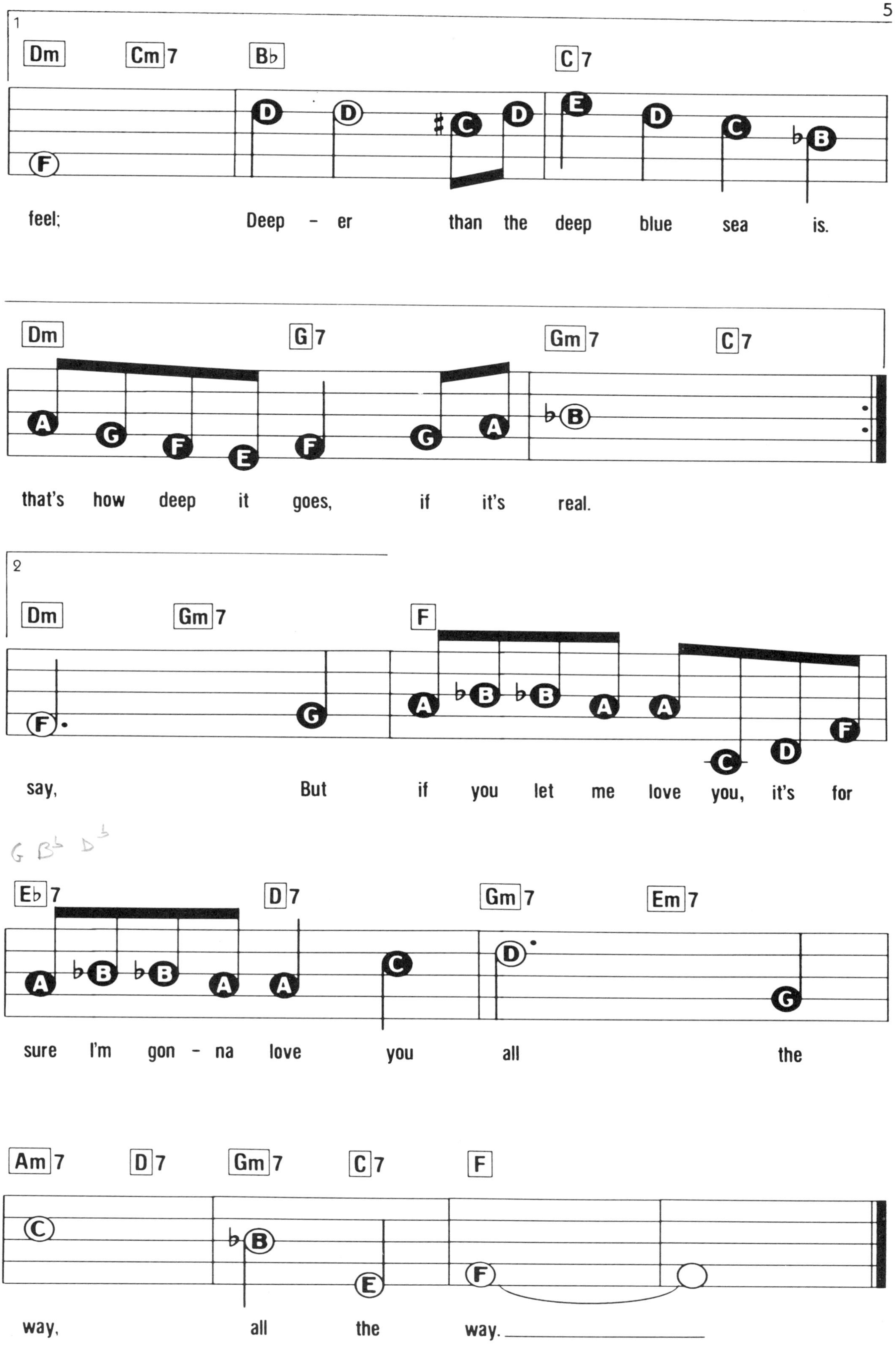
1
Dm Cm7 B♭ C7
feel; Deep - er than the deep blue sea is.
Dm G7 Gm7 C7
that's how deep it goes, if it's real.
2
Dm Gm7 F
say, But if you let me love you, it's for
E♭7 D7 Gm7 Em7
sure I'm gon - na love you all the
Am7 D7 Gm7 C7 F
way, all the way.

The Book

Regi-Sound Program: 6
Rhythm: Fox Trot or Ballad

Words by Paddy Roberts
Music by Hans Gotwald

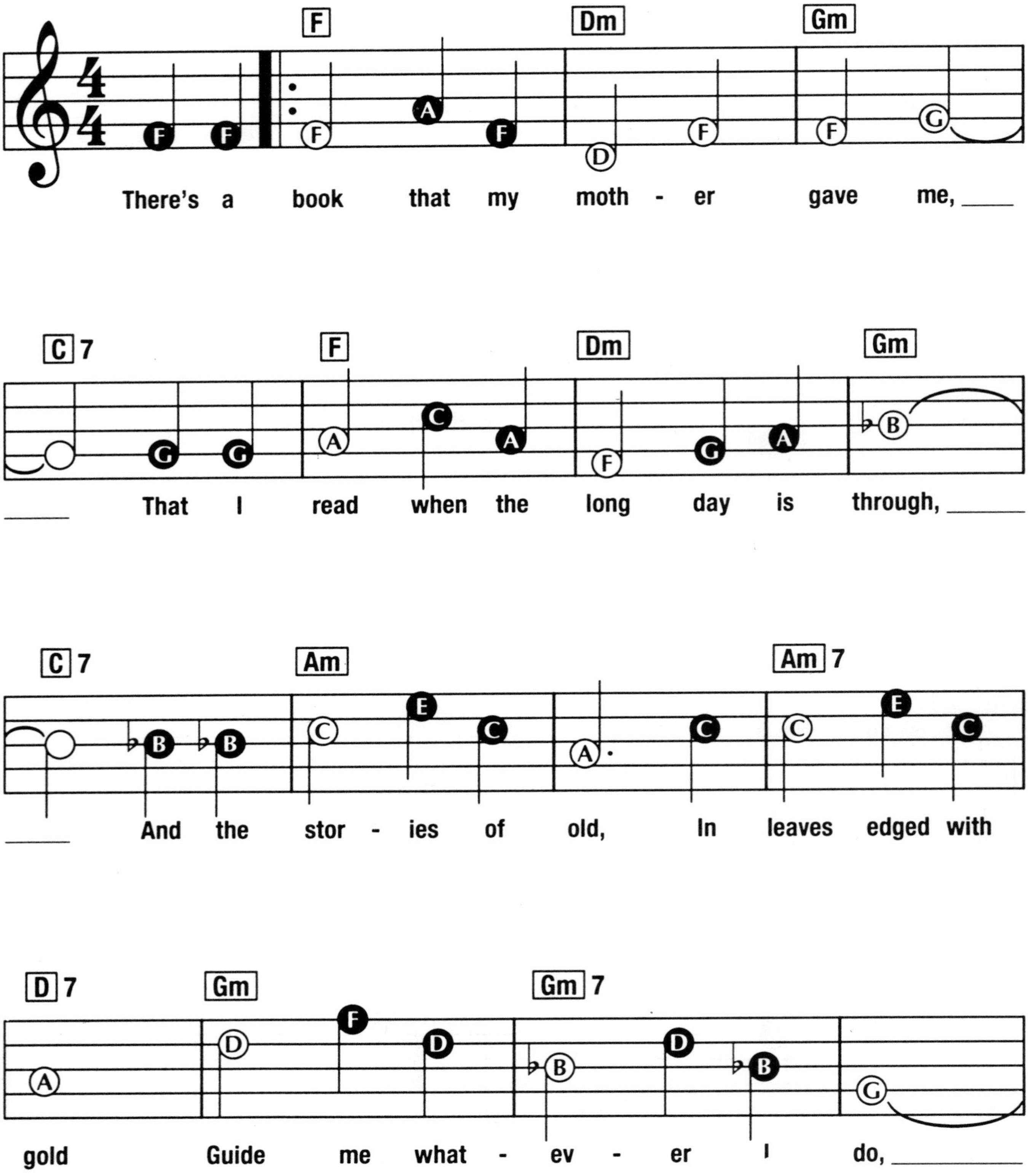
F Dm Gm
There's a book that my moth - er gave me,
C7 F Dm Gm
That I read when the long day is through,
C7 Am Am7
And the stor - ies of old, In leaves edged with
D7 Gm Gm7
gold Guide me what - ev - er I do,

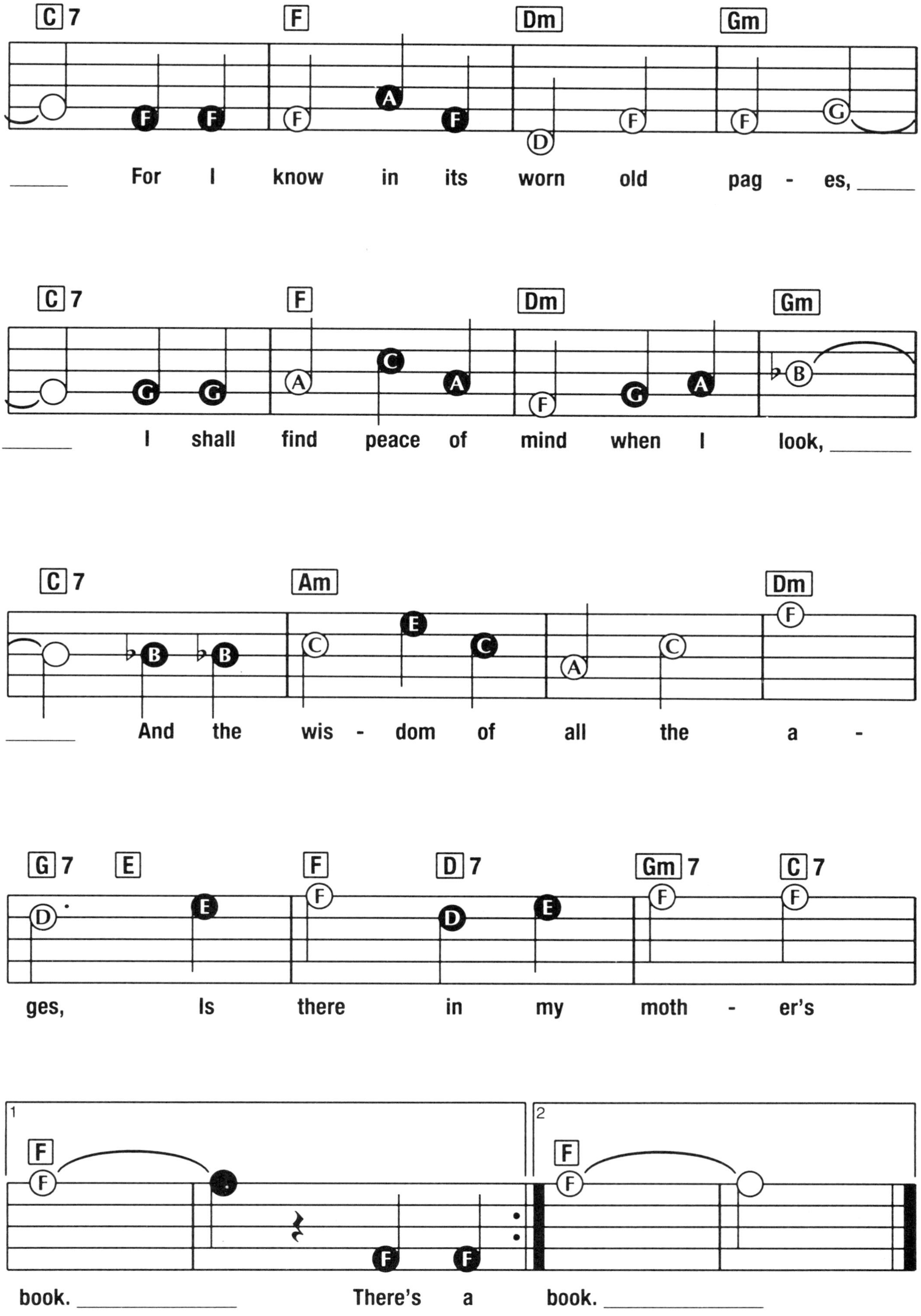
C7 F Dm Gm
For I know in its worn old pag - es,
C7 F Dm Gm
I shall find peace of mind when I look,
C7 Am Dm
And the wis - dom of all the a -
G7 E F D7 Gm7 C7
ges, Is there in my moth - er's
1 F
book. There's a
2 F
book.

Cry Me A River

Regi-Sound Program: 2
Rhythm: Fox Trot

Words and Music by
Arthur Hamilton

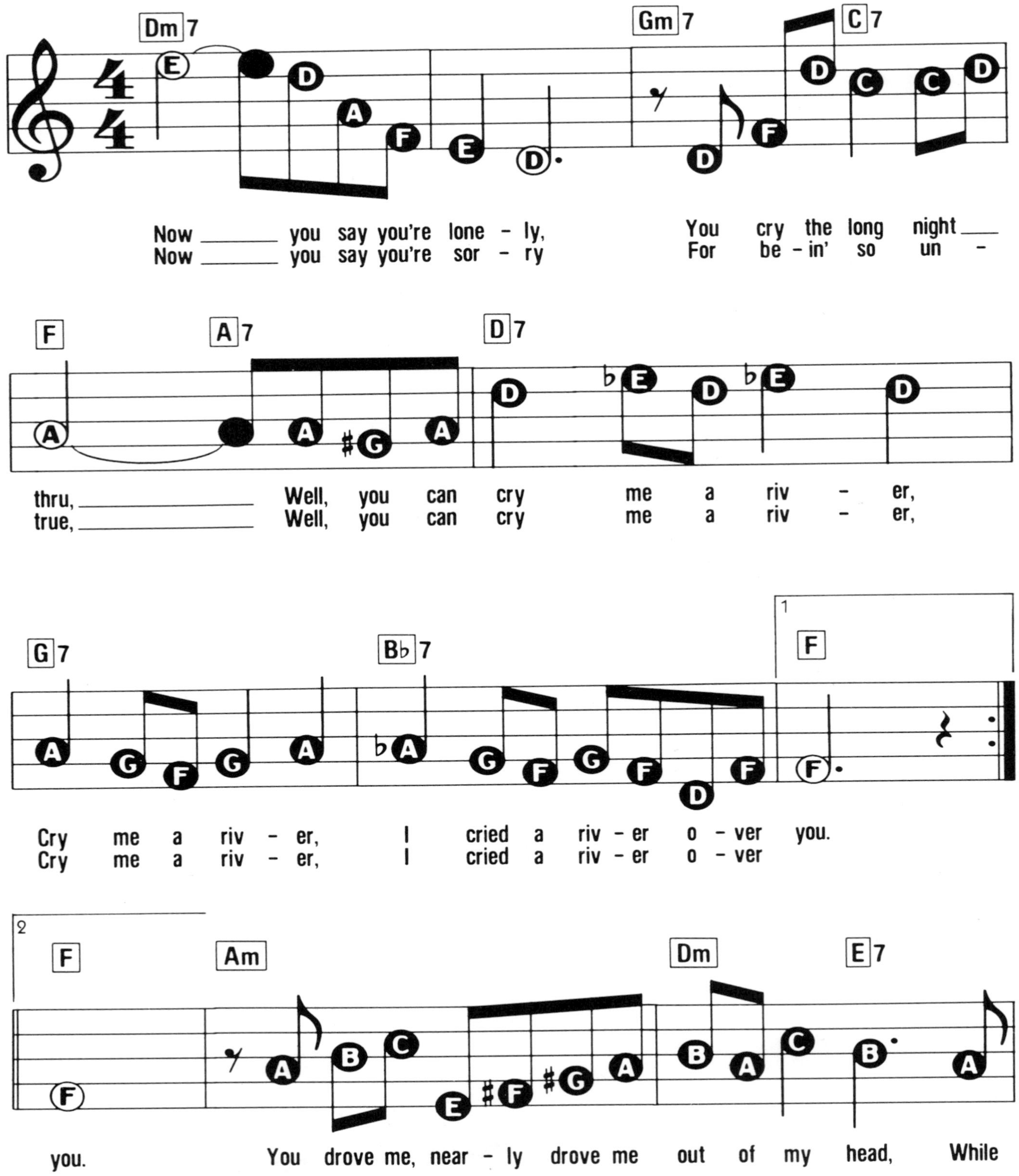

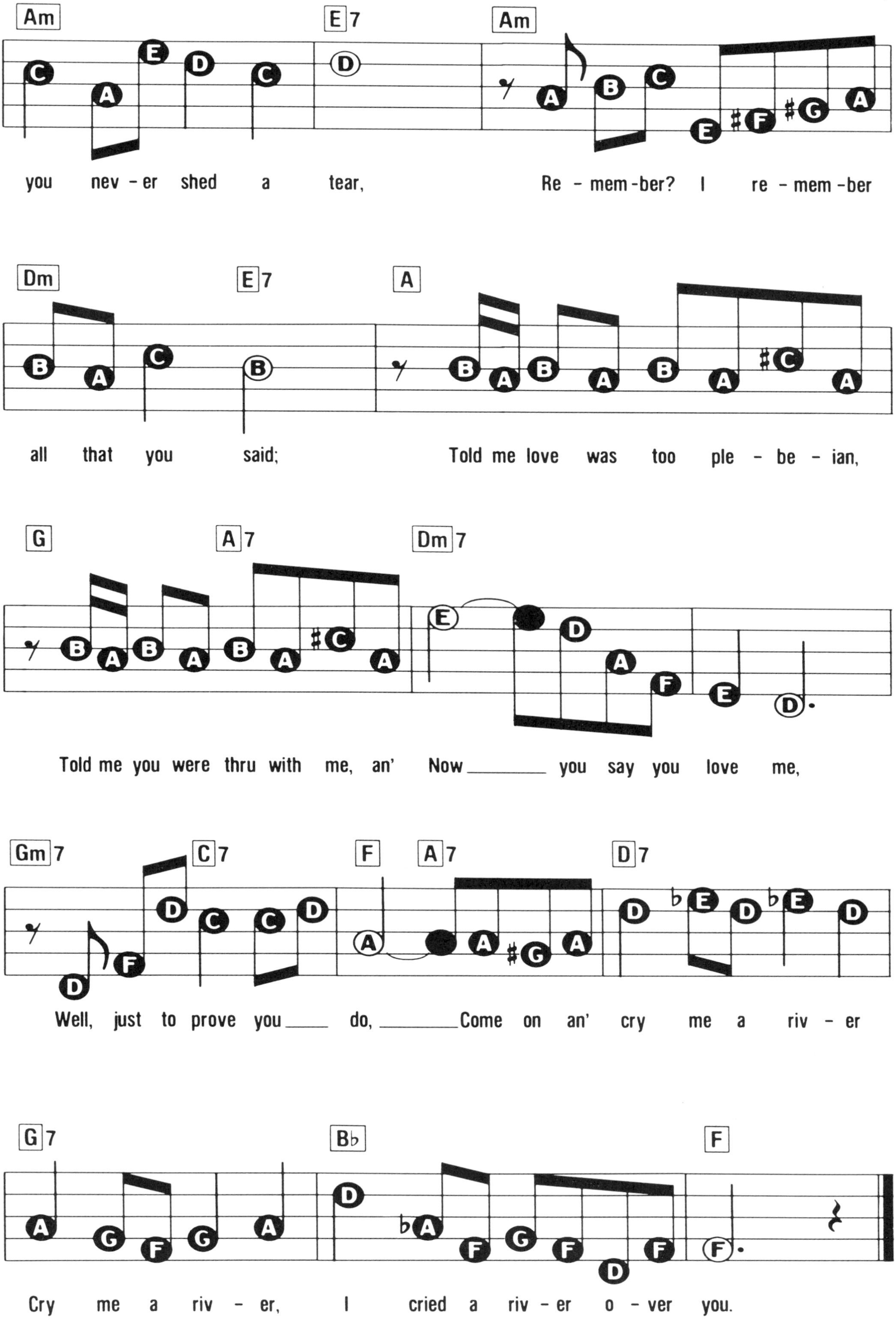
Am E7 Am
you nev - er shed a tear, Re - mem - ber? I re - mem - ber
Dm E7 A
all that you said; Told me love was too ple - be - ian,
G A7 Dm7
Told me you were thru with me, an' Now ____ you say you love me,
Gm7 C7 F A7 D7
Well, just to prove you ___ do, ______ Come on an' cry me a riv - er
G7 B♭ F
Cry me a riv - er, I cried a riv - er o - ver you.

Busy Line

Regi-Sound Program: 5
Rhythm: Swing or Rock

Words and Music by Murray Semos
and Frank Stanton

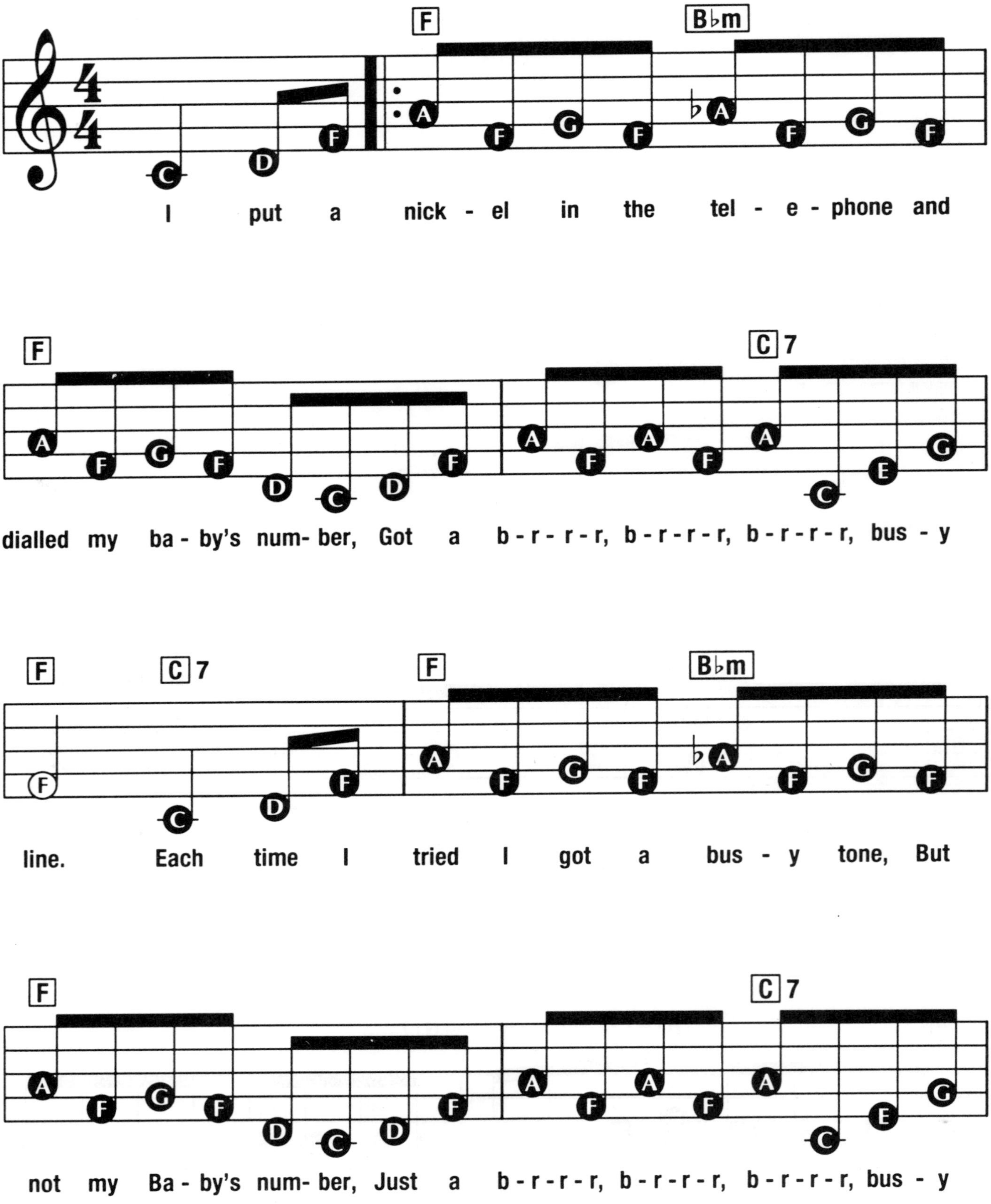
F
B♭m
I put a nick - el in the tel - e - phone and
F
C7
dialled my ba - by's num- ber, Got a b - r - r - r, b - r - r - r, b - r - r - r, bus - y
F
C7
F
B♭m
line. Each time I tried I got a bus - y tone, But
F
C7
not my Ba - by's num- ber, Just a b - r - r - r, b - r - r - r, b - r - r - r, bus - y

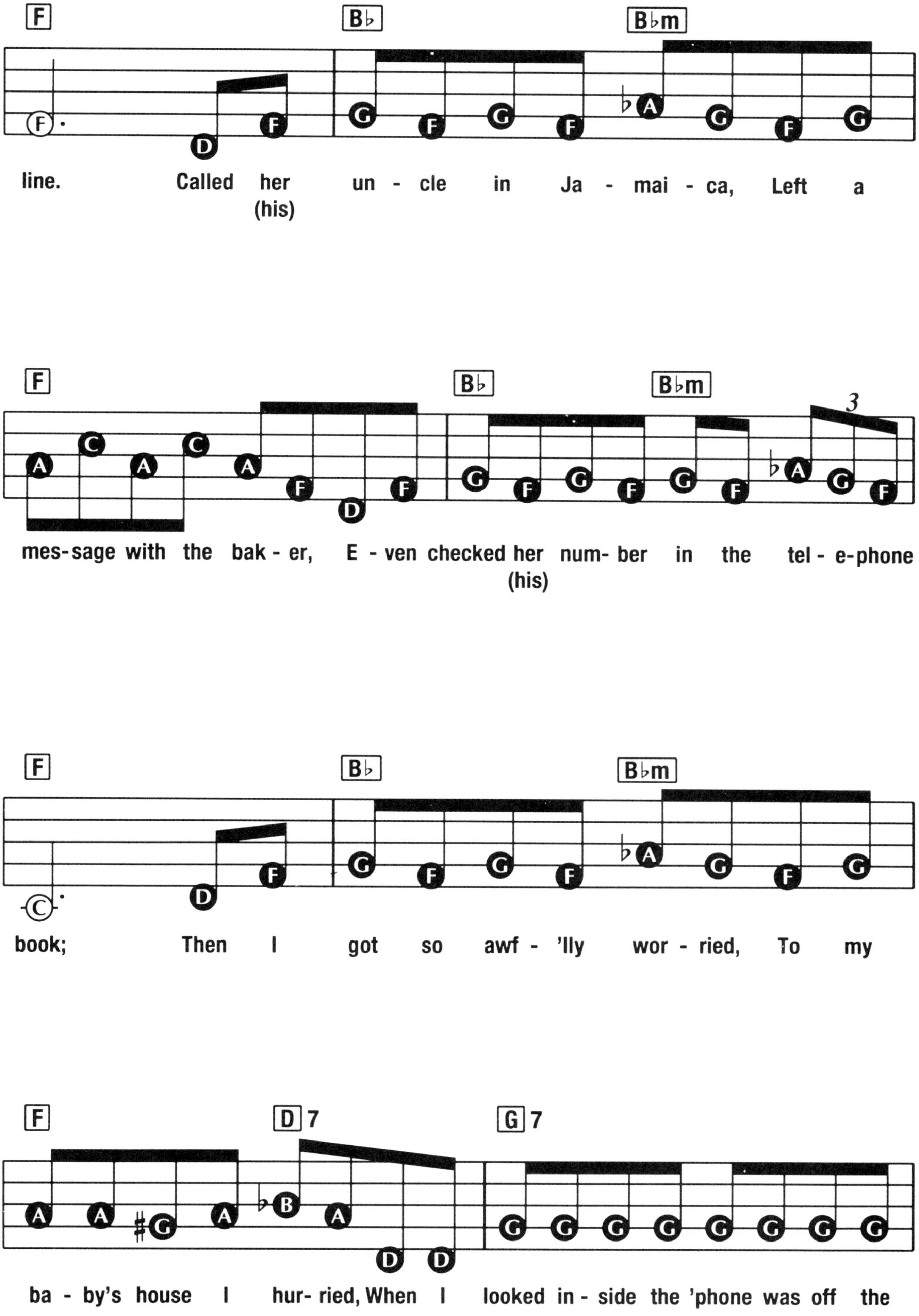
F
B♭
B♭m
line. Called her uncle in Jamaica, Left a
(his)
F
B♭
B♭m
3
mes-sage with the bak-er, E-ven checked her num-ber in the tel-e-phone
(his)
F
B♭
B♭m
book; Then I got so awf-'lly wor-ried, To my
F
D 7
G 7
ba-by's house I hur-ried, When I looked in-side the 'phone was off the

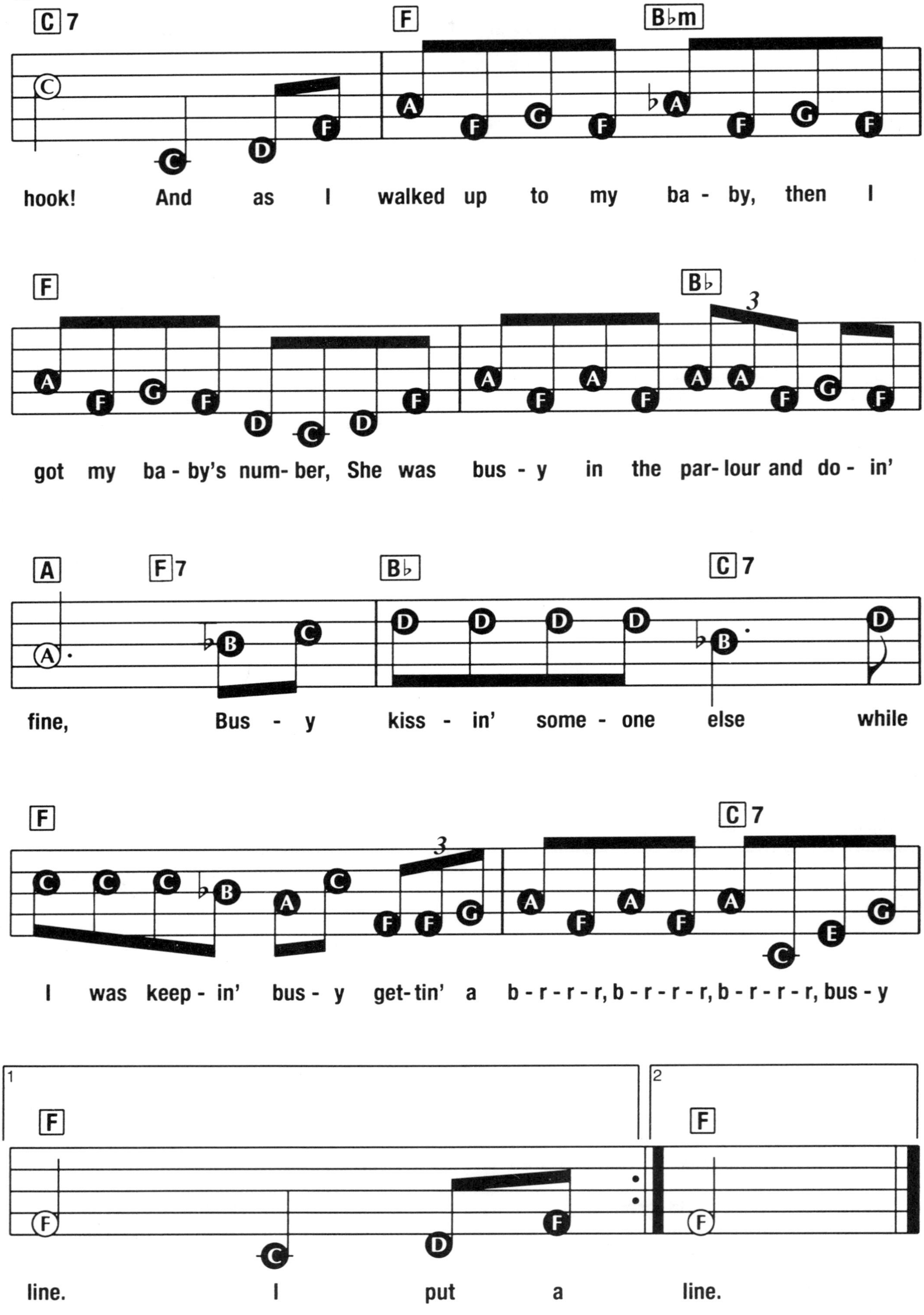
C7 F B♭m
hook! And as I walked up to my ba - by, then I
F B♭
got my ba - by's num- ber, She was bus - y in the par- lour and do - in'
A F7 B♭ C7
fine, Bus - y kiss - in' some - one else while
F C7
I was keep - in' bus - y get- tin' a b - r - r - r, b - r - r - r, b - r - r - r, bus - y
1 F 2 F
line. I put a line.

The Day The Rains Came

Regi-Sound Program: 1
Rhythm: Rock

English lyrics by Carl Sigman
French lyrics by Pierre Delanoe
Music by Gilbert Becaud

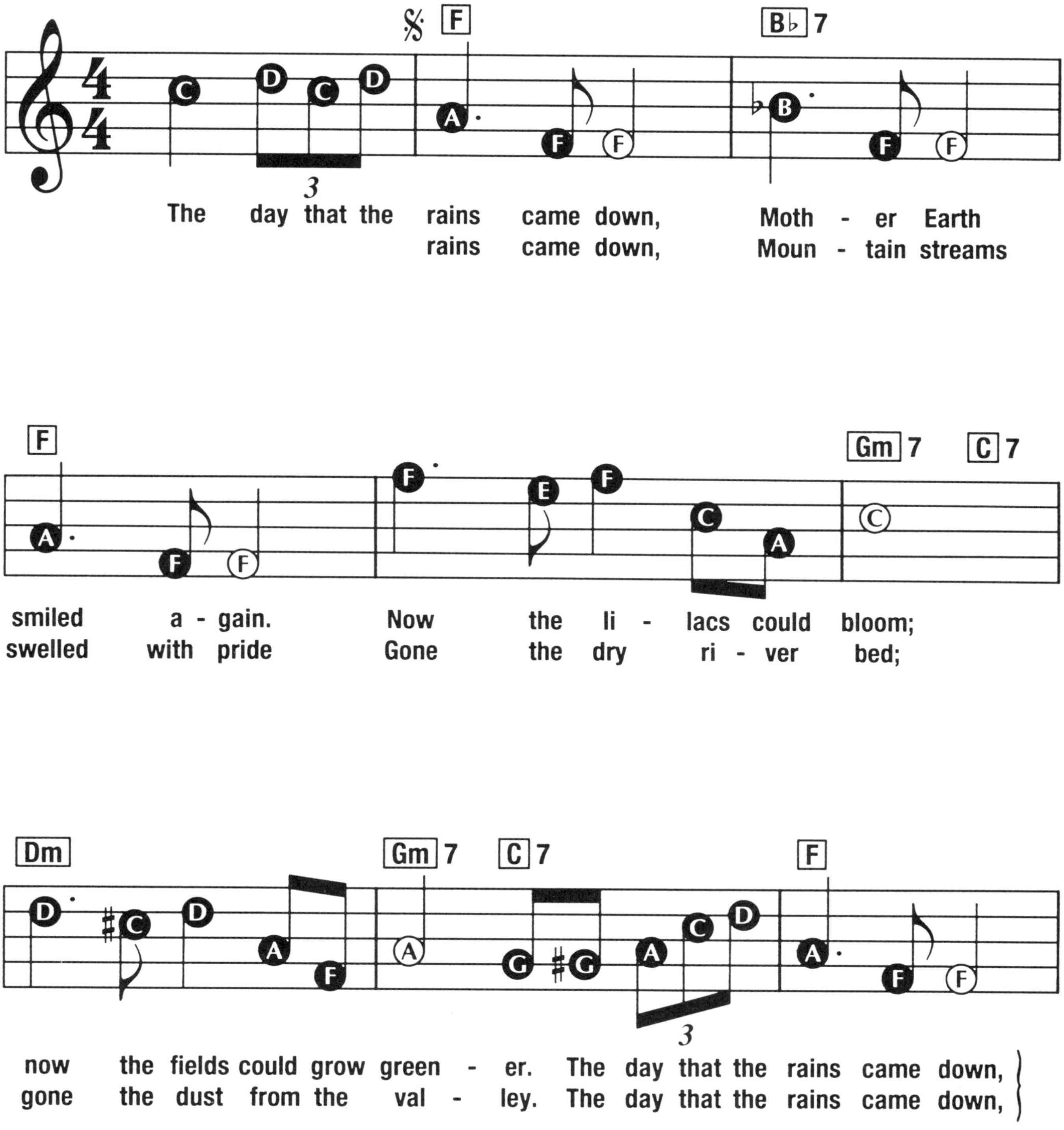
F
B♭7
The day that the rains came down, Moth - er Earth
rains came down, Moun - tain streams
F
Gm7 C7
smiled a - gain. Now the li - lacs could bloom;
swelled with pride Gone the dry ri - ver bed;
Dm
Gm7 C7
F
now the fields could grow green - er. The day that the rains came down,
gone the dust from the val - ley. The day that the rains came down,

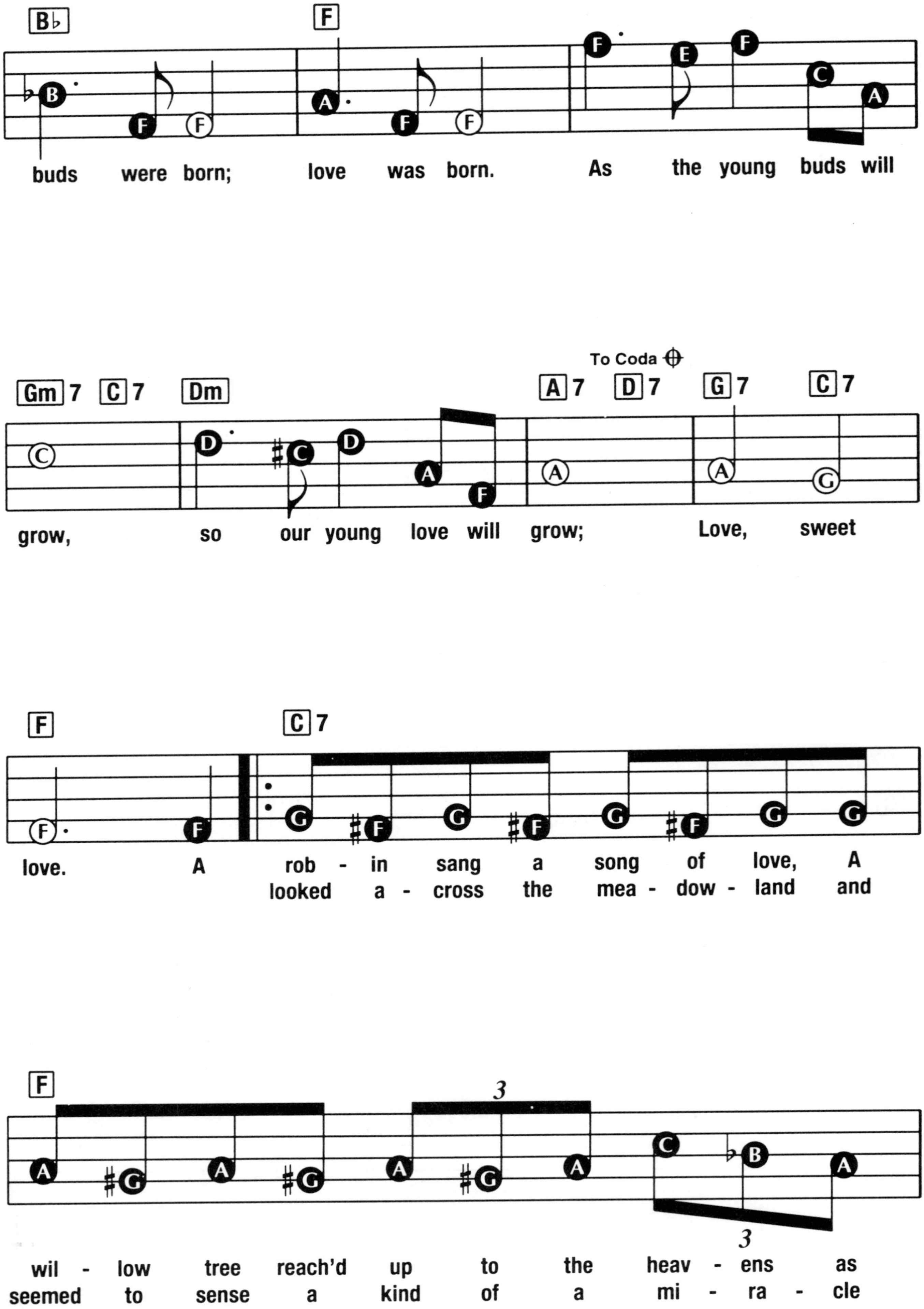
B♭
F
buds were born; love was born. As the young buds will
Gm7 C7 Dm
To Coda
A7 D7 G7 C7
grow, so our young love will grow; Love, sweet
F C7
love. A rob - in sang a song of love, A
looked a - cross the mea - dow - land and
F
3
wil - low tree reach'd up to the heav - ens as
seemed to sense a kind of a mi - ra - cle

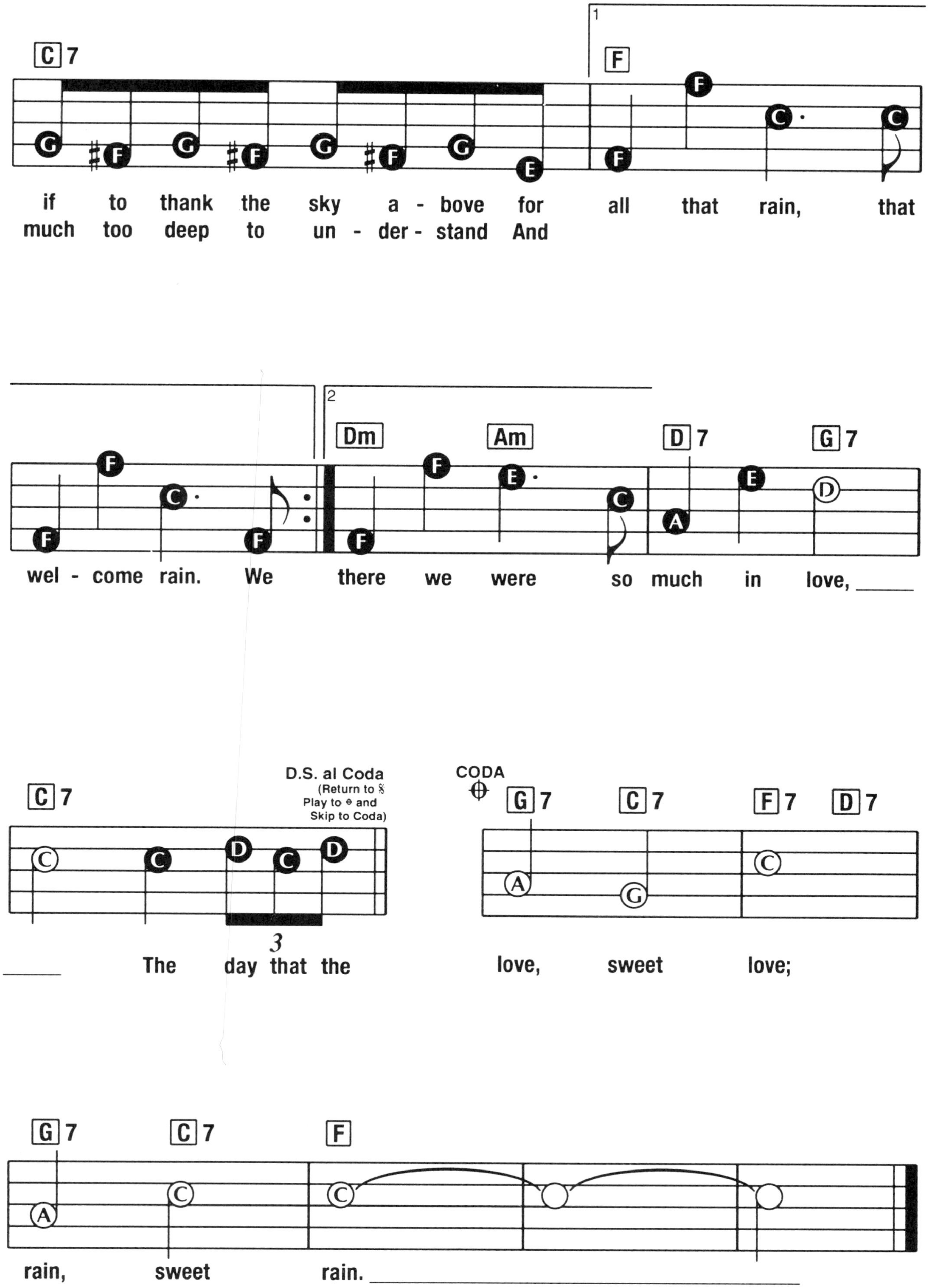
C7
1
F
if to thank the sky a - bove for all that rain, that
much too deep to un - der - stand And
wel - come rain. We
2
Dm
Am
D7
G7
there we were so much in love,
C7
D.S. al Coda
(Return to 𝄋
Play to ⊕ and
Skip to Coda)
The day that the
3
CODA
G7
C7
F7
D7
love, sweet love;
G7
C7
F
rain, sweet rain.

Dream Lover

Regi-Sound Program: 4
Rhythm: Rock

Words and Music by
Bobby Darin

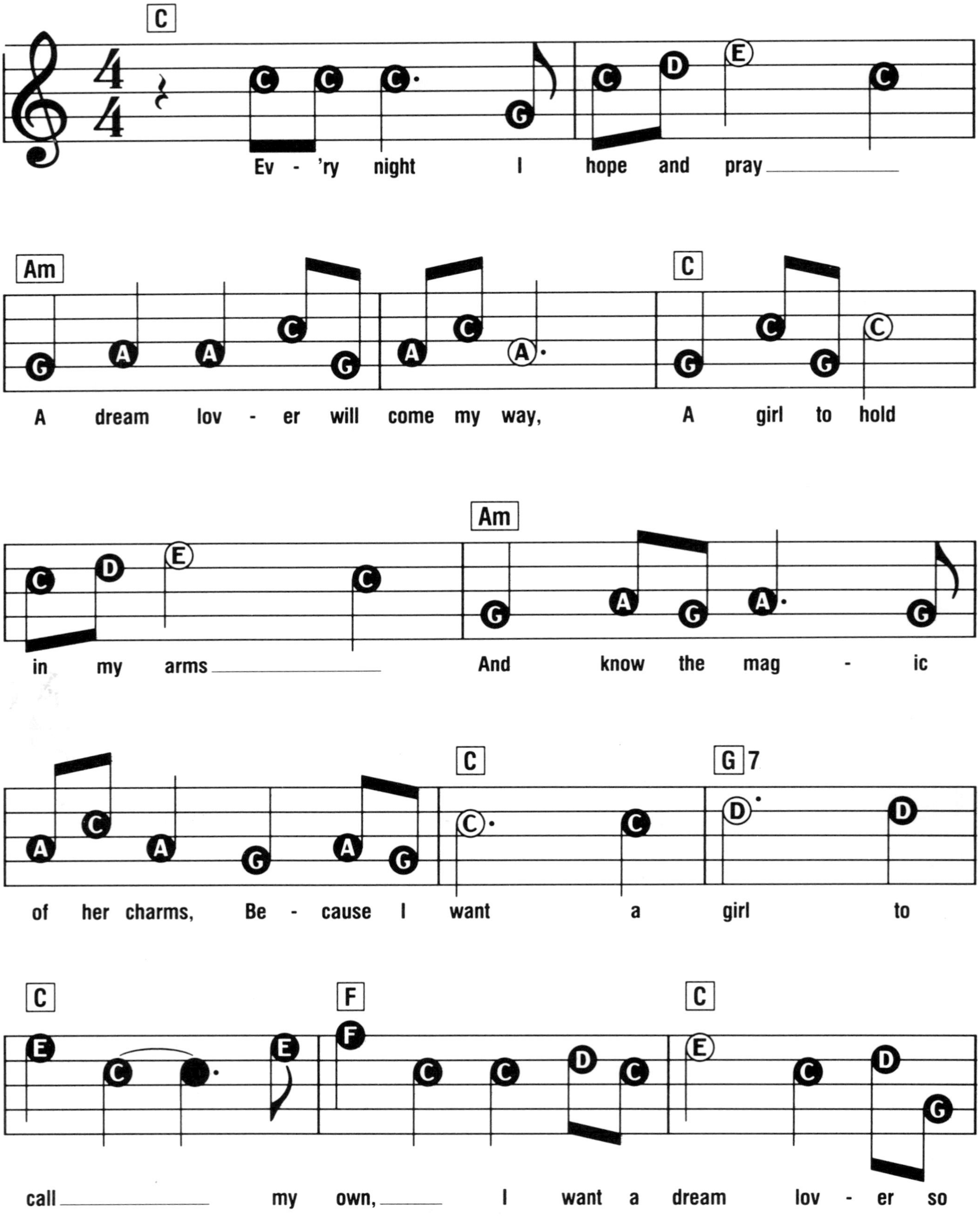

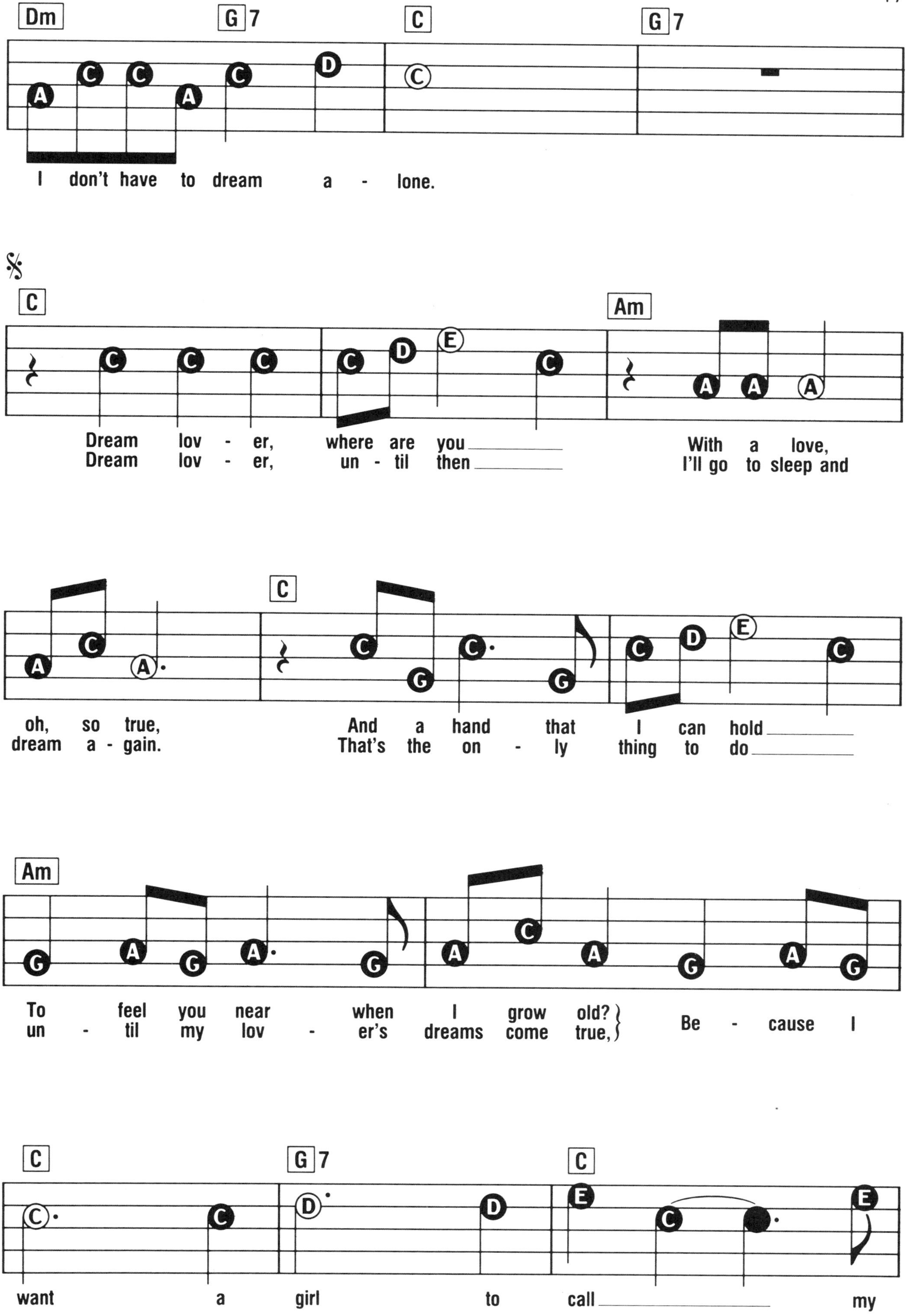
Dm G7 C G7
I don't have to dream a - lone.
C Am
Dream lov - er, where are you
Dream lov - er, un - til then
With a love,
I'll go to sleep and
C
oh, so true, And a hand that I can hold
dream a - gain. That's the on - ly thing to do
Am
To feel you near when I grow old?
un - til my lov - er's dreams come true,
Be - cause I
C G7 C
want a girl to call my

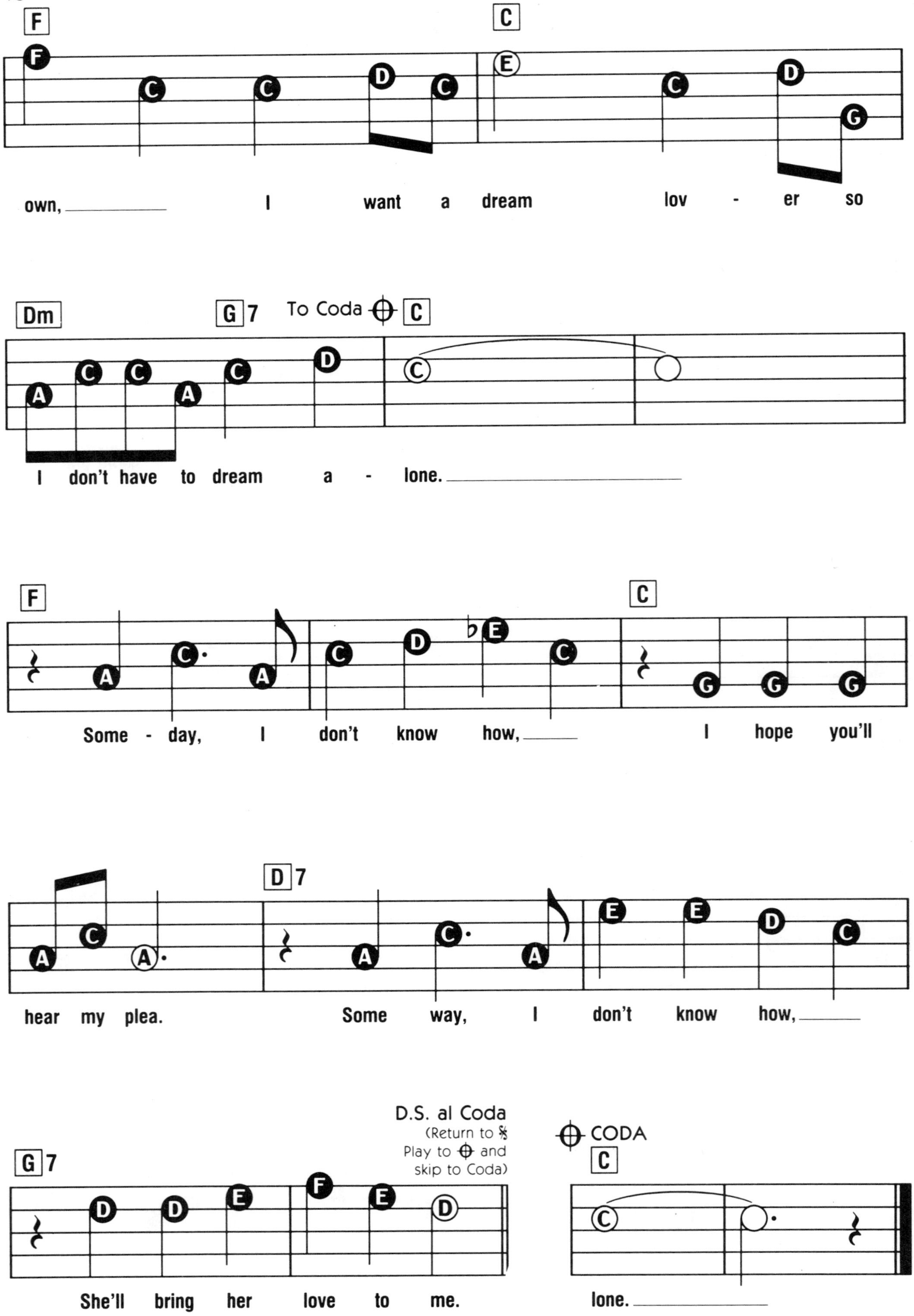
own, I want a dream lov - er so
I don't have to dream a - lone.
To Coda
Some - day, I don't know how, I hope you'll
hear my plea. Some way, I don't know how,
She'll bring her love to me.
D.S. al Coda
(Return to 𝄋
Play to ⊕ and
skip to Coda)
CODA
lone.

Friends And Neighbours

Regi-Sound Program: 9
Rhythm: Fox Trot or Ballad

Words and Music by Marvin Scott
& Malcolm Lockyer

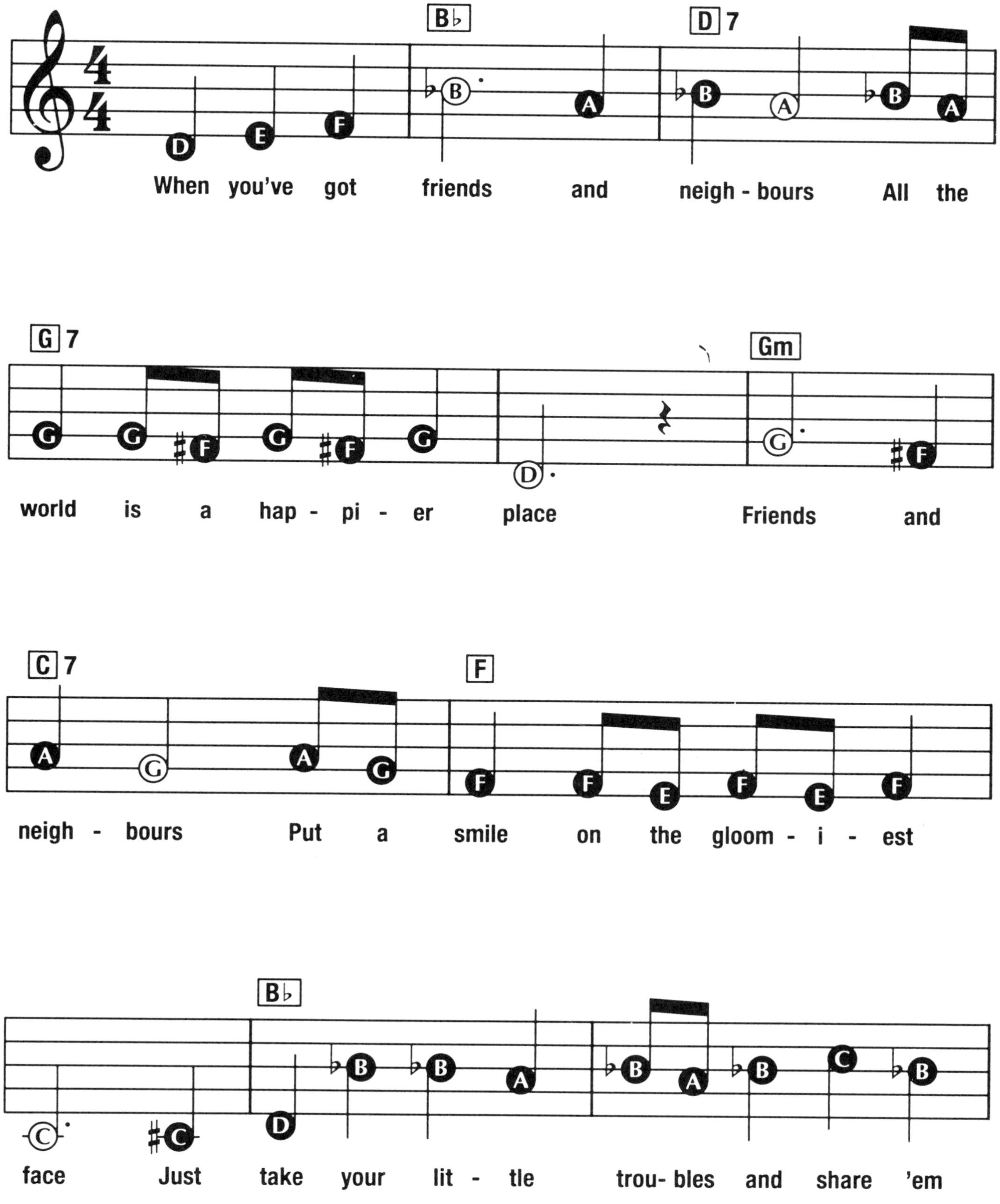
B♭
D 7
When you've got friends and neigh - bours All the
G 7
Gm
world is a hap - pi - er place Friends and
C 7
F
neigh - bours Put a smile on the gloom - i - est
B♭
face Just take your lit - tle trou- bles and share 'em

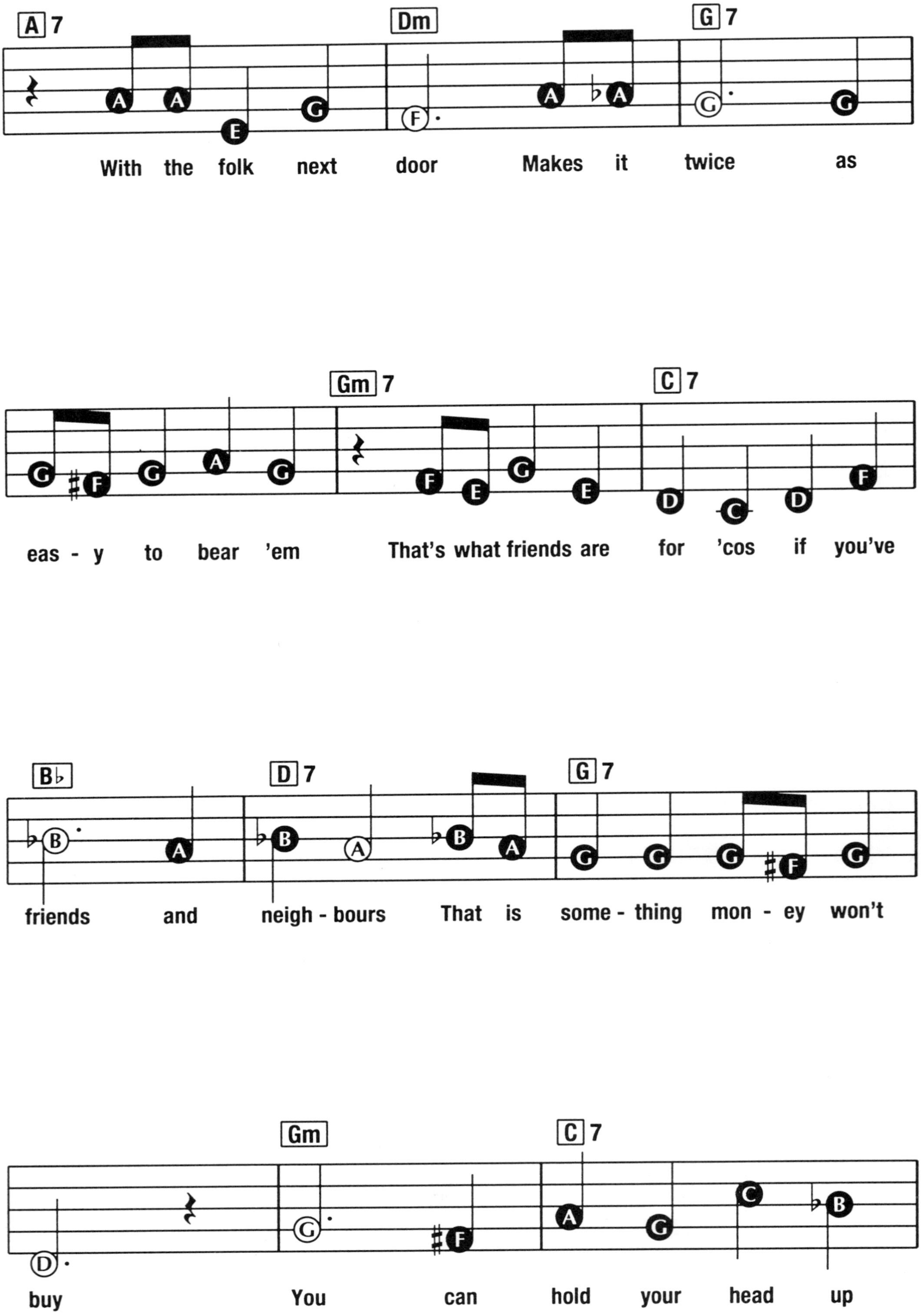
A7 Dm G7
With the folk next door Makes it twice as
Gm7 C7
eas - y to bear 'em That's what friends are for 'cos if you've
B♭ D7 G7
friends and neigh - bours That is some - thing mon - ey won't
Gm C7
buy You can hold your head up

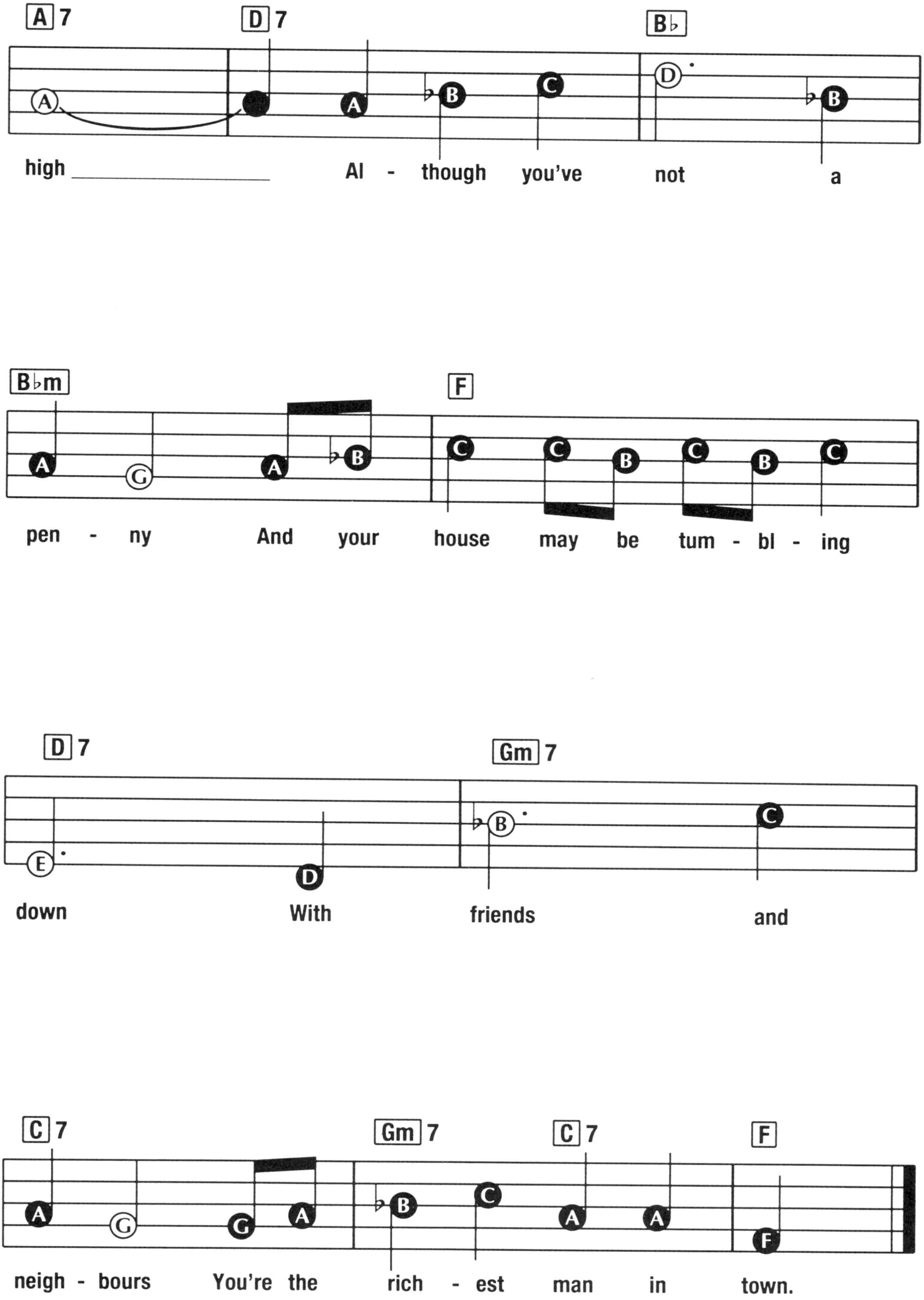
A7 D7 B♭
high ___ Al - though you've not a
B♭m F
pen - ny And your house may be tum - bl - ing
D7 Gm7
down With friends and
C7 Gm7 C7 F
neigh - bours You're the rich - est man in town.

Fever

Regi-Sound Program: 9
Rhythm: Ballad

Words and Music by John Davenport
and Eddie Cooley

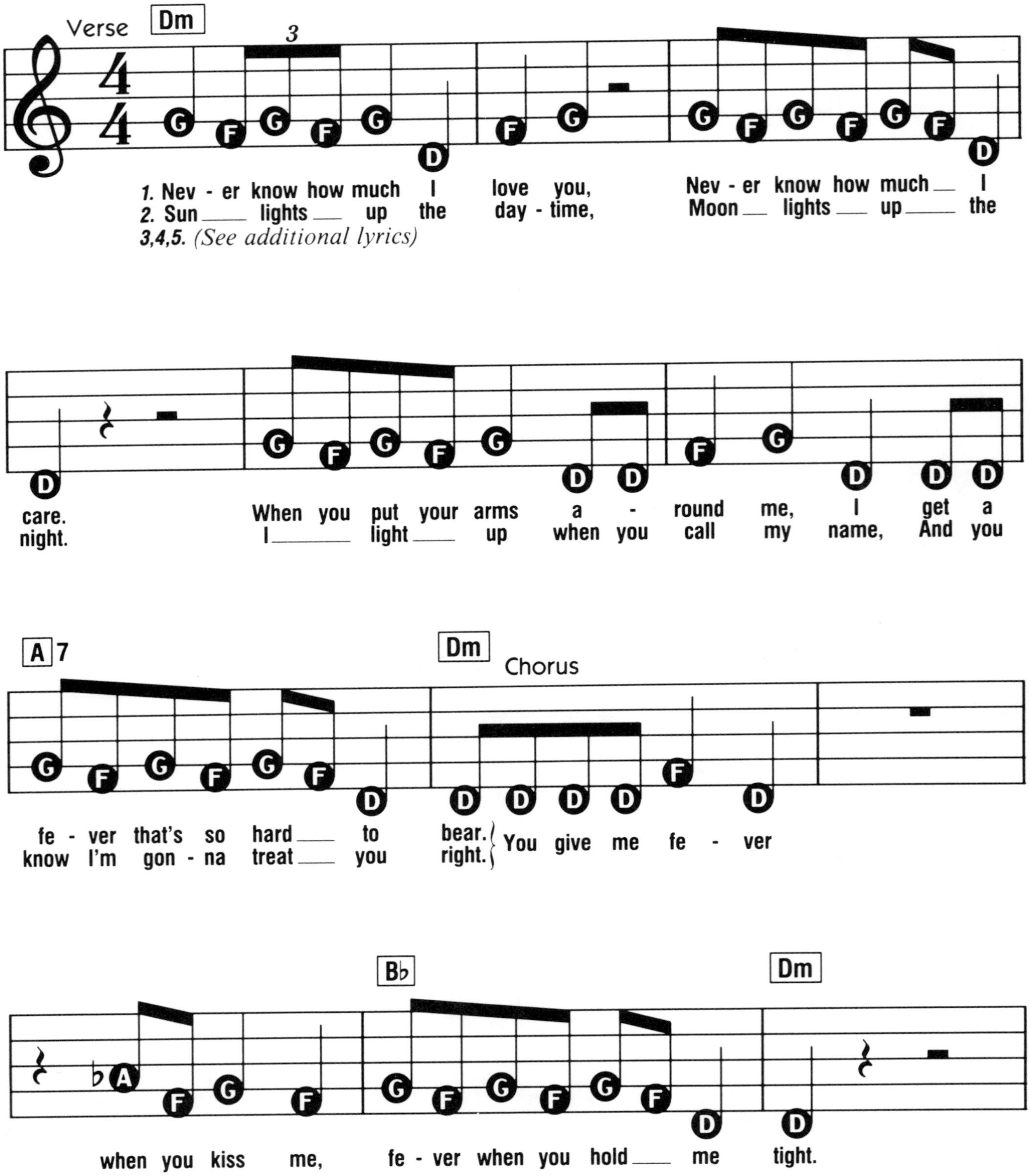
Verse
Dm
3
1. Nev - er know how much I love you, Nev - er know how much I care.
2. Sun lights up the day - time, Moon lights up the night.
3,4,5. (See additional lyrics)
When you put your arms a - round me, I get a fe - ver that's so hard to bear.
I light up when you call my name, And you know I'm gon - na treat you right.
A 7
Dm
Chorus
You give me fe - ver
B♭
Dm
when you kiss me, fe - ver when you hold me tight.

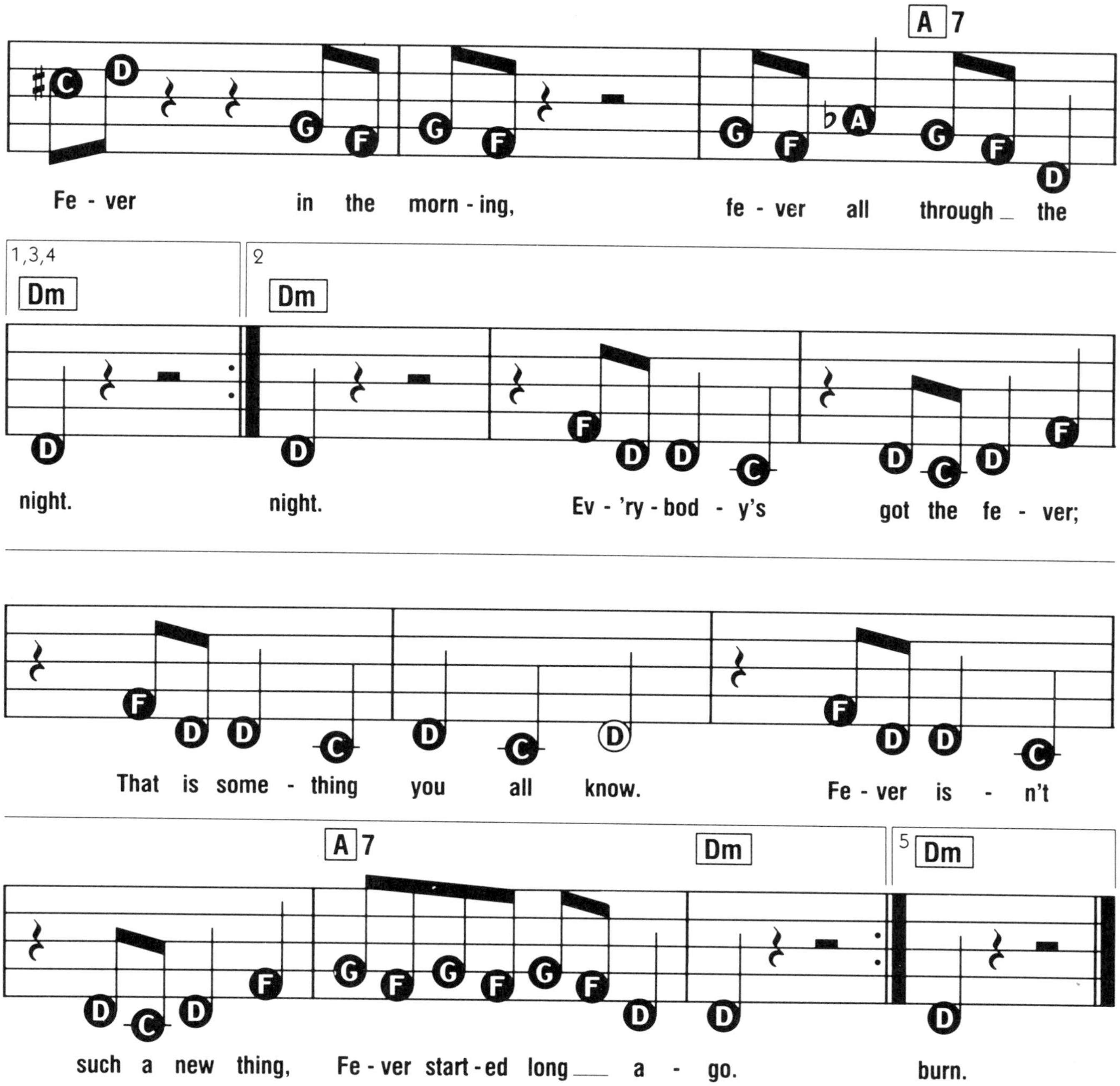

Additional Lyrics

Verse 3
Romeo loved Juliet,
Juliet she felt the same.
When he put his arms around her, he said,
"Julie, baby, you're my flame."

Chorus:
Thou givest fever, when we kisseth,
FEVER with thy flaming youth.
FEVER — I'm afire,
FEVER, yea I burn forsooth.

Verse 4
Captain Smith and Pocahantas
Had a very mad affair,
When her Daddy tried to kill him, she said,
"Daddy-o don't you dare."

Chorus:
Give me fever, with his kisses,
FEVER when he holds me tight.
FEVER — I'm his Missus,
Oh Daddy won't you treat him right.

Verse 5
Now you've listened to my story
Here's the point that I have made.
Chicks were born to give you FEVER
Be it fahrenheit or centigrade.

Chorus:
They give you FEVER, when you kiss them,
FEVER if you live and learn.
FEVER — till you sizzle,
What a lovely way to burn.

Freight Train

Regi-Sound Program: 9
Rhythm: Fox Trot or Swing

Words and Music by Paul James,
Fred Williams & Elizabeth Cotton

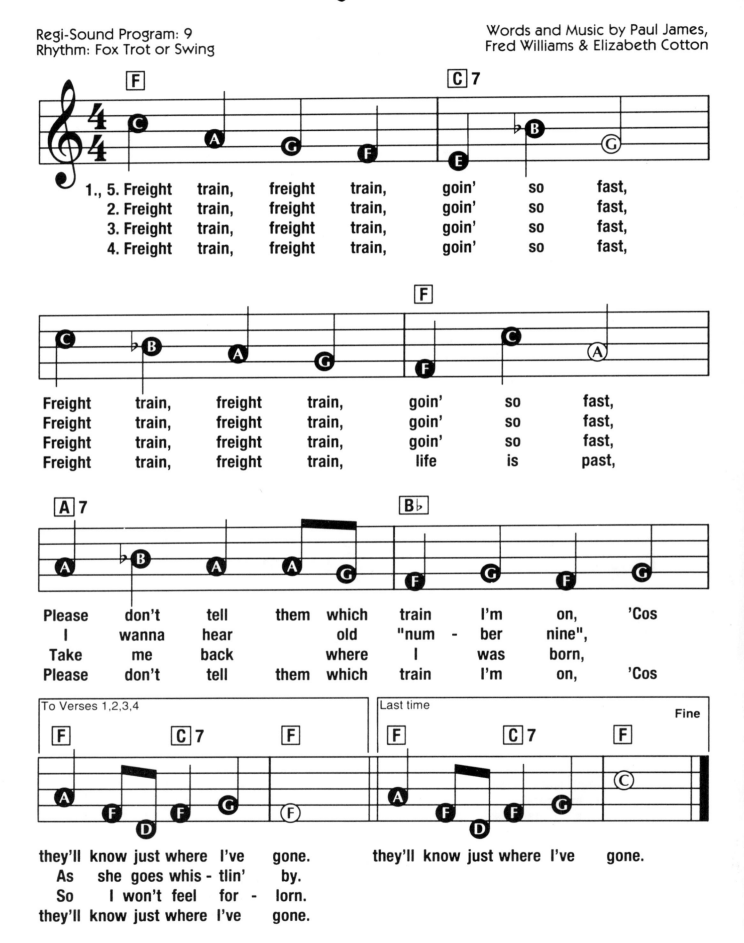

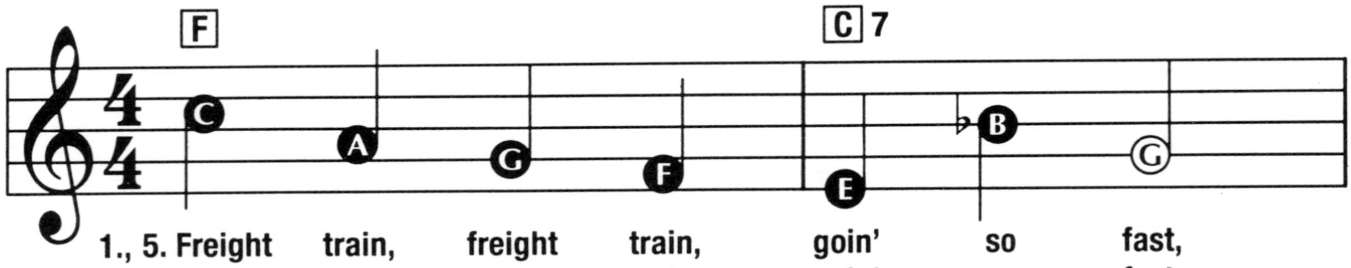

1., 5. Freight train, freight train, goin' so fast,
2. Freight train, freight train, goin' so fast,
3. Freight train, freight train, goin' so fast,
4. Freight train, freight train, goin' so fast,

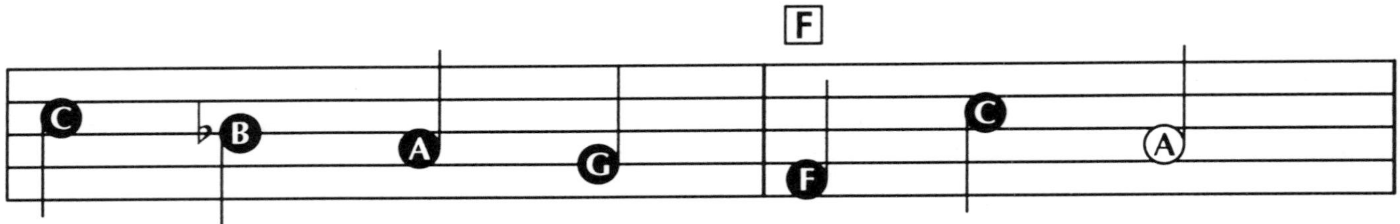

Freight train, freight train, goin' so fast,
Freight train, freight train, goin' so fast,
Freight train, freight train, goin' so fast,
Freight train, freight train, life is past,

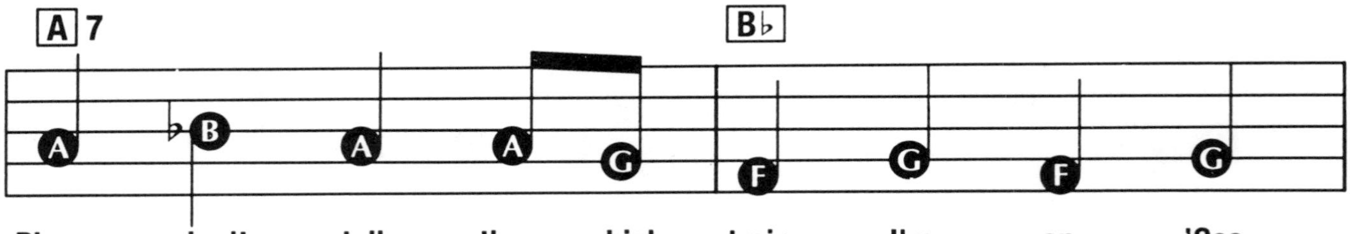

Please don't tell them which train I'm on, 'Cos
I wanna hear old "num - ber nine",
Take me back where I was born,
Please don't tell them which train I'm on, 'Cos

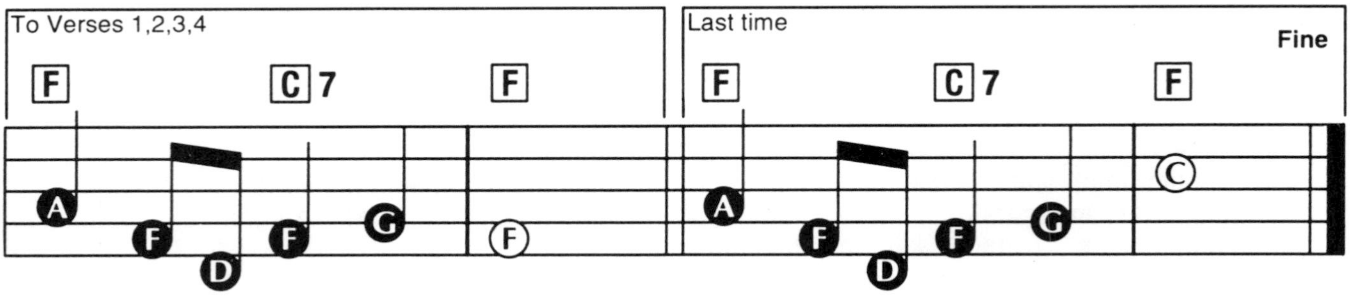

To Verses 1,2,3,4:
they'll know just where I've gone.
As she goes whis - tlin' by.
So I won't feel for - lorn.
they'll know just where I've gone.

Last time:
they'll know just where I've gone.

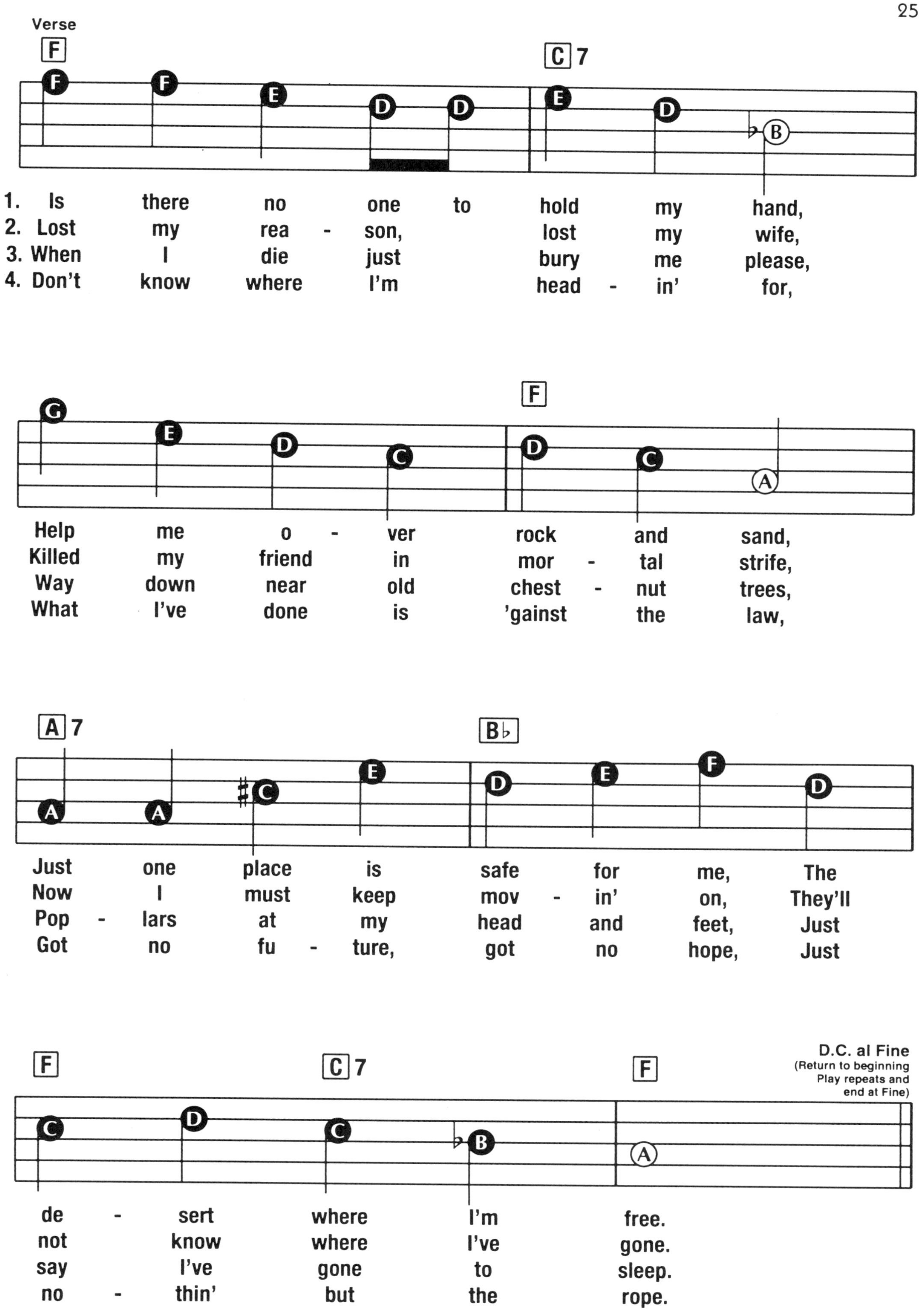
Verse
F
C7
1. Is there no one to hold my hand,
2. Lost my rea - son, lost my wife,
3. When I die just bury me please,
4. Don't know where I'm head - in' for,
F
Help me o - ver rock and sand,
Killed my friend in mor - tal strife,
Way down near old chest - nut trees,
What I've done is 'gainst the law,
A7
B♭
Just one place is safe for me, The
Now I must keep mov - in' on, They'll
Pop - lars at my head and feet, Just
Got no fu - ture, got no hope, Just
F
C7
F
D.C. al Fine
(Return to beginning
Play repeats and
end at Fine)
de - sert where I'm free.
not know where I've gone.
say I've gone to sleep.
no - thin' but the rope.

Here In My Heart

Regi-Sound Program: 3
Rhythm: Swing

Words and Music by Pat Genaro,
Lou Levinson and Bill Borrelli

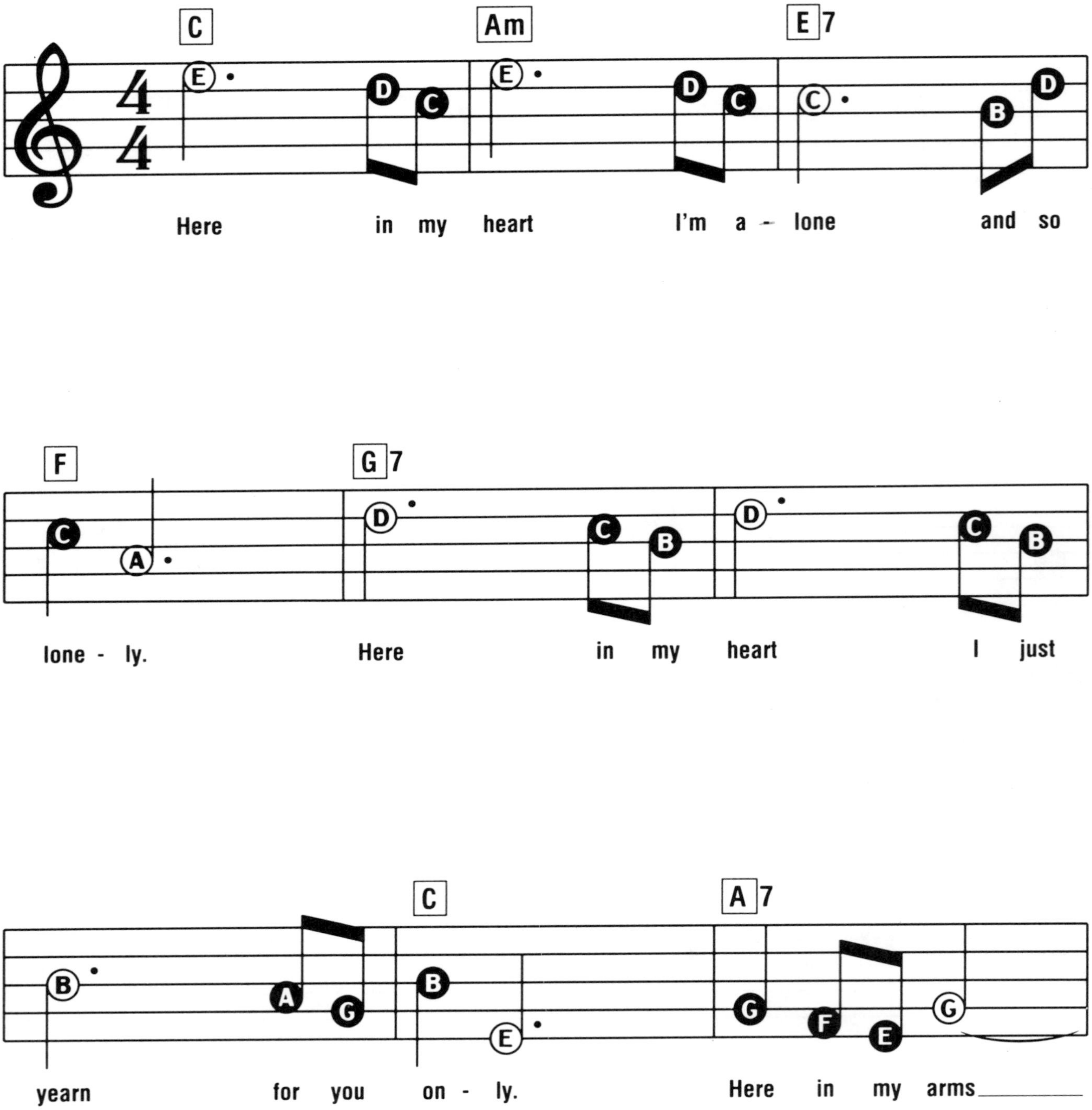
C
Am
E7
Here in my heart I'm a - lone and so
F
G7
lone - ly. Here in my heart I just
C
A7
yearn for you on - ly. Here in my arms

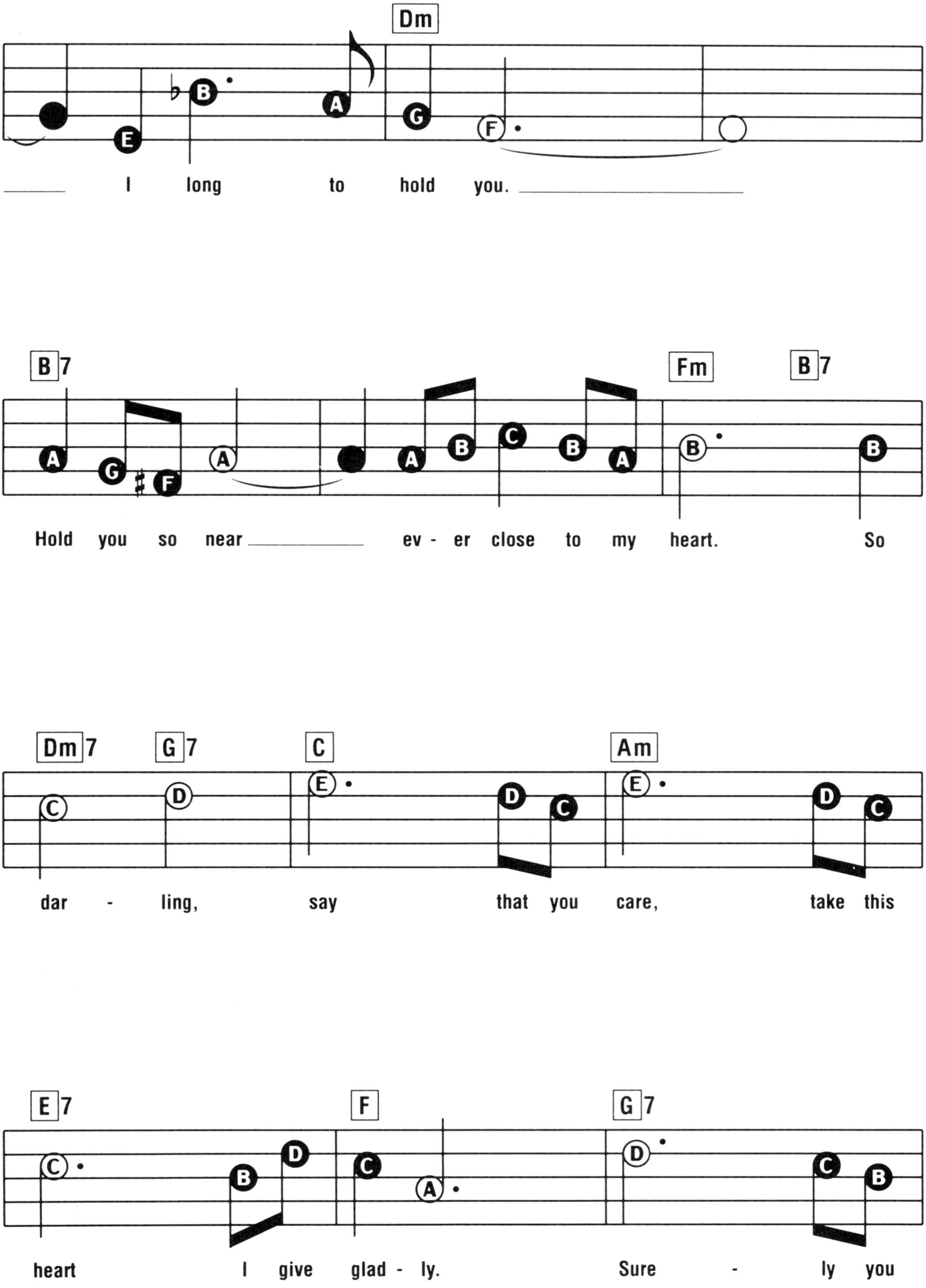
Dm
I long to hold you.
B 7 Fm B 7
Hold you so near ever close to my heart. So
Dm 7 G 7 C Am
dar - ling, say that you care, take this
E 7 F G 7
heart I give glad - ly. Sure - ly you

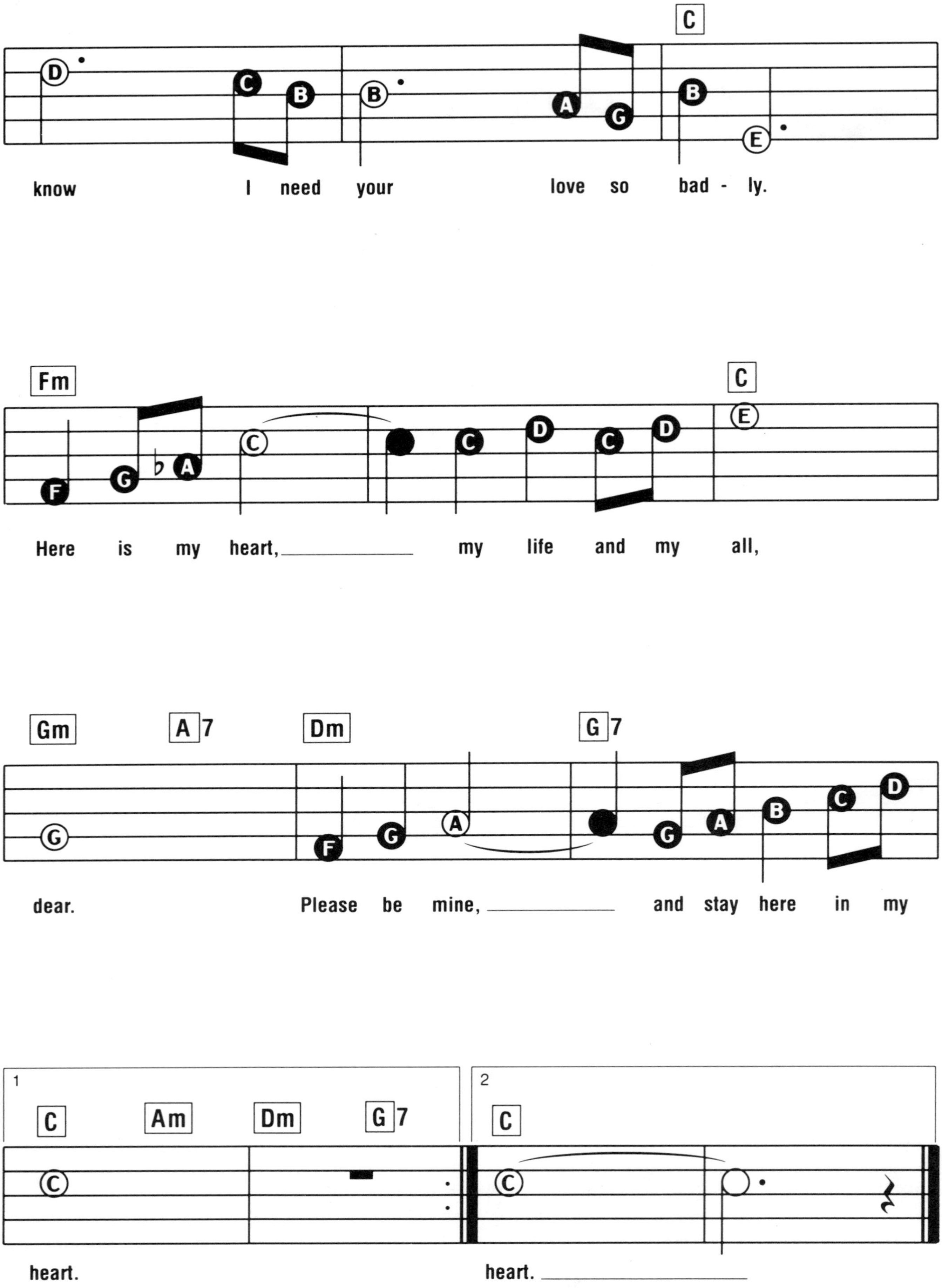
C
know I need your love so bad - ly.
Fm
C
Here is my heart, my life and my all,
Gm
A7
Dm
G7
dear. Please be mine, and stay here in my
1
C
Am
Dm
G7
heart.
2
C
heart.

High Hopes

Regi-Sound Program: 8
Rhythm: Fox Trot or Swing

Words by Sammy Cahn
Music by James Van Heusen

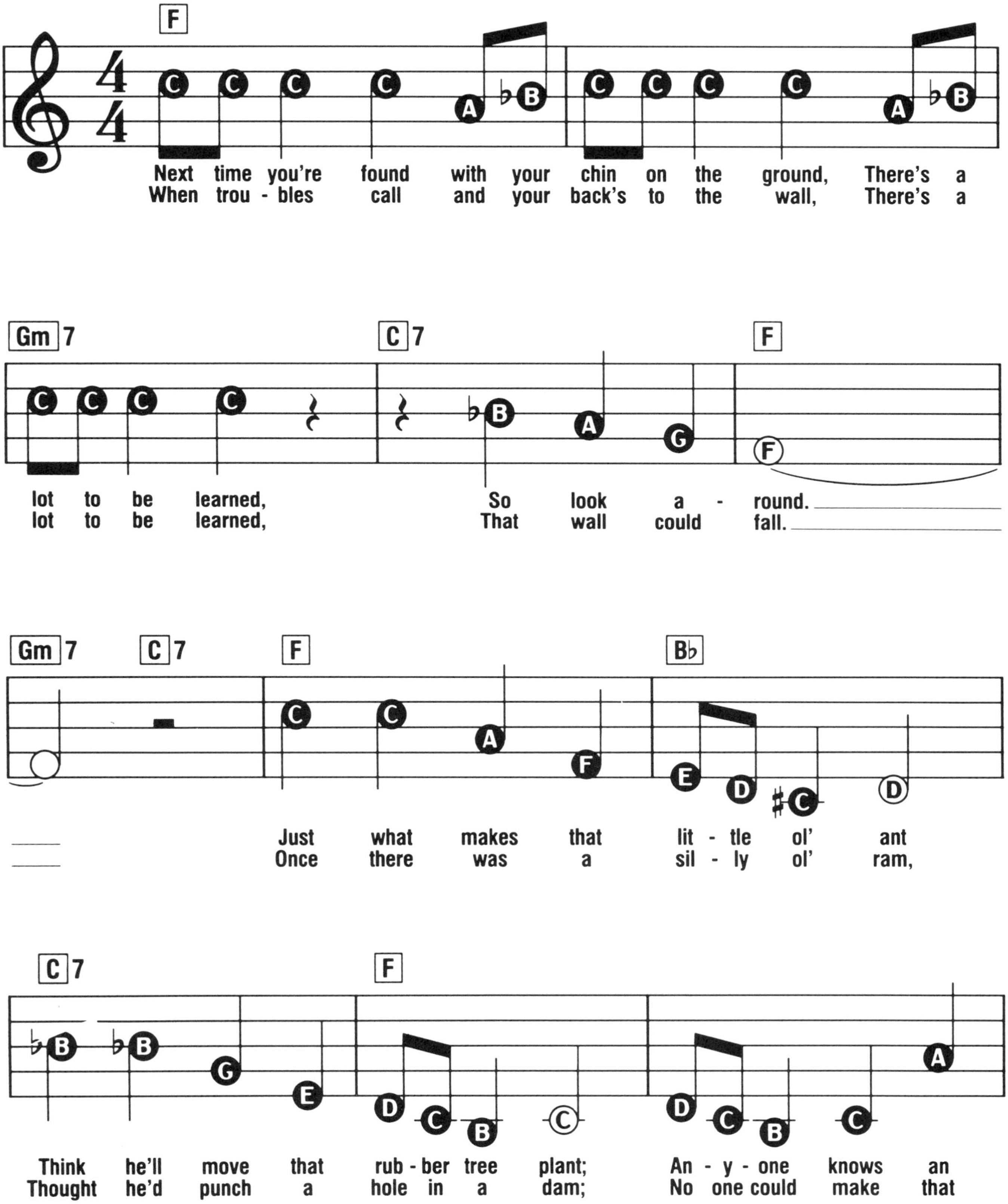
F
Next time you're found with your chin on the ground, There's a
When trou - bles call and your back's to the wall, There's a
Gm7 C7 F
lot to be learned, So look a - round.
lot to be learned, That wall could fall.
Gm7 C7 F B♭
Just what makes that lit - tle ol' ant
Once there was a sil - ly ol' ram,
C7 F
Think he'll move that rub - ber tree plant; An - y - one knows an
Thought he'd punch a hole in a dam; No one could make that

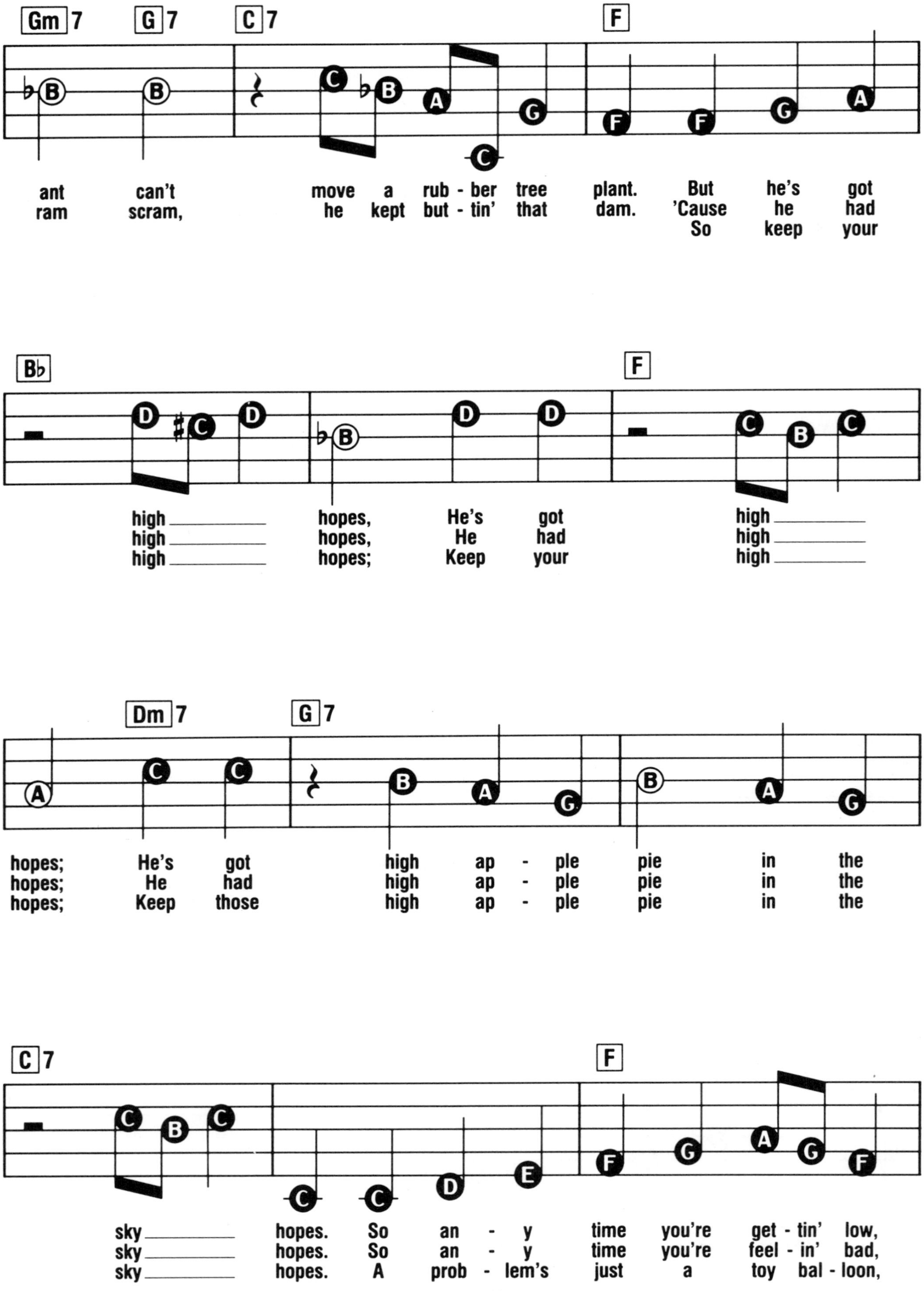
Gm7 G7 C7 F
ant can't move a rub - ber tree plant. But he's got
ram scram, he kept but - tin' that dam. 'Cause he had
So keep your
B♭ F
high hopes, He's got high
high hopes, He had high
high hopes; Keep your high
Dm7 G7
hopes; He's got high ap - ple pie in the
hopes; He had high ap - ple pie in the
hopes; Keep those high ap - ple pie in the
C7 F
sky hopes. So an - y time you're get - tin' low,
sky hopes. So an - y time you're feel - in' bad,
sky hopes. A prob - lem's just a toy bal - loon,

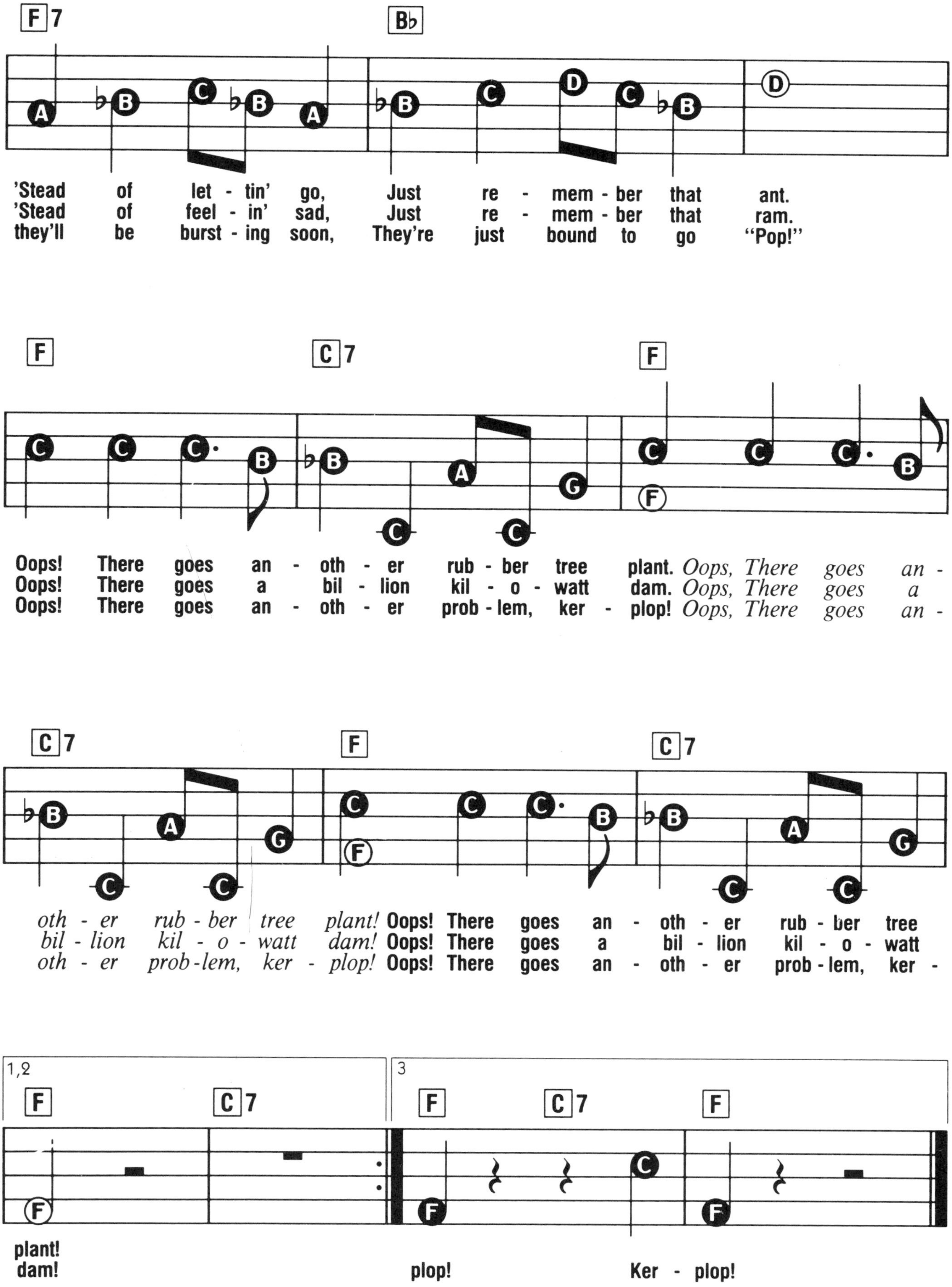
F7
B♭
'Stead of let - tin' go, Just re - mem - ber that ant.
'Stead of feel - in' sad, Just re - mem - ber that ram.
they'll be burst - ing soon, They're just bound to go "Pop!"
F
C7
F
Oops! There goes an - oth - er rub - ber tree plant. Oops, There goes an -
Oops! There goes a bil - lion kil - o - watt dam. Oops, There goes a
Oops! There goes an - oth - er prob - lem, ker - plop! Oops, There goes an -
C7
F
C7
oth - er rub - ber tree plant! Oops! There goes an - oth - er rub - ber tree
bil - lion kil - o - watt dam! Oops! There goes a bil - lion kil - o - watt
oth - er prob - lem, ker - plop! Oops! There goes an - oth - er prob - lem, ker -
1,2
F
C7
plant!
dam!
3
F
C7
F
plop! Ker - plop!

How Lucky You Are

Regi-Sound Program: 1
Rhythm: Waltz

Words by Desmond O'Connor
Music by Eddie Cassen

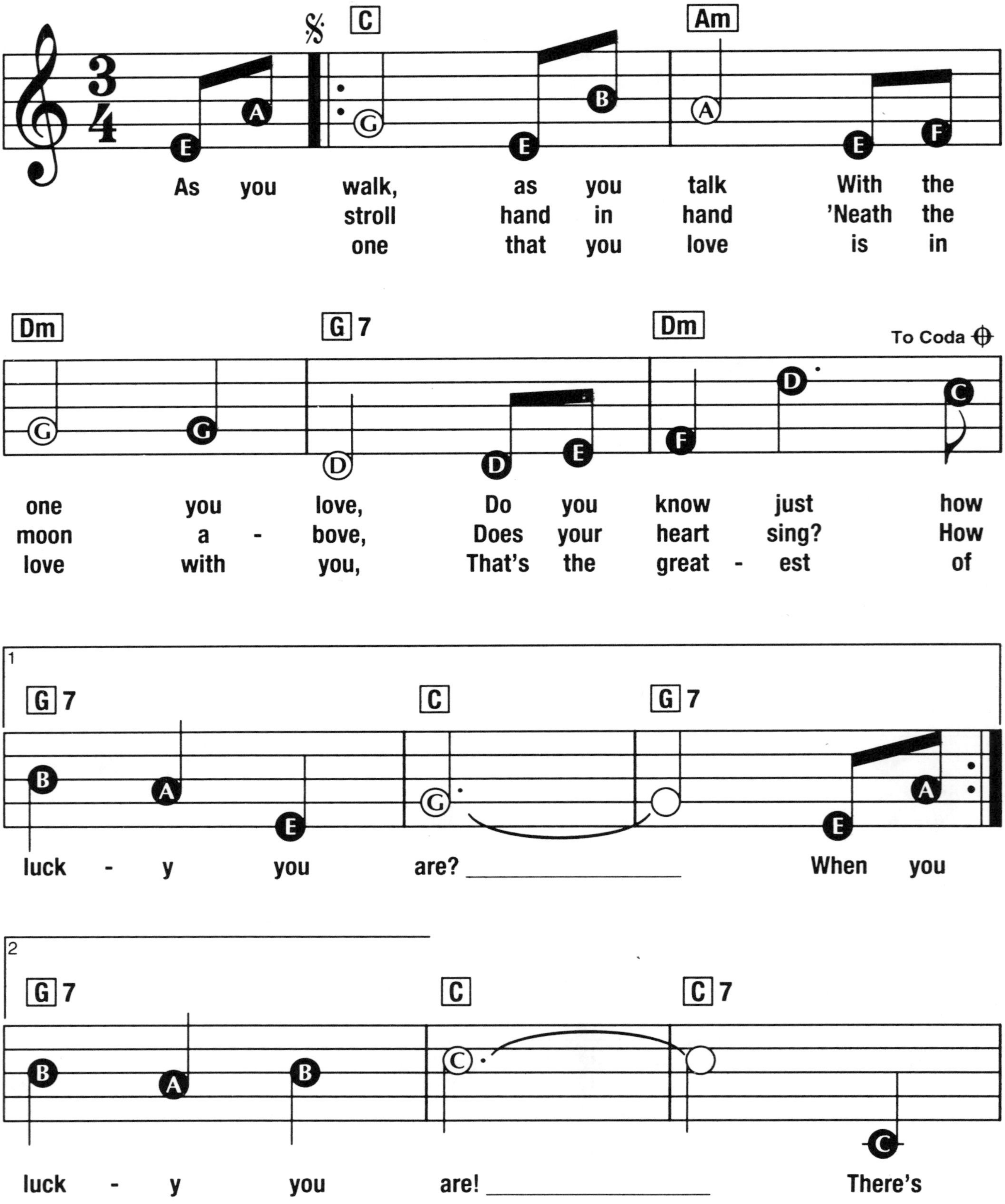

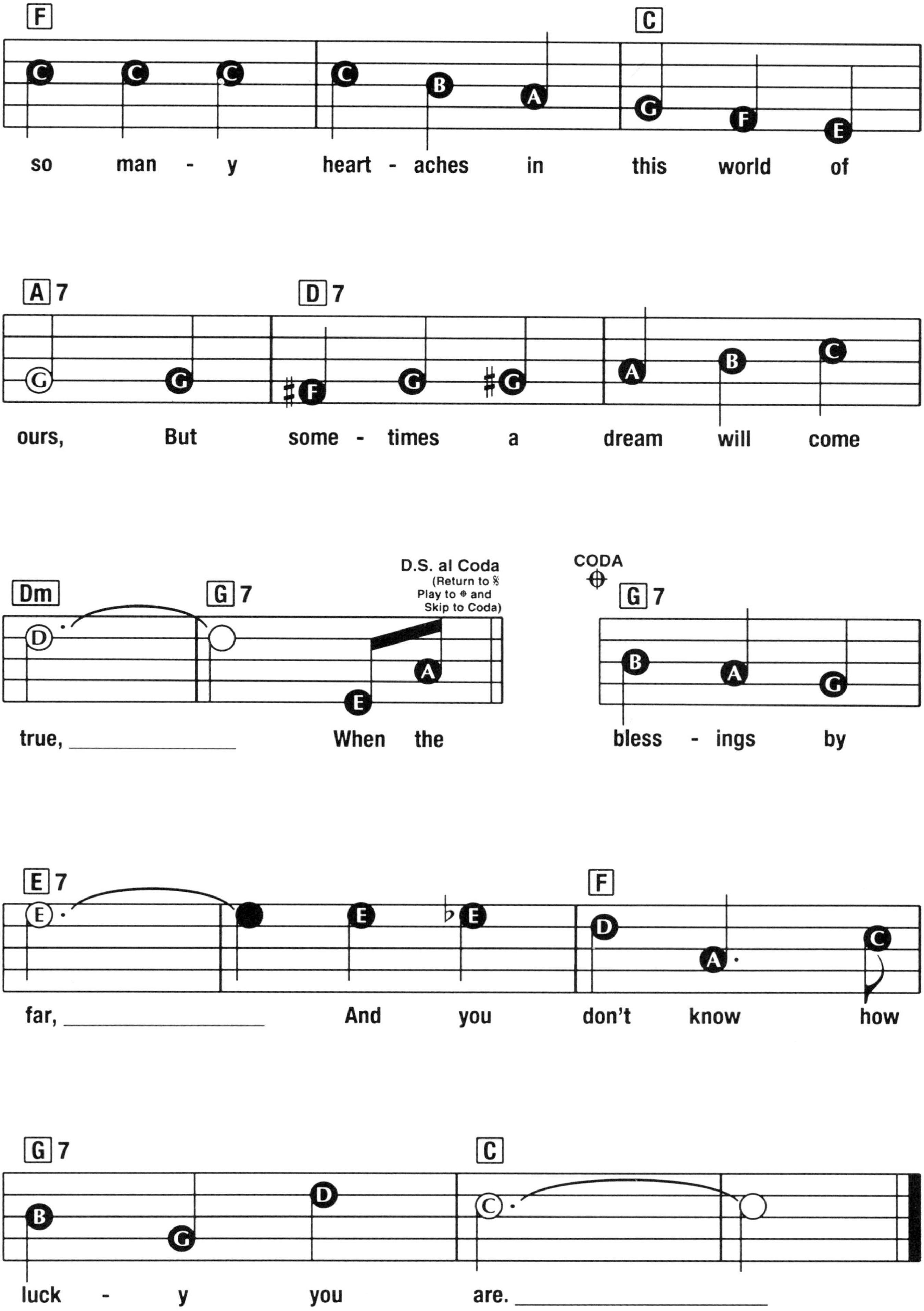
F
C
so many - y heart - aches in this world of
A7
D7
ours, But some - times a dream will come
Dm
G7
D.S. al Coda
(Return to 𝄋
Play to ⊕ and
Skip to Coda)
true, When the
CODA
G7
bless - ings by
E7
F
far, And you don't know how
G7
C
luck - y you are.

How Wonderful To Know

Regi-Sound Program: 10
Rhythm: Ballad or Fox Trot

English Words by Kermit Goell
Music by Salve D'Esposito

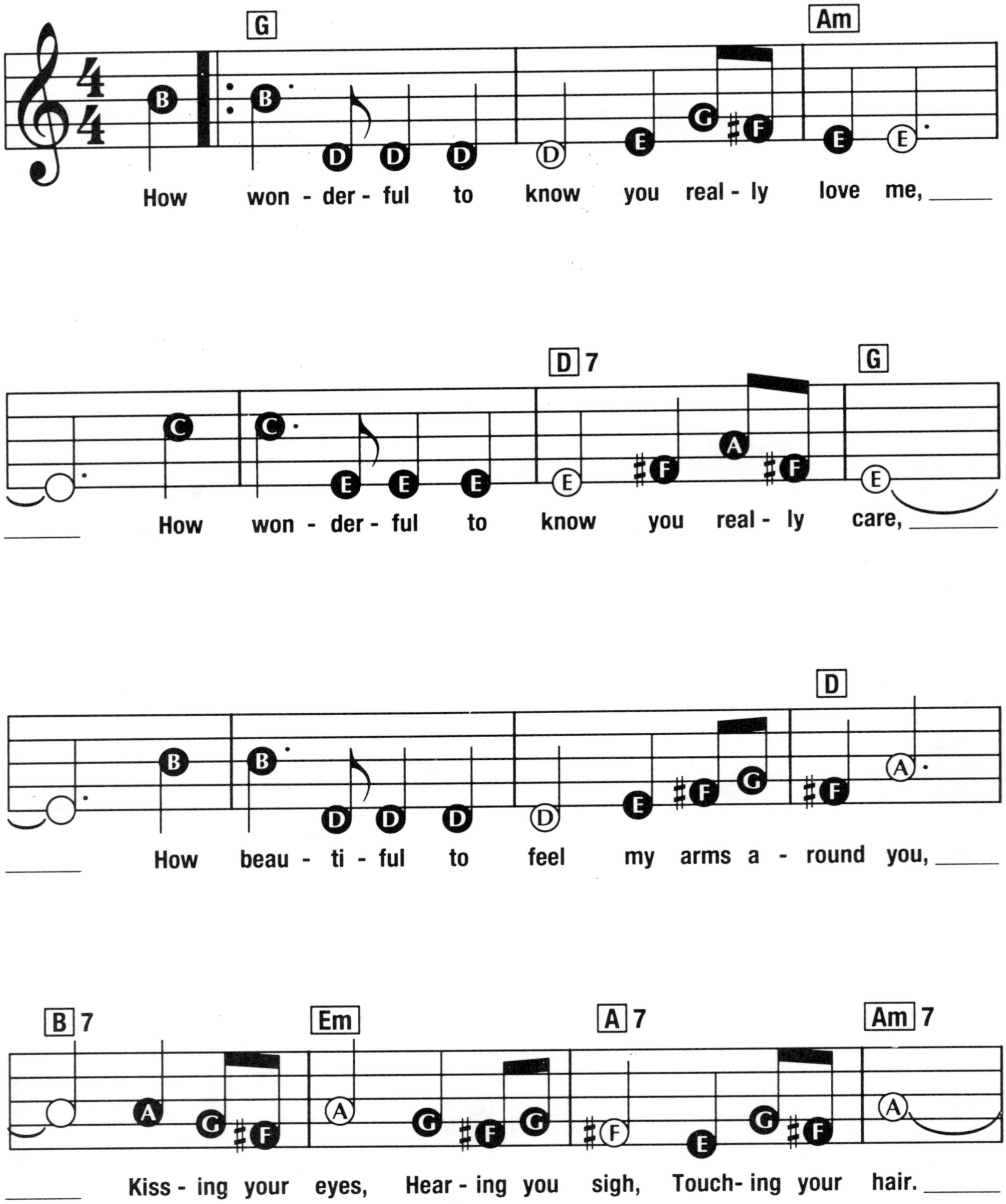
G Am
How won - der - ful to know you real - ly love me,
D7 G
How won - der - ful to know you real - ly care,
D
How beau - ti - ful to feel my arms a - round you,
B7 Em A7 Am7
Kiss - ing your eyes, Hear - ing you sigh, Touch - ing your hair.

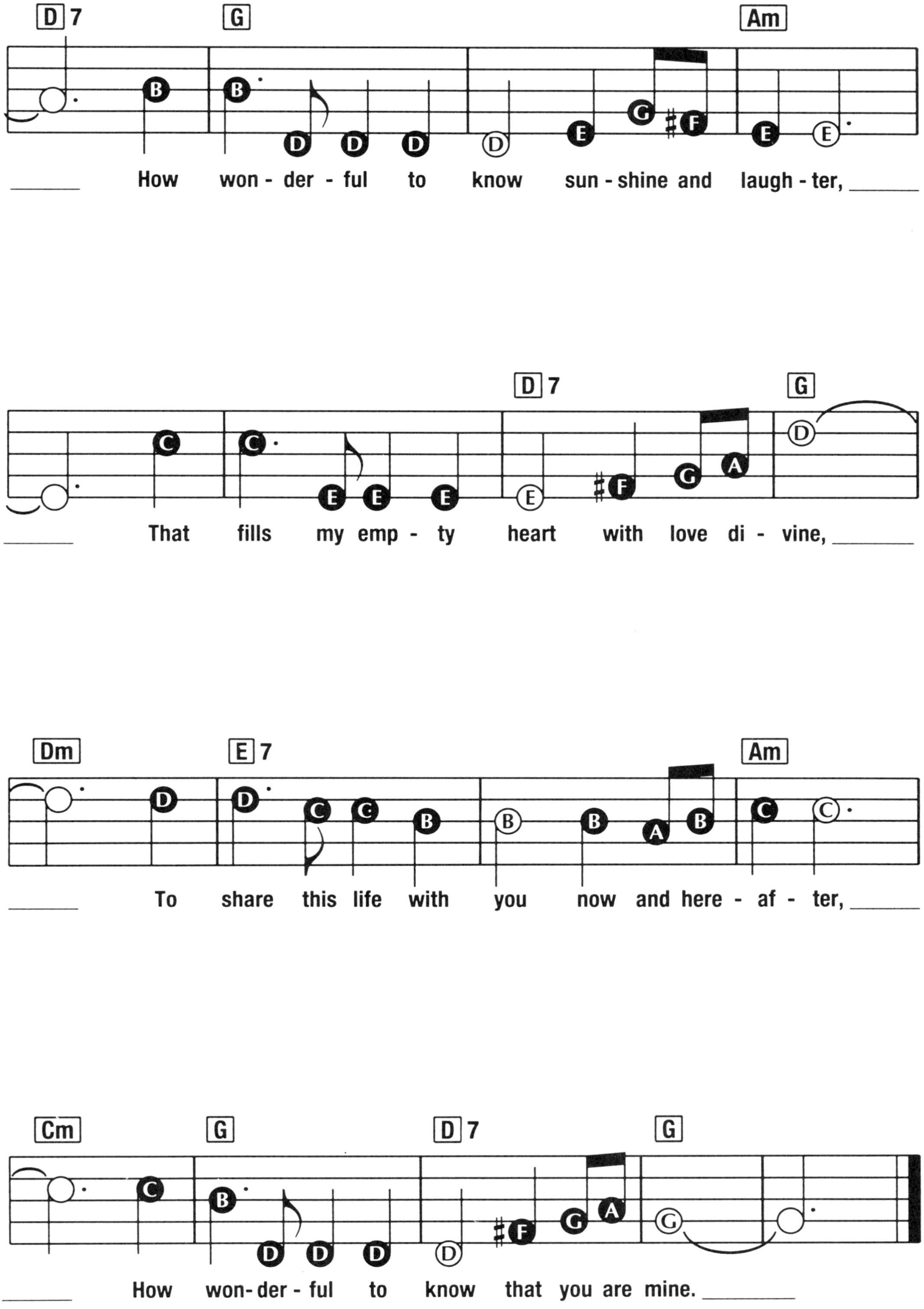
D7 G Am
How won - der - ful to know sun - shine and laugh - ter,
D7 G
That fills my emp - ty heart with love di - vine,
Dm E7 Am
To share this life with you now and here - af - ter,
Cm G D7 G
How won - der - ful to know that you are mine.

In The Wee Small Hours Of The Morning

Regi-Sound Program: 2
Rhythm: Ballad or Fox Trot

Words by Bob Hilliard
Music by David Mann

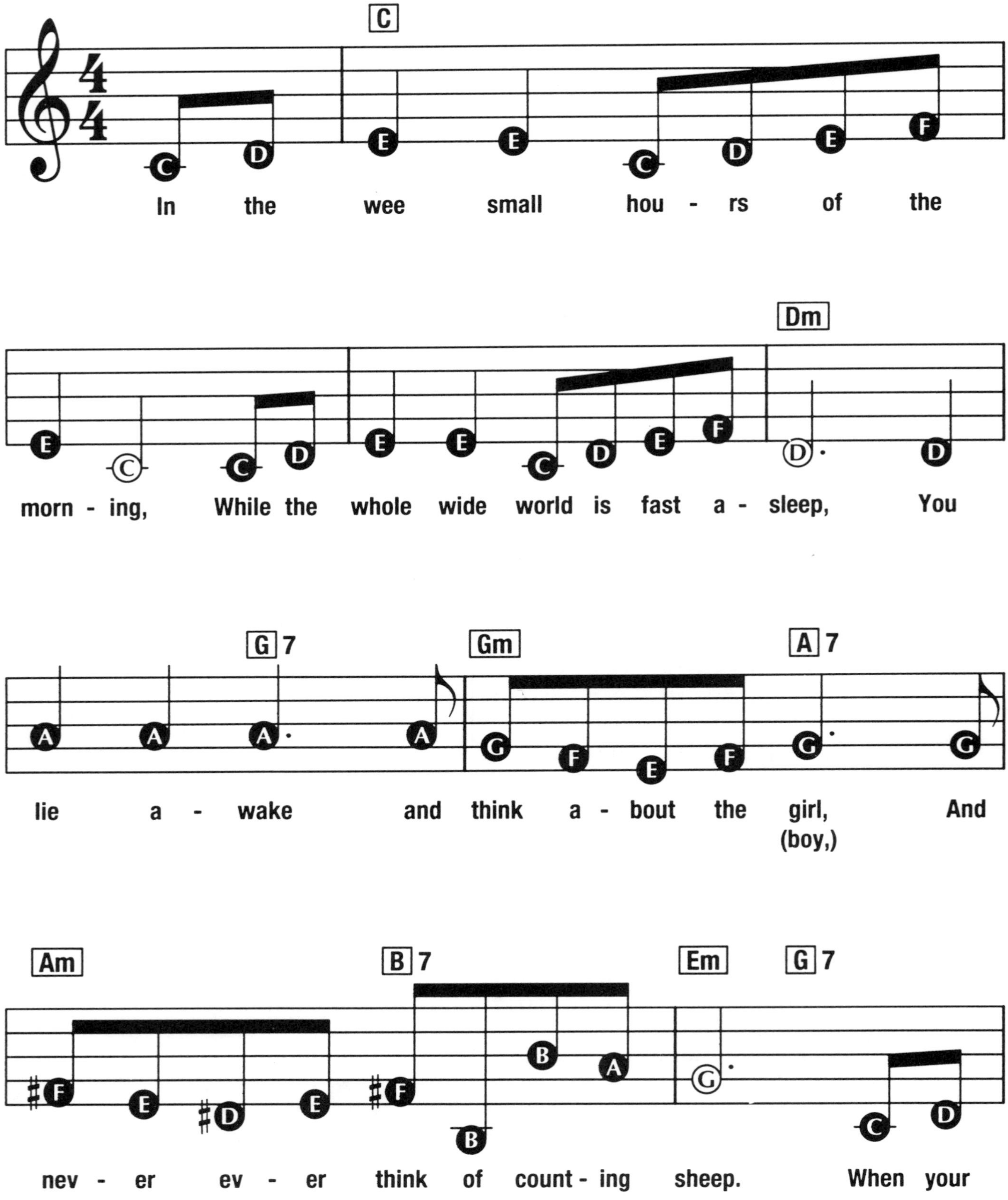

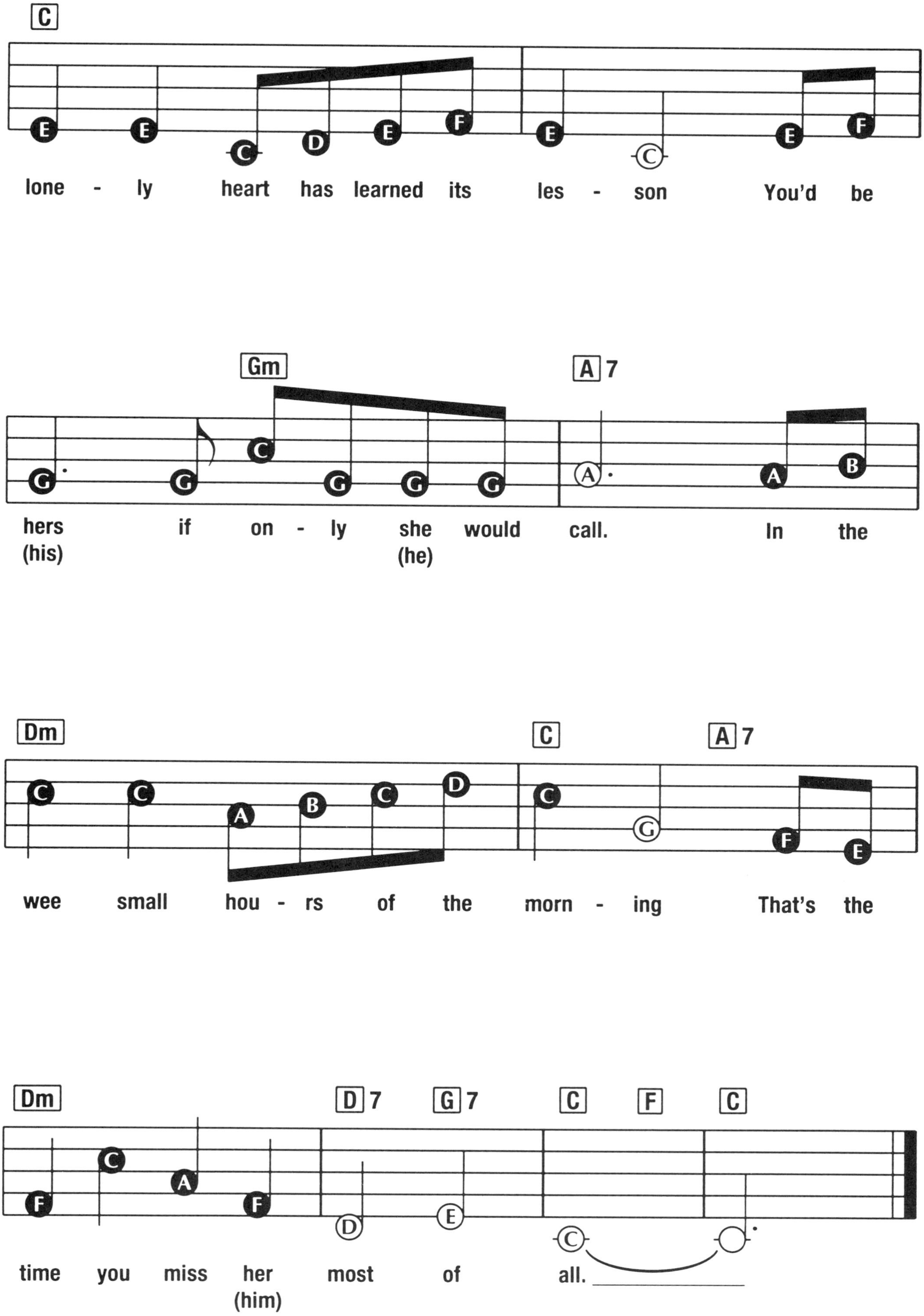
C
lone - ly heart has learned its les - son You'd be
Gm
A 7
hers if on - ly she would call. In the
(his) (he)
Dm
C
A 7
wee small hou - rs of the morn - ing That's the
Dm
D 7
G 7
C
F
C
time you miss her most of all.
(him)

I Wanna Be Around

Regi-Sound Program: 4
Rhythm: Swing

Words and Music by Johnny Mercer
and Sadie Vimmerstedt

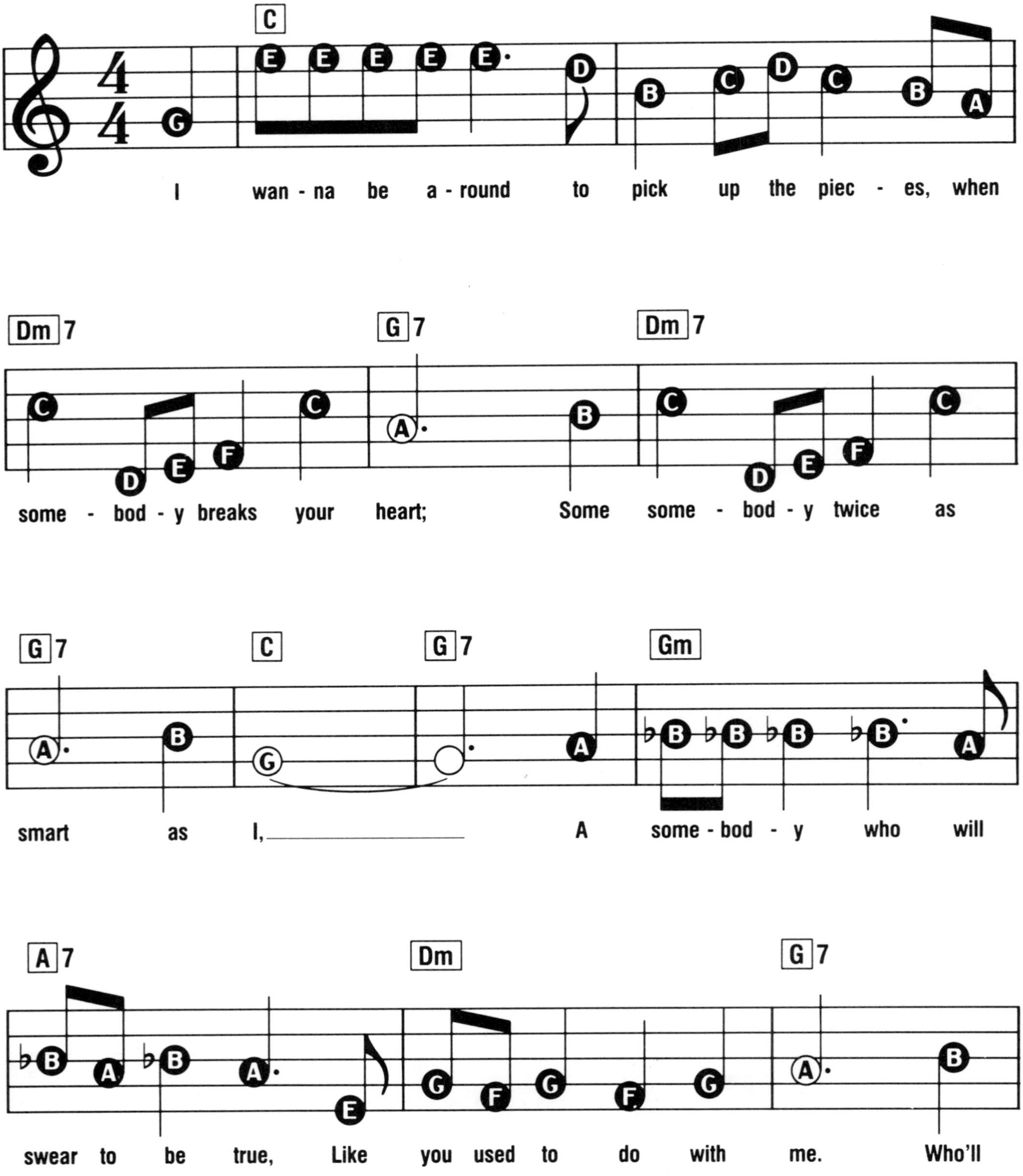
C
I wan - na be a - round to pick up the piec - es, when
Dm7 G7 Dm7
some - bod - y breaks your heart; Some some - bod - y twice as
G7 C G7 Gm
smart as I, A some - bod - y who will
A7 Dm G7
swear to be true, Like you used to do with me. Who'll

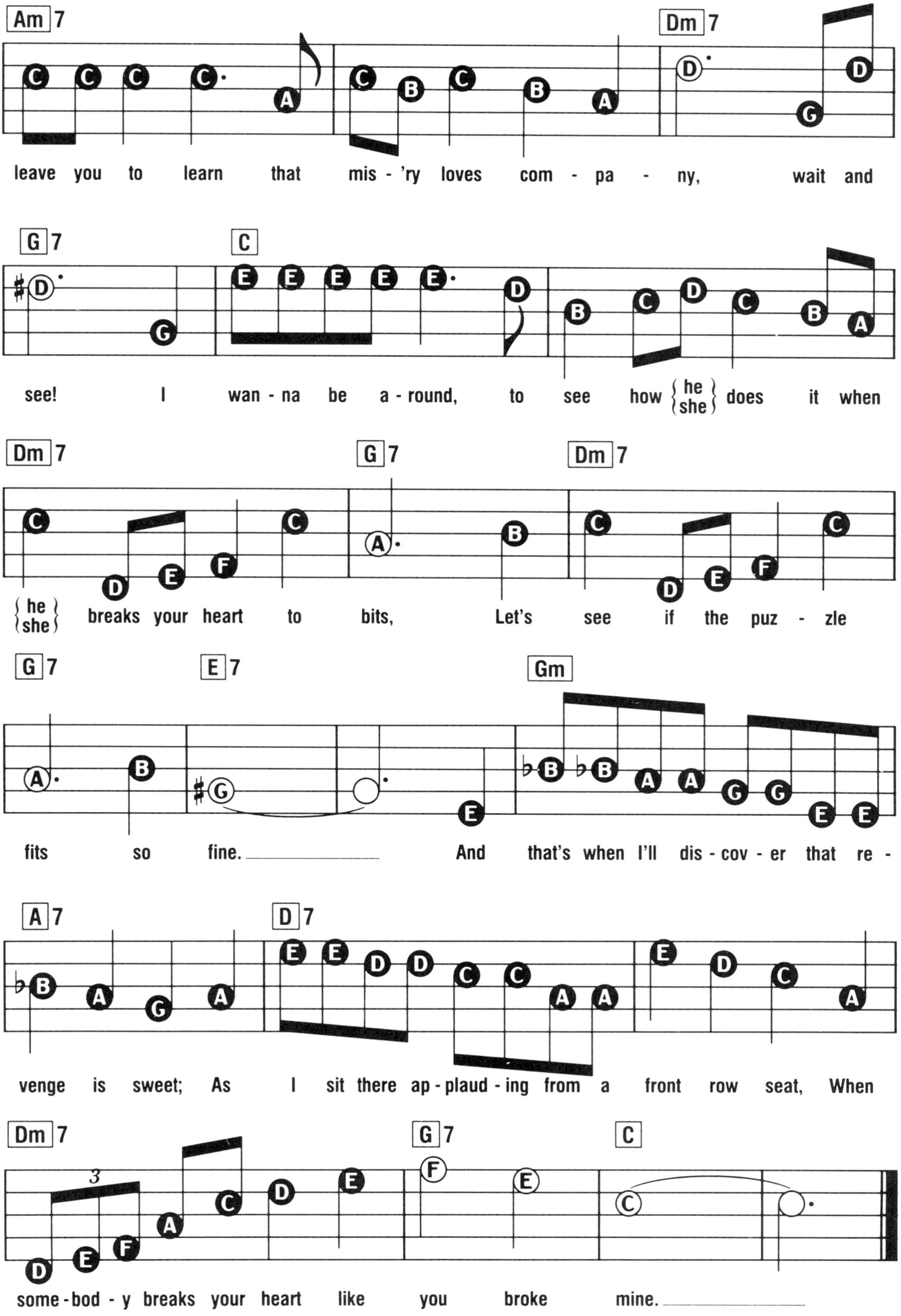
Am7 Dm7
leave you to learn that mis - 'ry loves com - pa - ny, wait and
G7 C
see! I wan - na be a - round, to see how {he / she} does it when
Dm7 G7 Dm7
{he / she} breaks your heart to bits, Let's see if the puz - zle
G7 E7 Gm
fits so fine. And that's when I'll dis - cov - er that re -
A7 D7
venge is sweet; As I sit there ap - plaud - ing from a front row seat, When
Dm7 G7 C
some - bod - y breaks your heart like you broke mine.

It Doesn't Matter Any More

Regi-Sound Program: 2
Rhythm: Fox Trot or Ballad

Words and Music by
Paul Anka

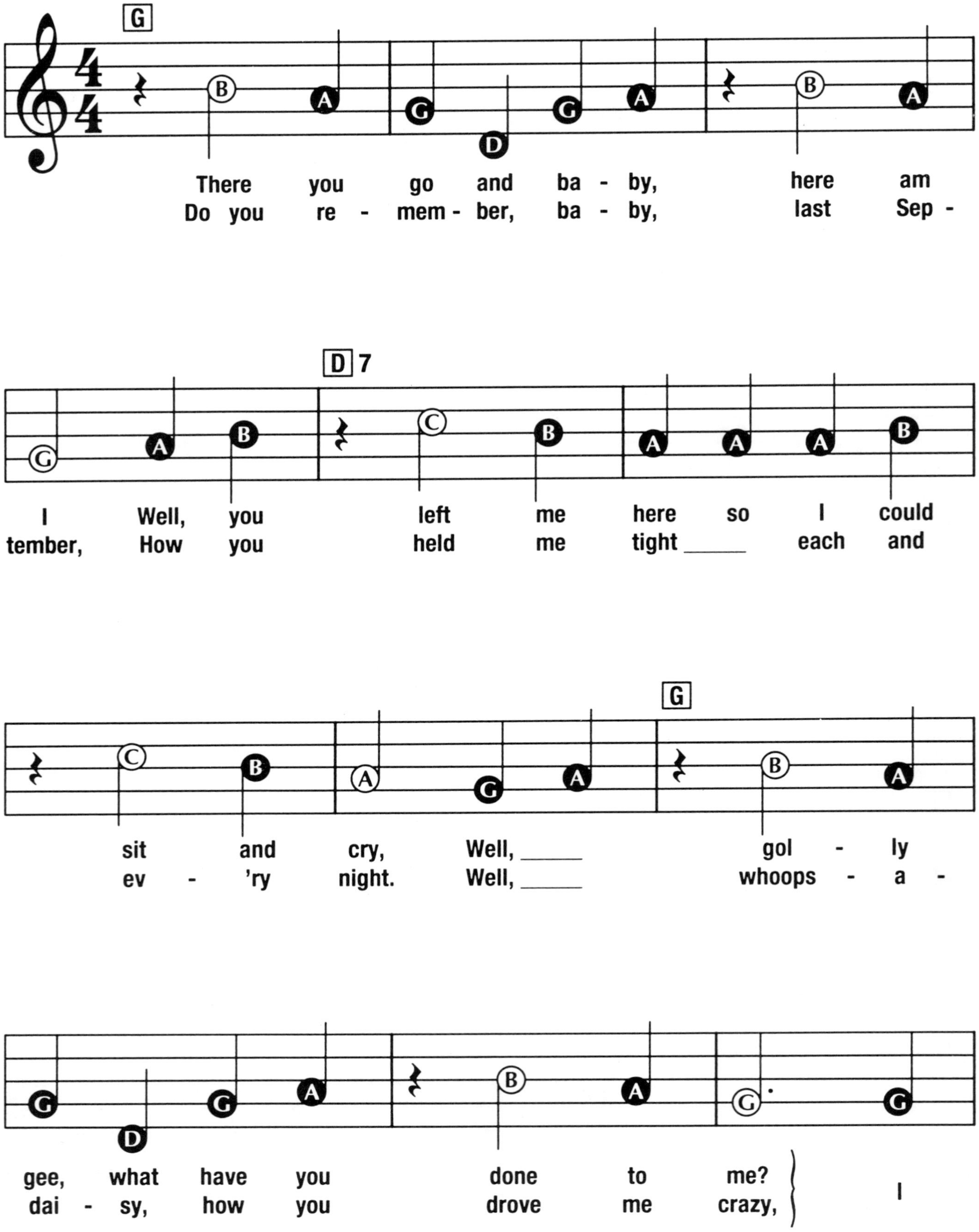
G
There you go and ba - by, here am I Well, you
Do you re - mem - ber, ba - by, last Sep - tember, How you
D7
left me here so I could sit and cry, Well, ____
held me tight ____ each and ev - 'ry night. Well, ____
G
gol - ly gee, what have you done to me?
whoops - a - dai - sy, how you drove me crazy,
I

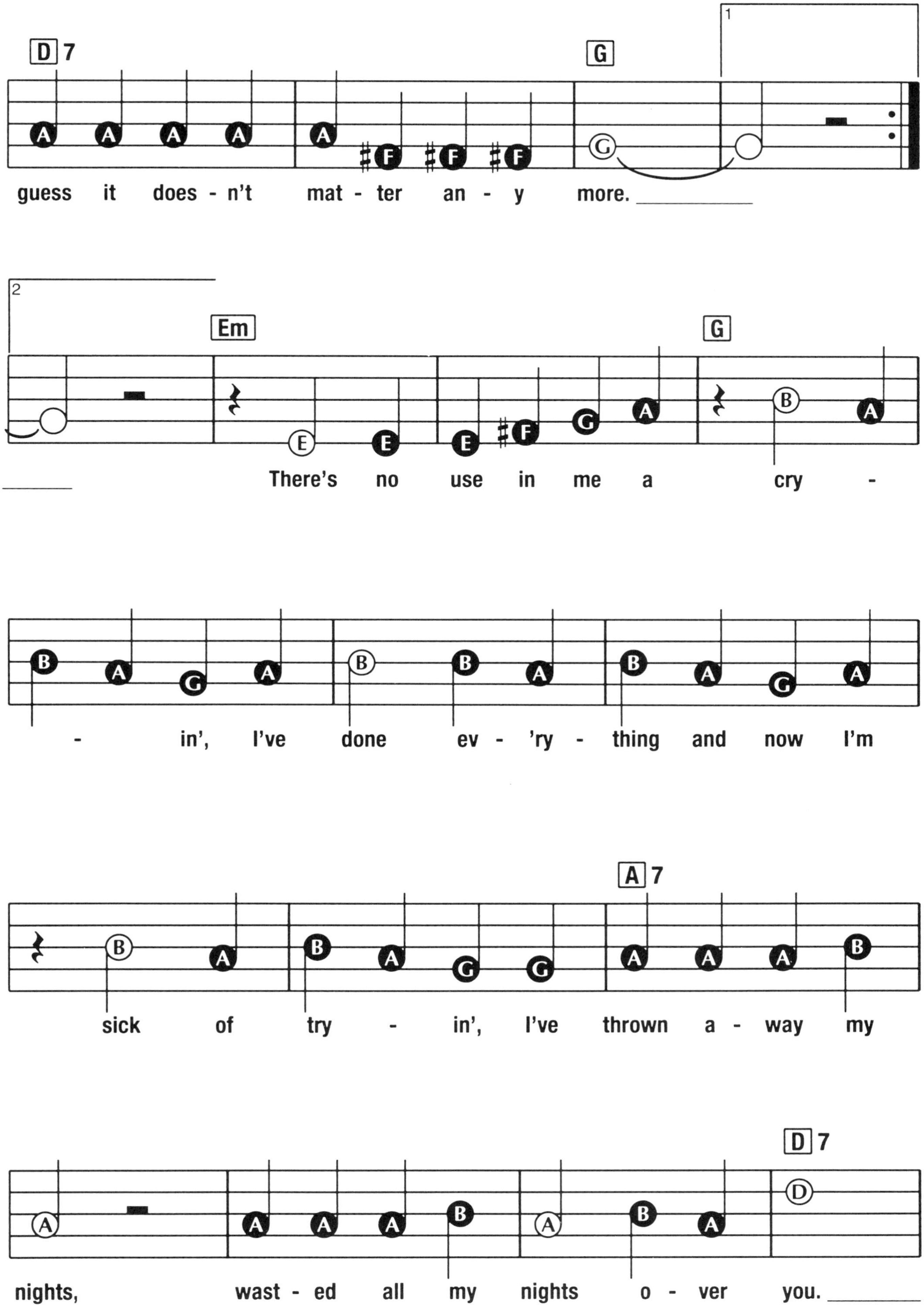
D 7
G
1
guess it does - n't mat - ter an - y more.
2
Em
G
There's no use in me a cry -
- in', I've done ev - 'ry - thing and now I'm
A 7
sick of try - in', I've thrown a - way my
D 7
nights, wast - ed all my nights o - ver you.

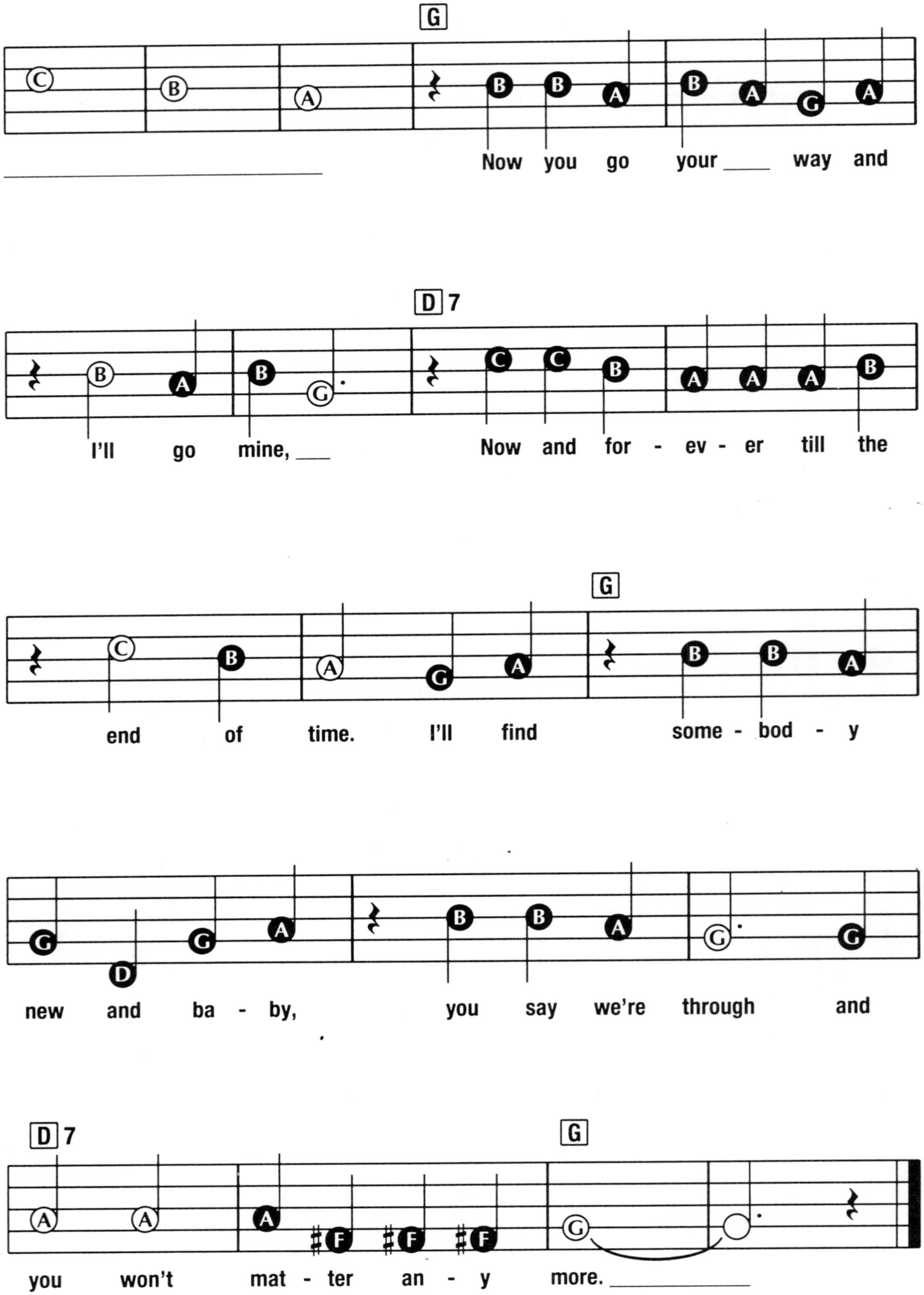
G
Now you go your ___ way and
D7
I'll go mine, ___ Now and for - ev - er till the
G
end of time. I'll find some - bod - y
new and ba - by, you say we're through and
D7
G
you won't mat - ter an - y more. ___

Little White Bull

Regi-Sound Program: 4
Rhythm: Fox Trot or Swing

Words and Music by Michael Pratt,
Lionel Bart & Jimmy Bennett

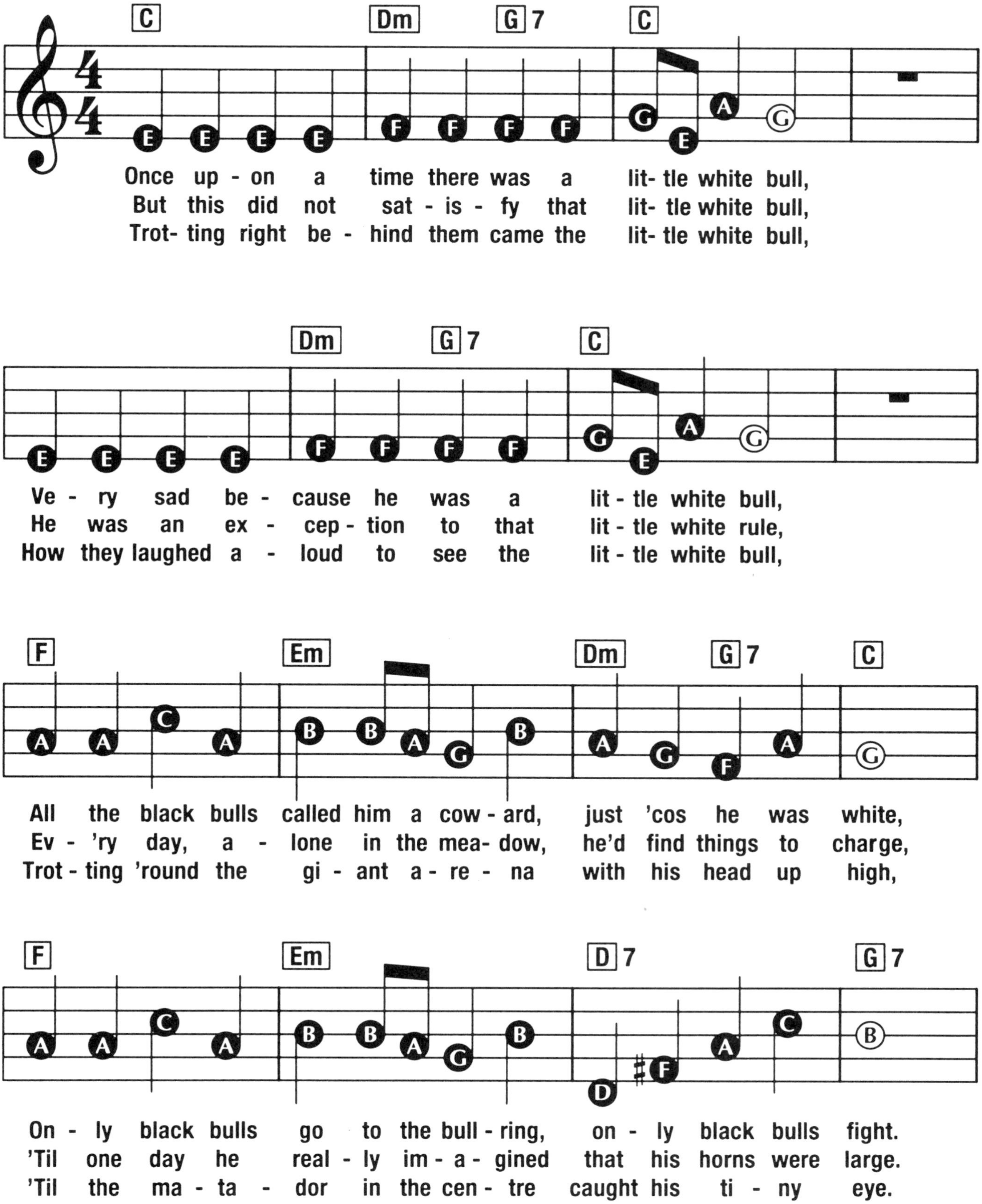
C Dm G7 C
Once up - on a time there was a lit- tle white bull,
But this did not sat - is - fy that lit- tle white bull,
Trot- ting right be - hind them came the lit- tle white bull,
Dm G7 C
Ve - ry sad be - cause he was a lit - tle white bull,
He was an ex - cep - tion to that lit - tle white rule,
How they laughed a - loud to see the lit - tle white bull,
F Em Dm G7 C
All the black bulls called him a cow - ard, just 'cos he was white,
Ev - 'ry day, a - lone in the mea- dow, he'd find things to charge,
Trot - ting 'round the gi - ant a - re - na with his head up high,
F Em D7 G7
On - ly black bulls go to the bull - ring, on - ly black bulls fight.
'Til one day he real - ly im - a - gined that his horns were large.
'Til the ma - ta - dor in the cen - tre caught his ti - ny eye.

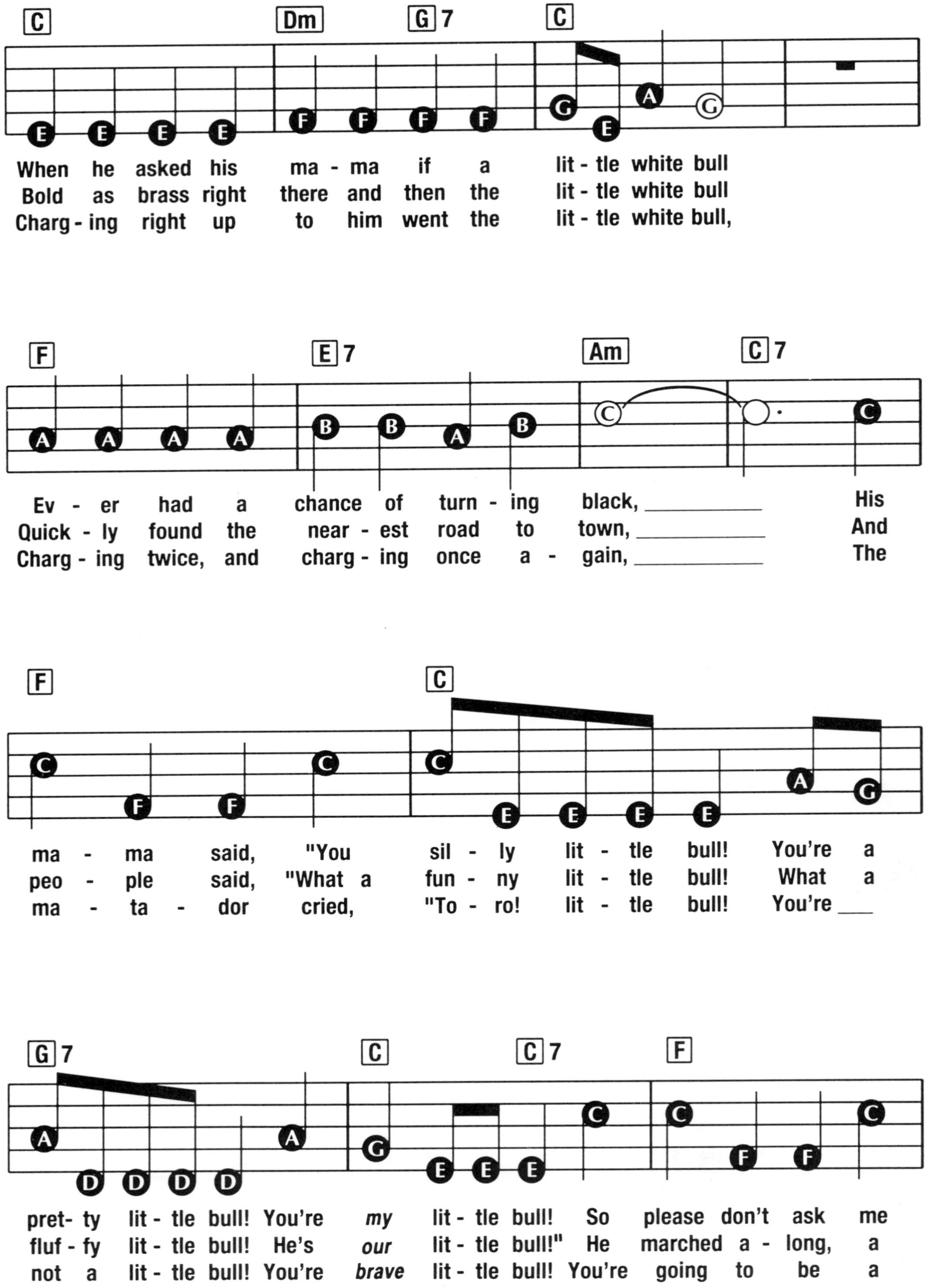
C Dm G7 C
When he asked his ma - ma if a lit - tle white bull
Bold as brass right there and then the lit - tle white bull
Charg - ing right up to him went the lit - tle white bull,
F E7 Am C7
Ev - er had a chance of turn - ing black, His
Quick - ly found the near - est road to town, And
Charg - ing twice, and charg - ing once a - gain, The
F C
ma - ma said, "You sil - ly lit - tle bull! You're a
peo - ple said, "What a fun - ny lit - tle bull! What a
ma - ta - dor cried, "To - ro! lit - tle bull! You're
G7 C C7 F
pret- ty lit - tle bull! You're my lit - tle bull! So please don't ask me
fluf - fy lit - tle bull! He's our lit - tle bull!" He marched a - long, a
not a lit - tle bull! You're brave lit - tle bull! You're going to be a

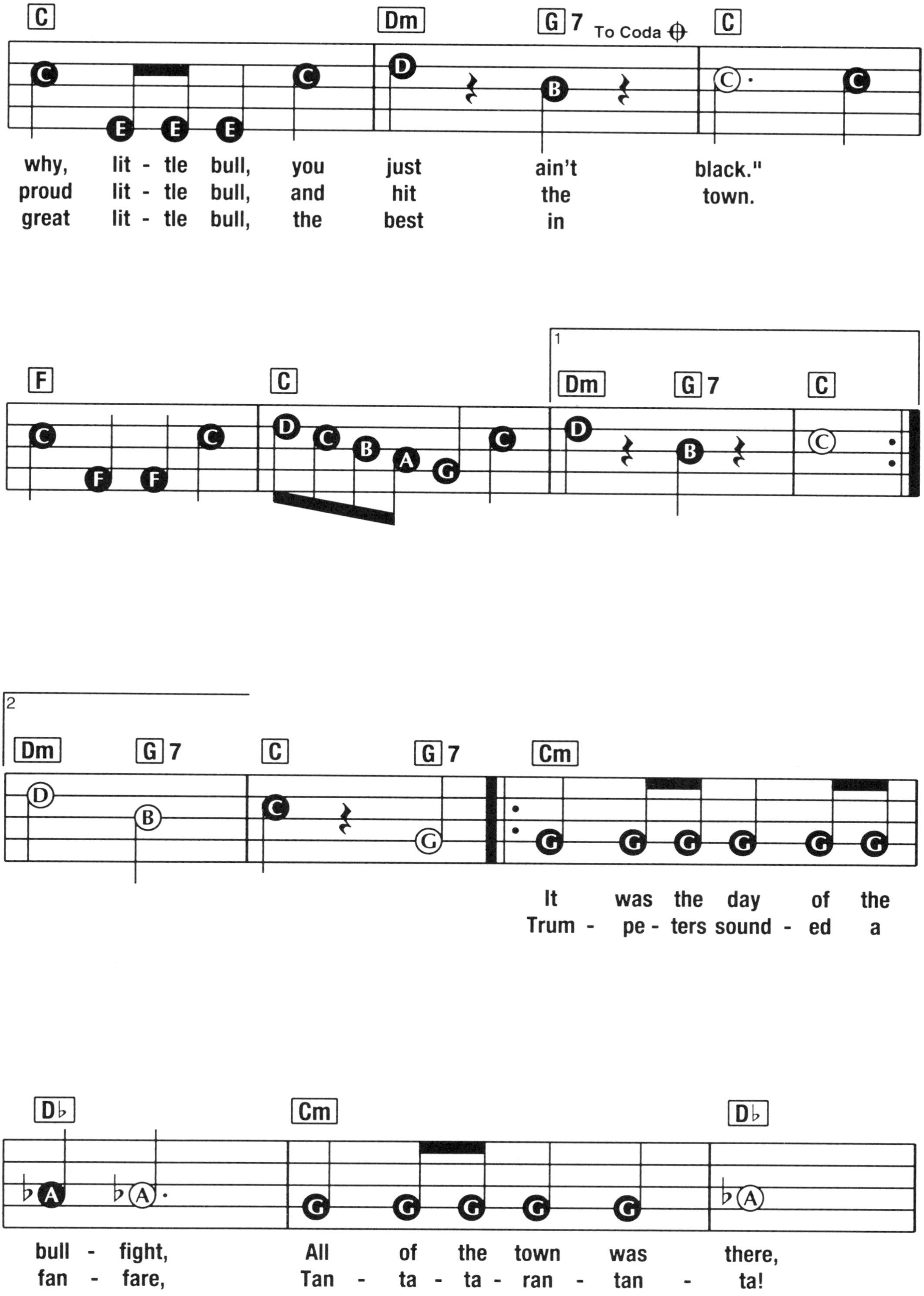
C
Dm
G 7
To Coda
C
why, lit - tle bull, you just ain't black."
proud lit - tle bull, and hit the town.
great lit - tle bull, the best in
F
C
1
Dm
G 7
C
2
Dm
G 7
C
G 7
Cm
It was the day of the
Trum - pe - ters sound - ed a
D♭
Cm
D♭
bull - fight, All of the town was there,
fan - fare, Tan - ta - ta - ran - tan - ta!

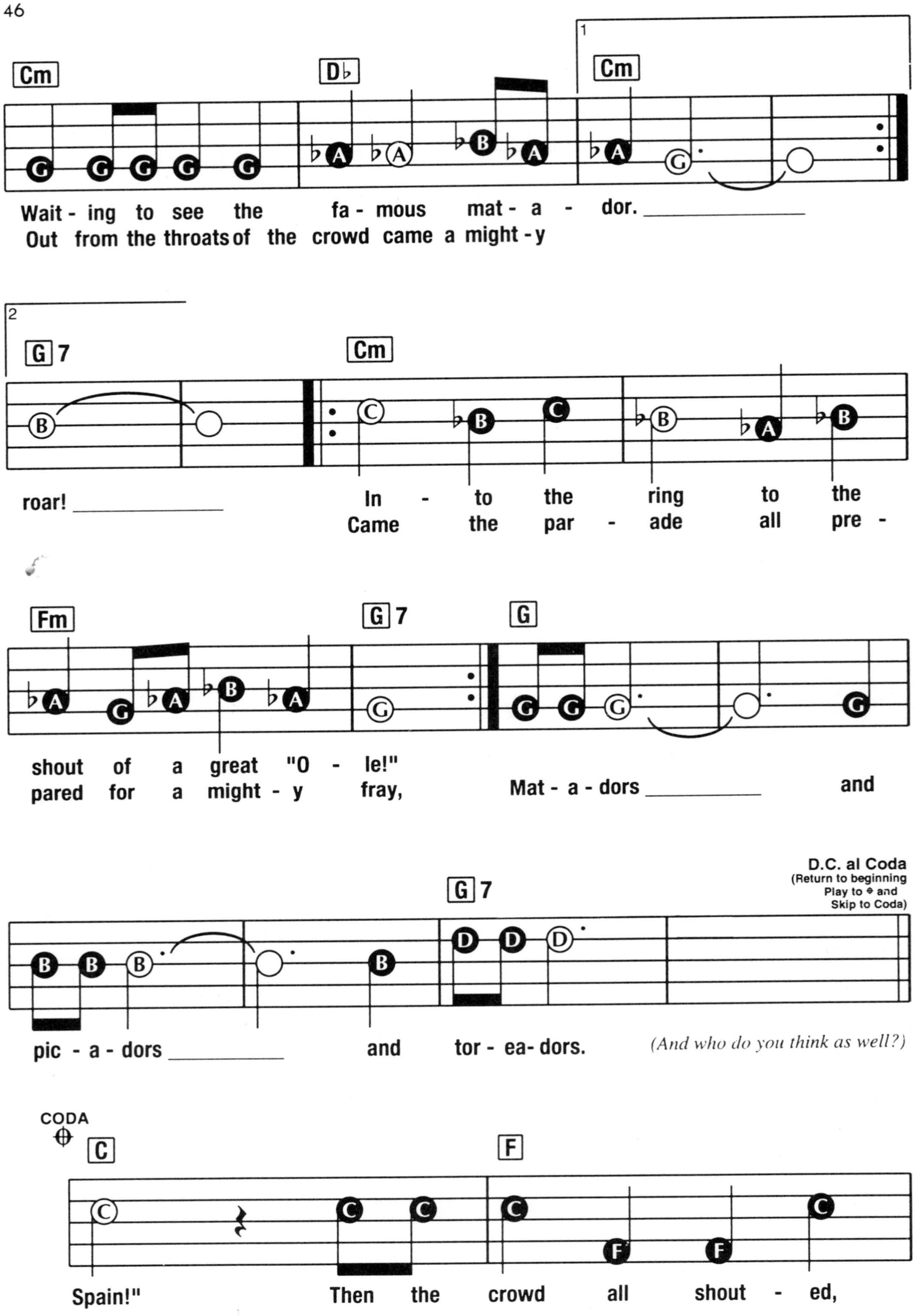
Cm
D♭
1
Cm
Wait - ing to see the fa - mous mat - a - dor.
Out from the throats of the crowd came a might - y
2
G 7
Cm
roar!
In - to the ring to the
Came the par - ade all pre -
Fm
G 7
G
shout of a great "O - le!"
pared for a might - y fray,
Mat - a - dors and
D.C. al Coda
(Return to beginning
Play to ⊕ and
Skip to Coda)
G 7
pic - a - dors and tor - ea - dors.
(And who do you think as well?)
CODA
C
F
Spain!" Then the crowd all shout - ed,

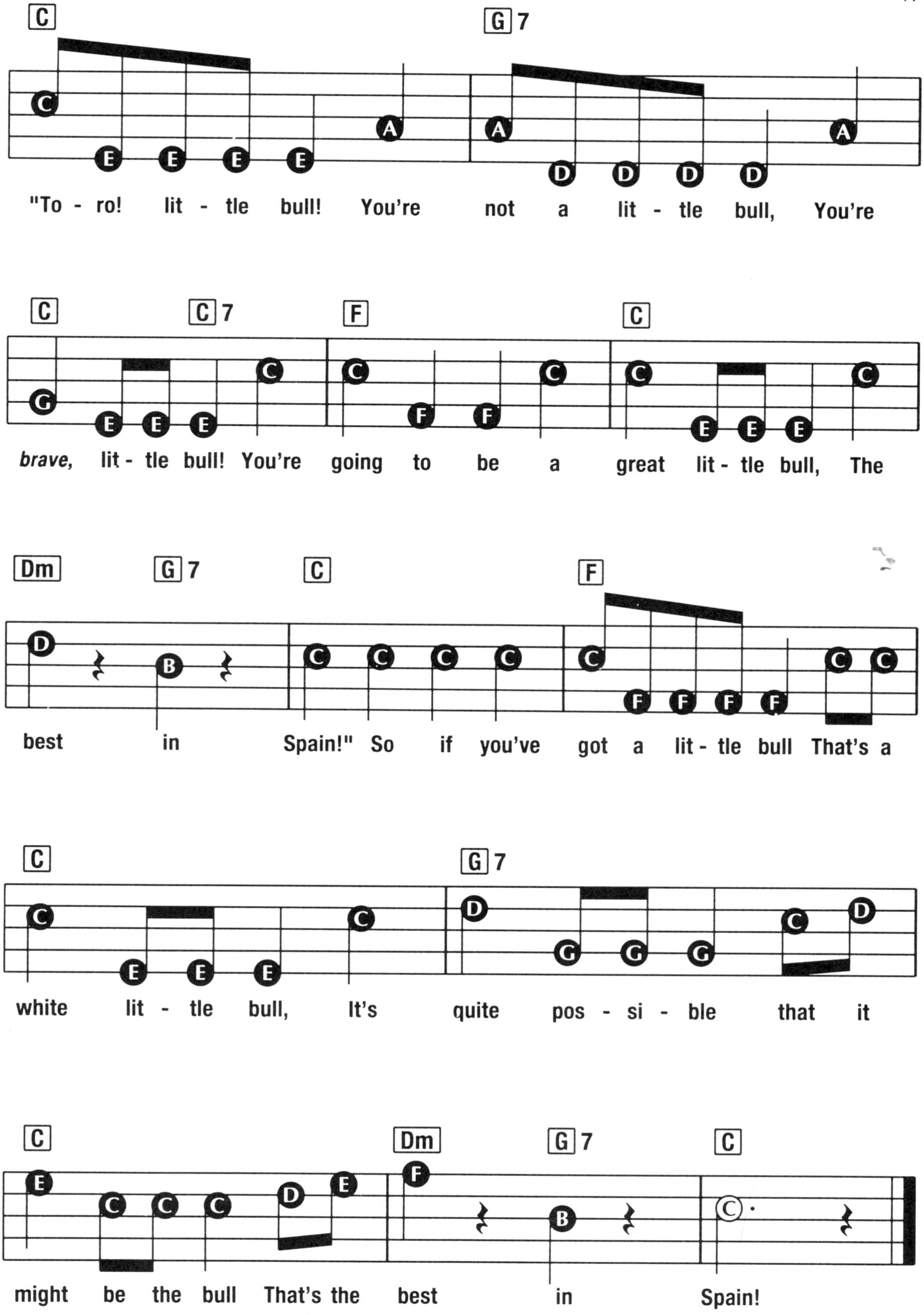
C G7
"To - ro! lit - tle bull! You're not a lit - tle bull, You're
C C7 F C
brave, lit - tle bull! You're going to be a great lit - tle bull, The
Dm G7 C F
best in Spain!" So if you've got a lit - tle bull That's a
C G7
white lit - tle bull, It's quite pos - si - ble that it
C Dm G7 C
might be the bull That's the best in Spain!

La Bamba

Regi-Sound Program: 4
Rhythm: Latin

Arranged by Ritchie Valens

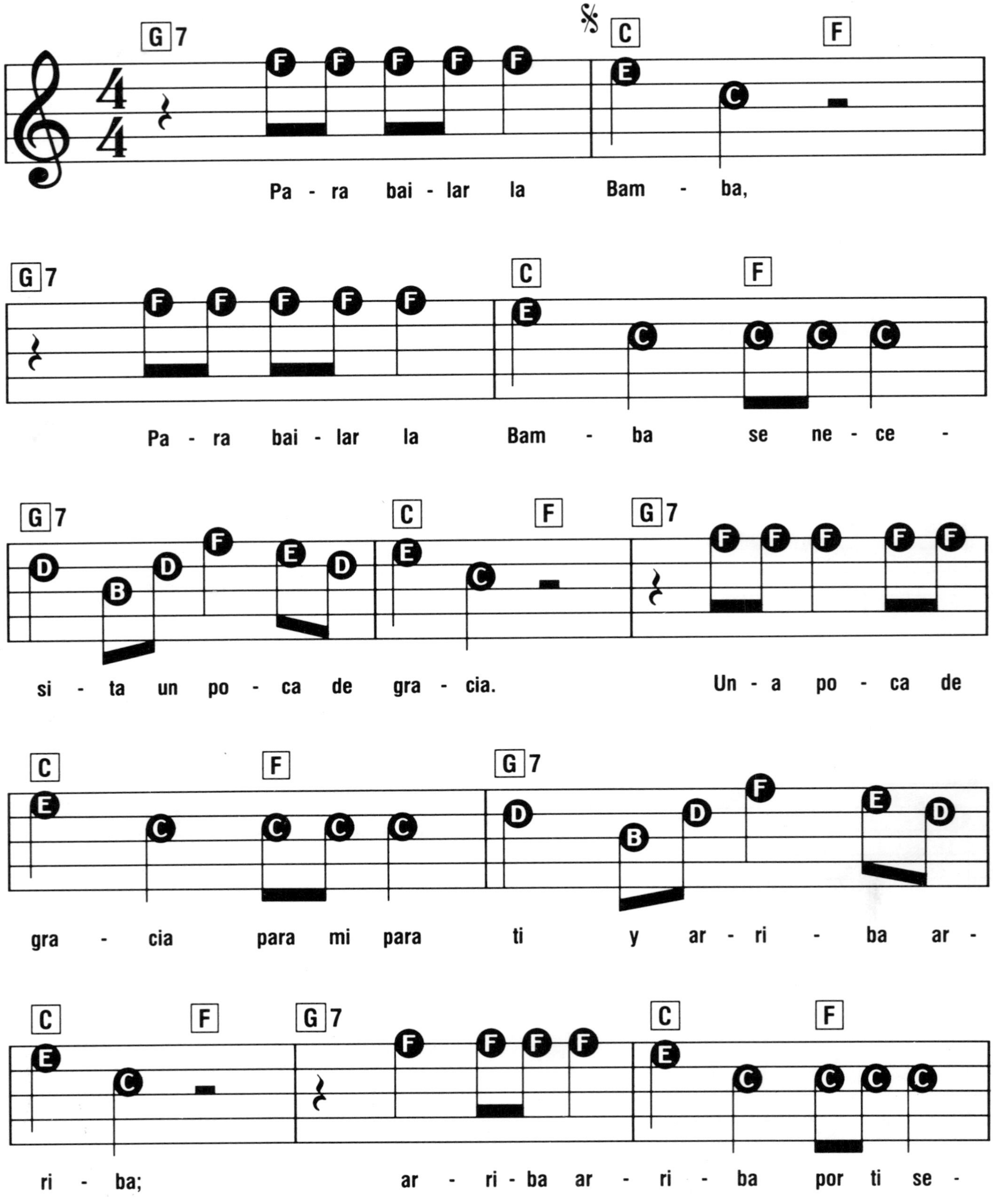

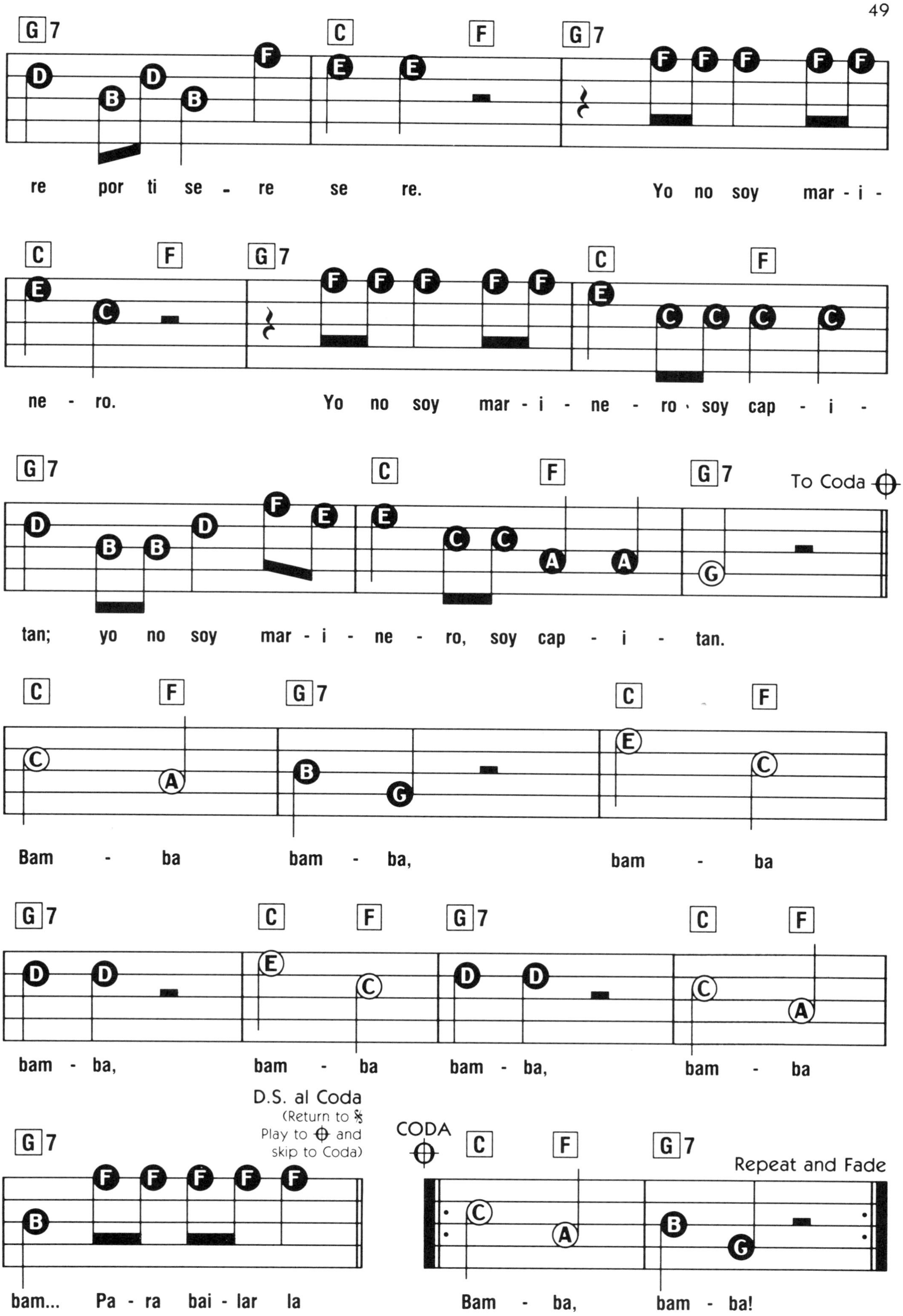
re por ti se - re se re. Yo no soy mar - i -
ne - ro. Yo no soy mar - i - ne - ro, soy cap - i -
tan; yo no soy mar - i - ne - ro, soy cap - i - tan.
To Coda
Bam - ba bam - ba, bam - ba
bam - ba, bam - ba bam - ba, bam - ba
bam... Pa - ra bai - lar la
D.S. al Coda
(Return to 𝄋 Play to 𝄌 and skip to Coda)
CODA
Repeat and Fade
Bam - ba, bam - ba!

Let Me Go, Lover!

Regi-Sound Program: 10
Rhythm: Waltz

Special Lyric by Al Hill
Words and Music by Jenny Lou Carson

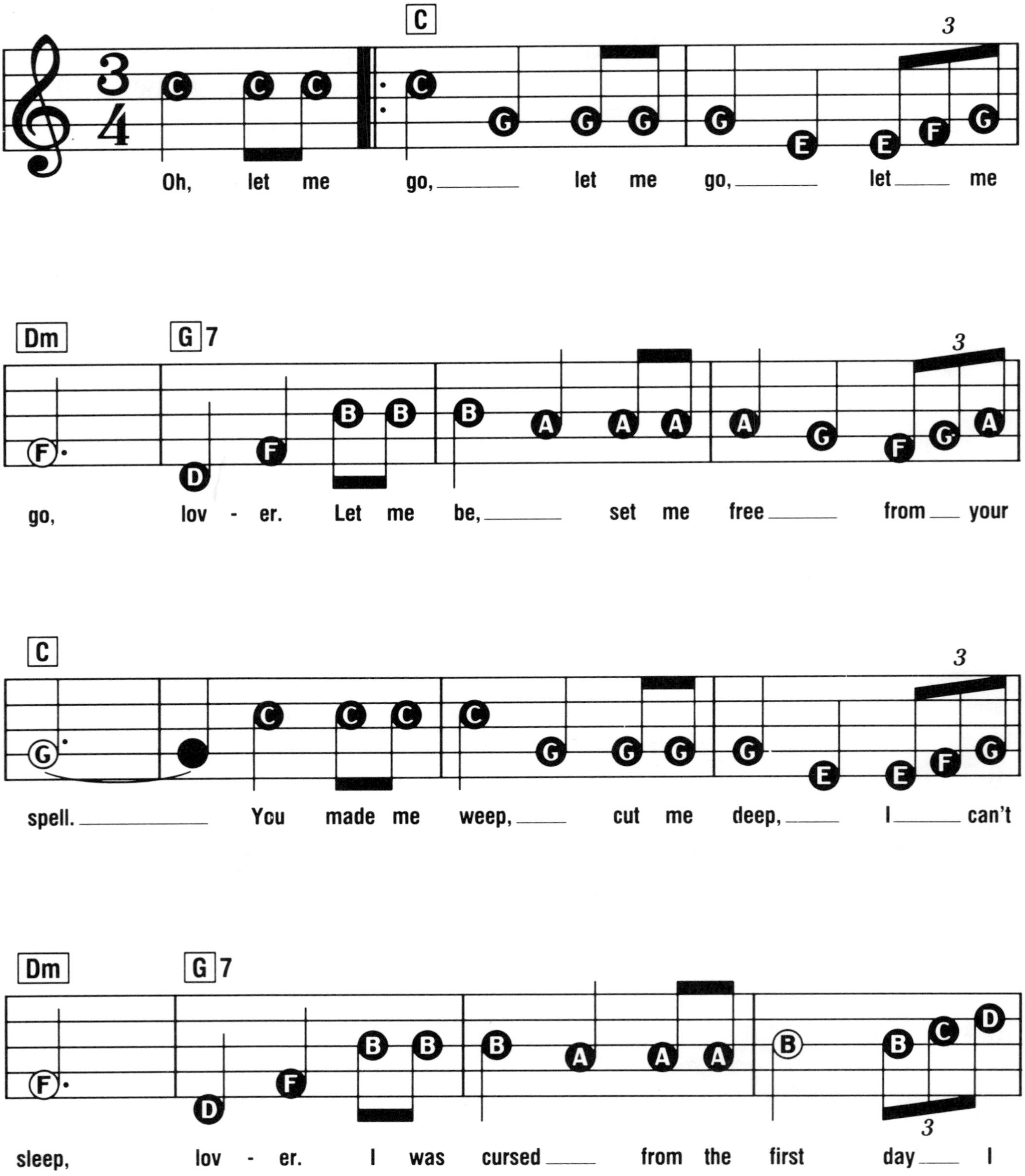
C
Oh, let me go, let me go, let me
Dm G7
go, lov - er. Let me be, set me free from your
C
spell. You made me weep, cut me deep, I can't
Dm G7
sleep, lov - er. I was cursed from the first day I

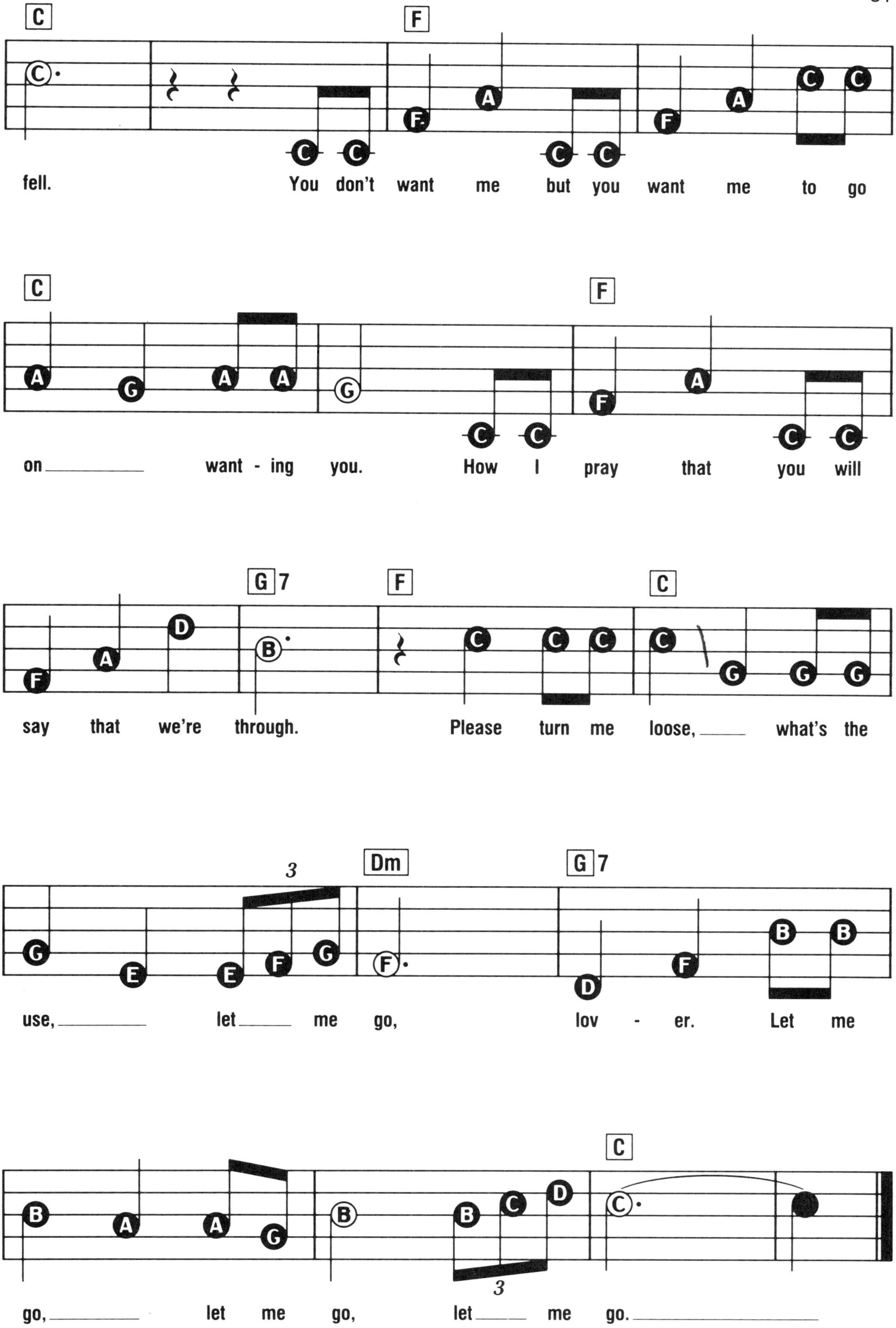
C F
fell. You don't want me but you want me to go
C F
on want - ing you. How I pray that you will
G7 F C
say that we're through. Please turn me loose, what's the
Dm G7
use, let me go, lov - er. Let me
C
go, let me go, let me go.

Living Doll

Regi-Sound Program: 9
Rhythm: Rock

Words and Music by
Lionel Bart

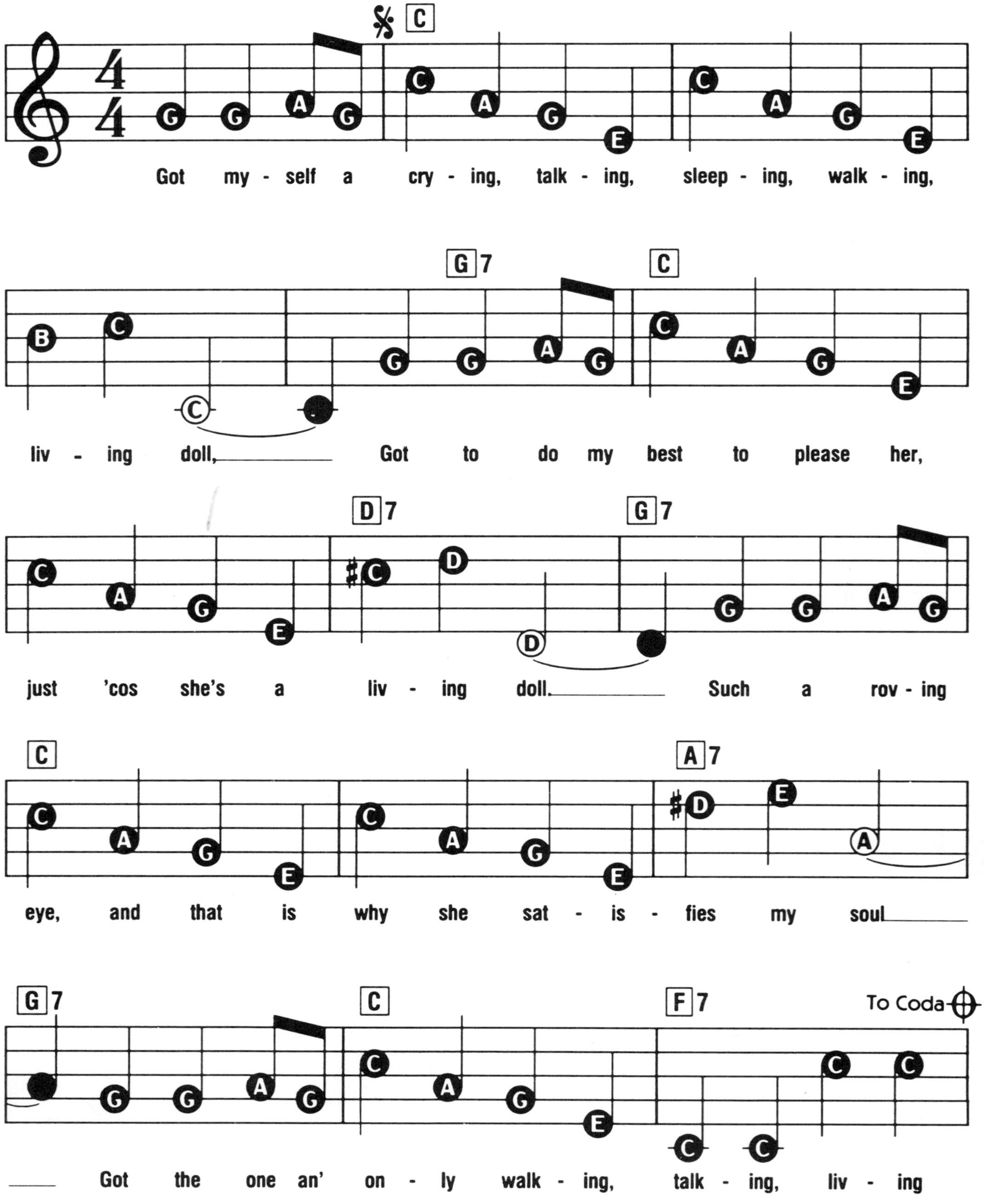

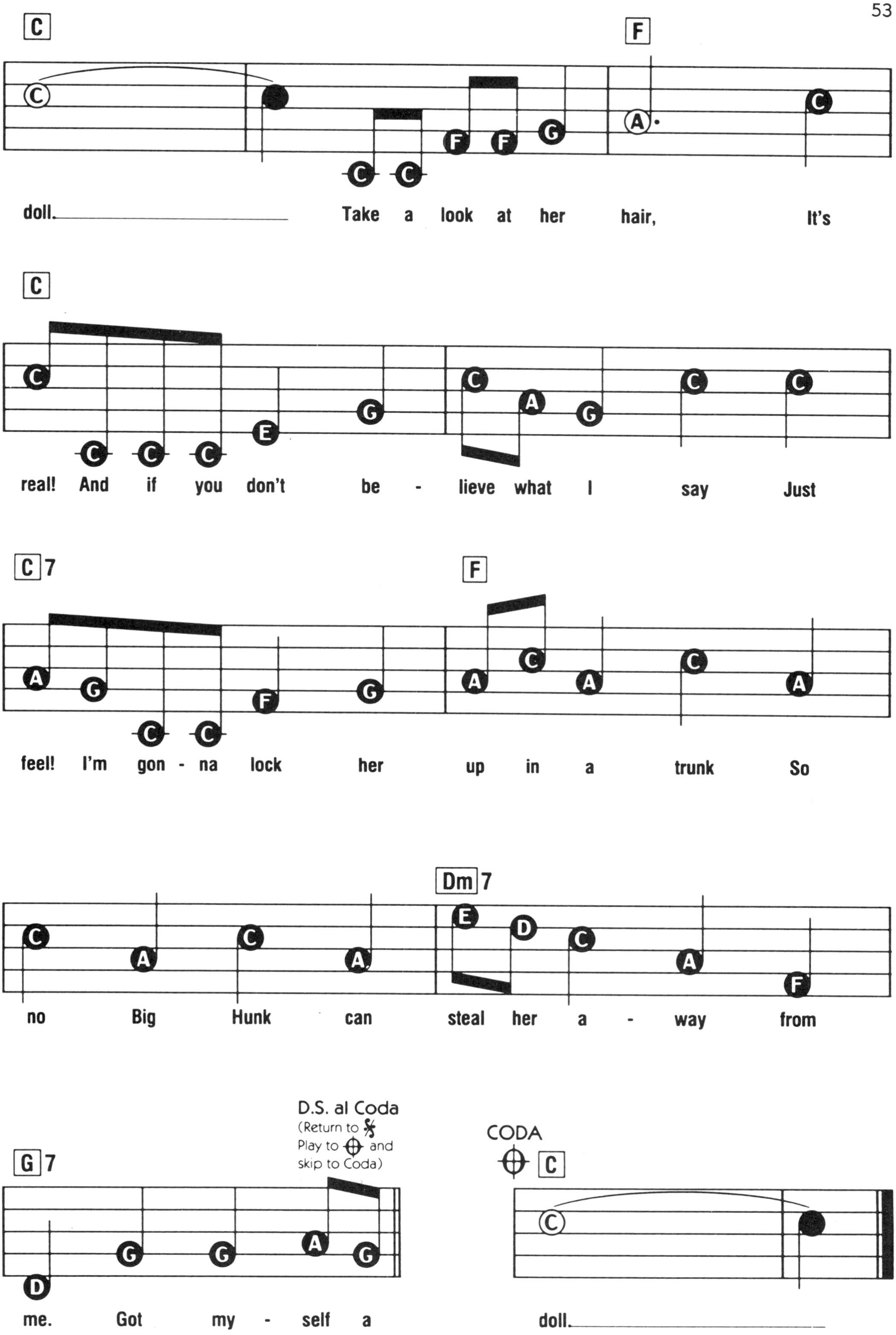
C
F
C C C C F F G A C
doll. Take a look at her hair, It's
C
C C C C E G C A G C C
real! And if you don't be - lieve what I say Just
C 7
F
A G C C F G A C A C A
feel! I'm gon - na lock her up in a trunk So
Dm 7
C A C A E D C A F
no Big Hunk can steal her a - way from
D.S. al Coda
(Return to 𝄋
Play to ⊕ and
skip to Coda)
G 7
D G G A G
me. Got my - self a
CODA
C
C
doll.

Love Is A Many Splendoured Thing

Regi-Sound Program: 9
Rhythm: Swing

Words by Paul Francis Webster
Music by Sammy Fain

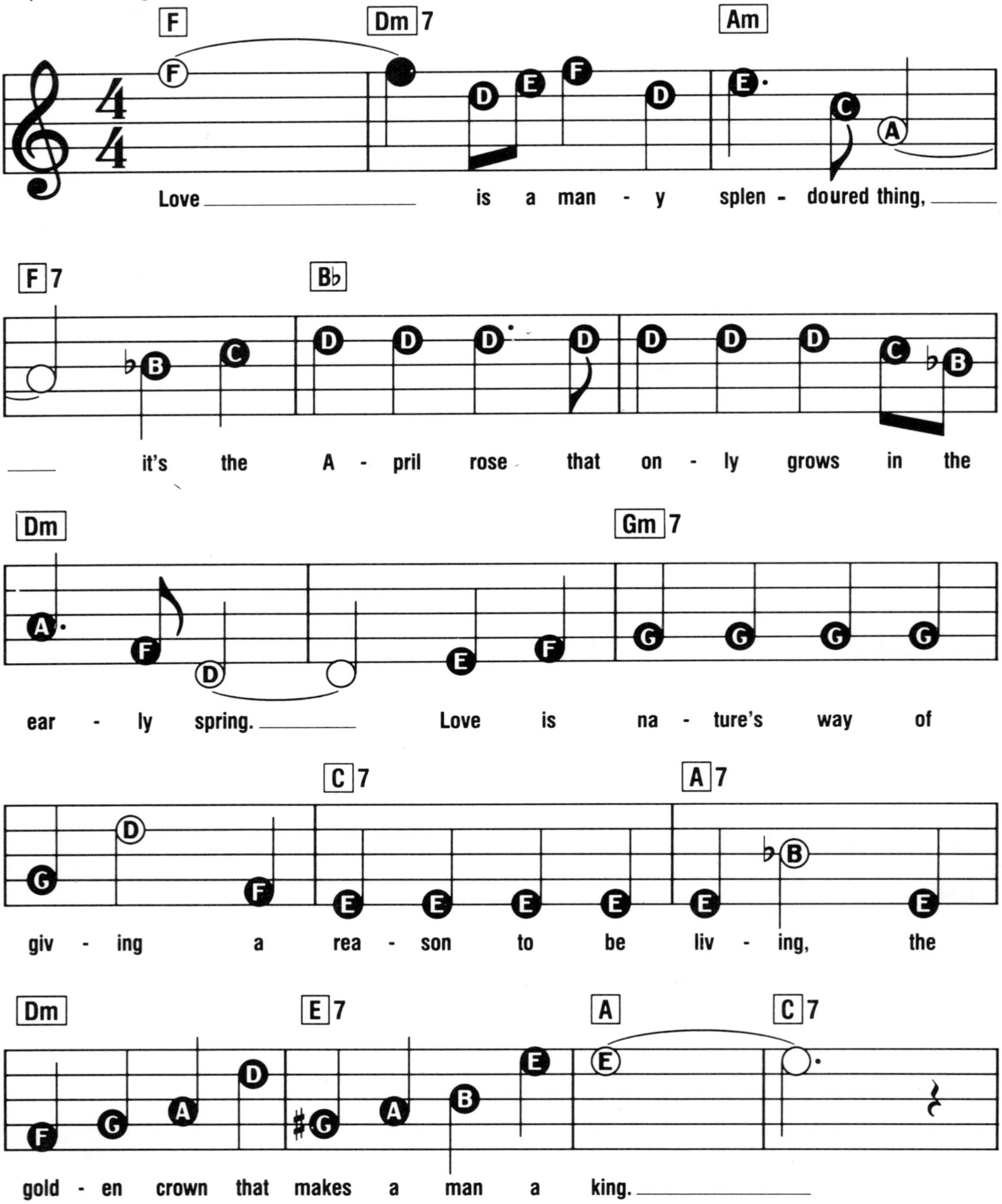

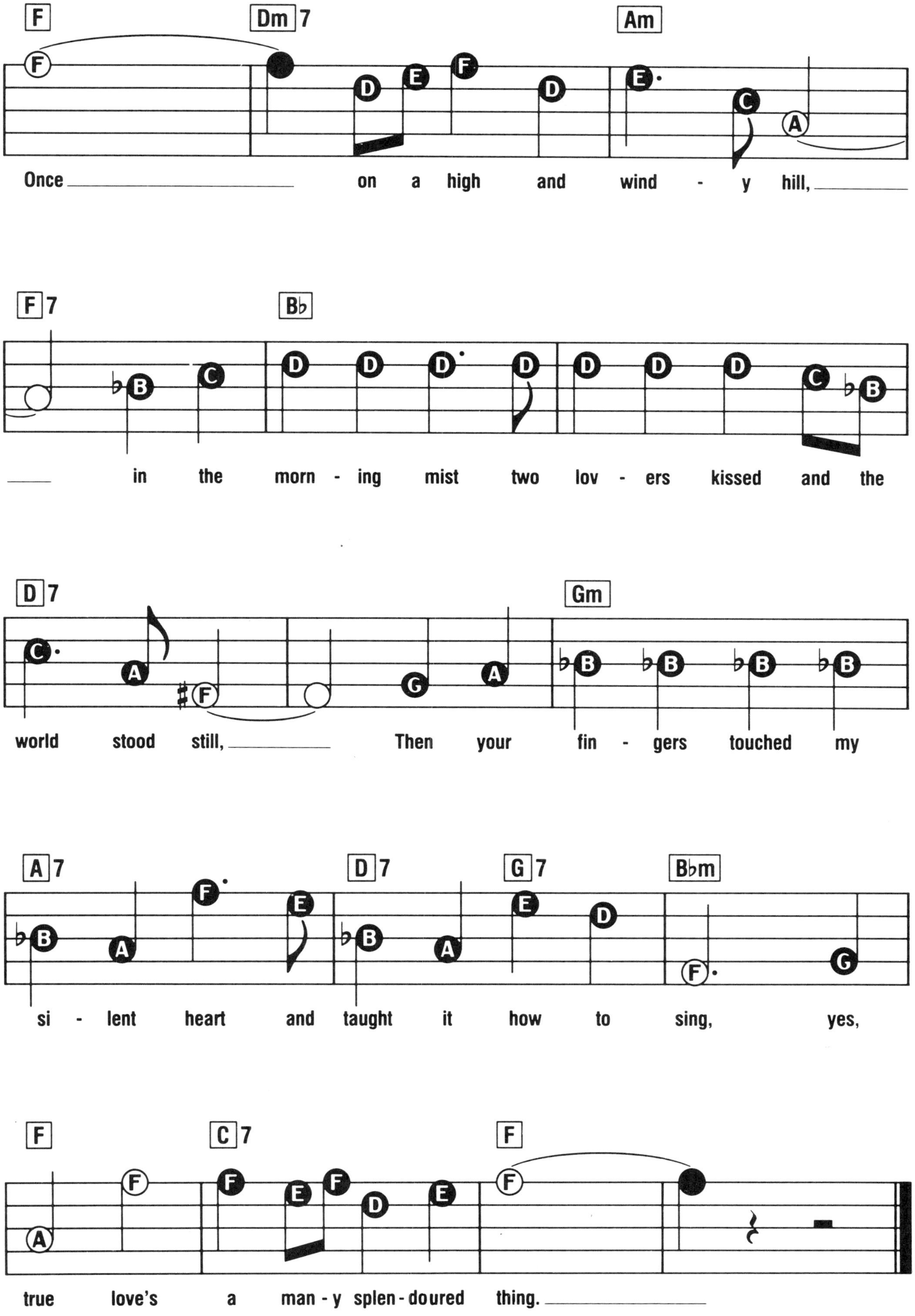
F Dm7 Am
Once on a high and wind - y hill,
F7 B♭
in the morn - ing mist two lov - ers kissed and the
D7 Gm
world stood still, Then your fin - gers touched my
A7 D7 G7 B♭m
si - lent heart and taught it how to sing, yes,
F C7 F
true love's a man - y splen - doured thing.

Love Me Tender

Regi-Sound Program: 9
Rhythm: Fox Trot

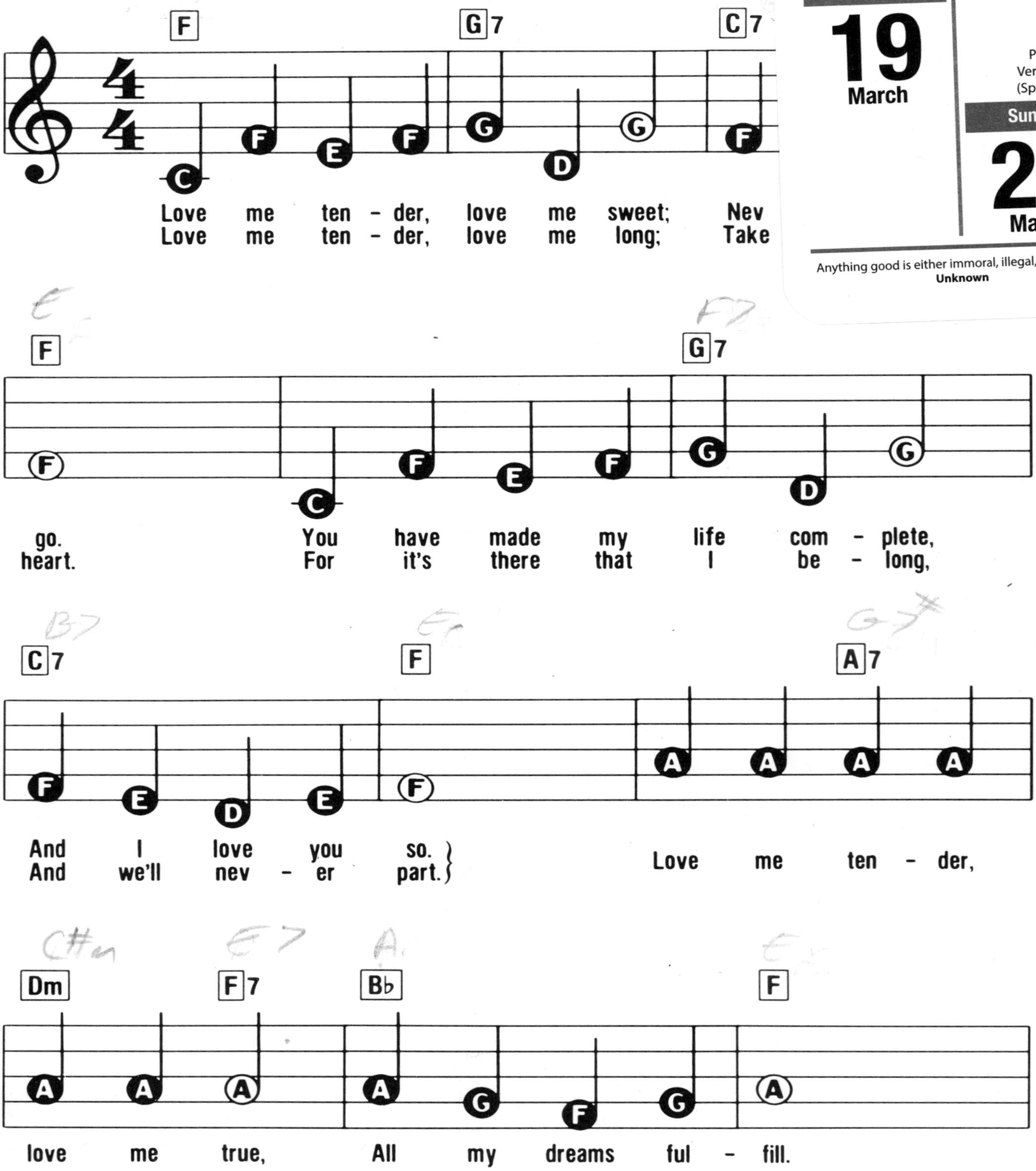

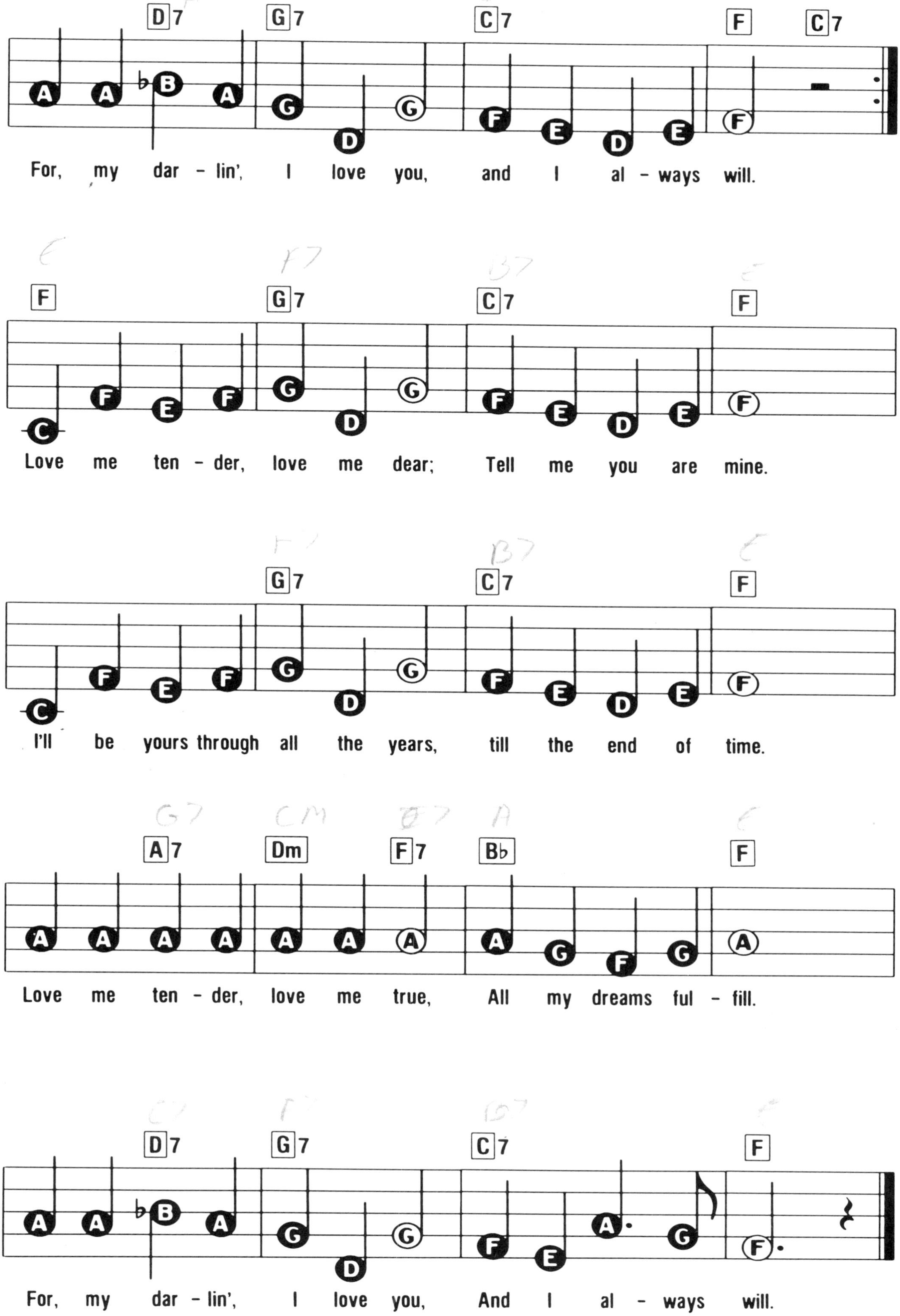
D7 G7 C7 F C7
For, my dar - lin', I love you, and I al - ways will.
F G7 C7 F
Love me ten - der, love me dear; Tell me you are mine.
G7 C7 F
I'll be yours through all the years, till the end of time.
A7 Dm F7 B♭ F
Love me ten - der, love me true, All my dreams ful - fill.
D7 G7 C7 F
For, my dar - lin', I love you, And I al - ways will.

Loving You

Regi-Sound Program: 4
Rhythm: Ballad or Slow Rock

Words and Music by
Mike Stoller and Jerry Leiber

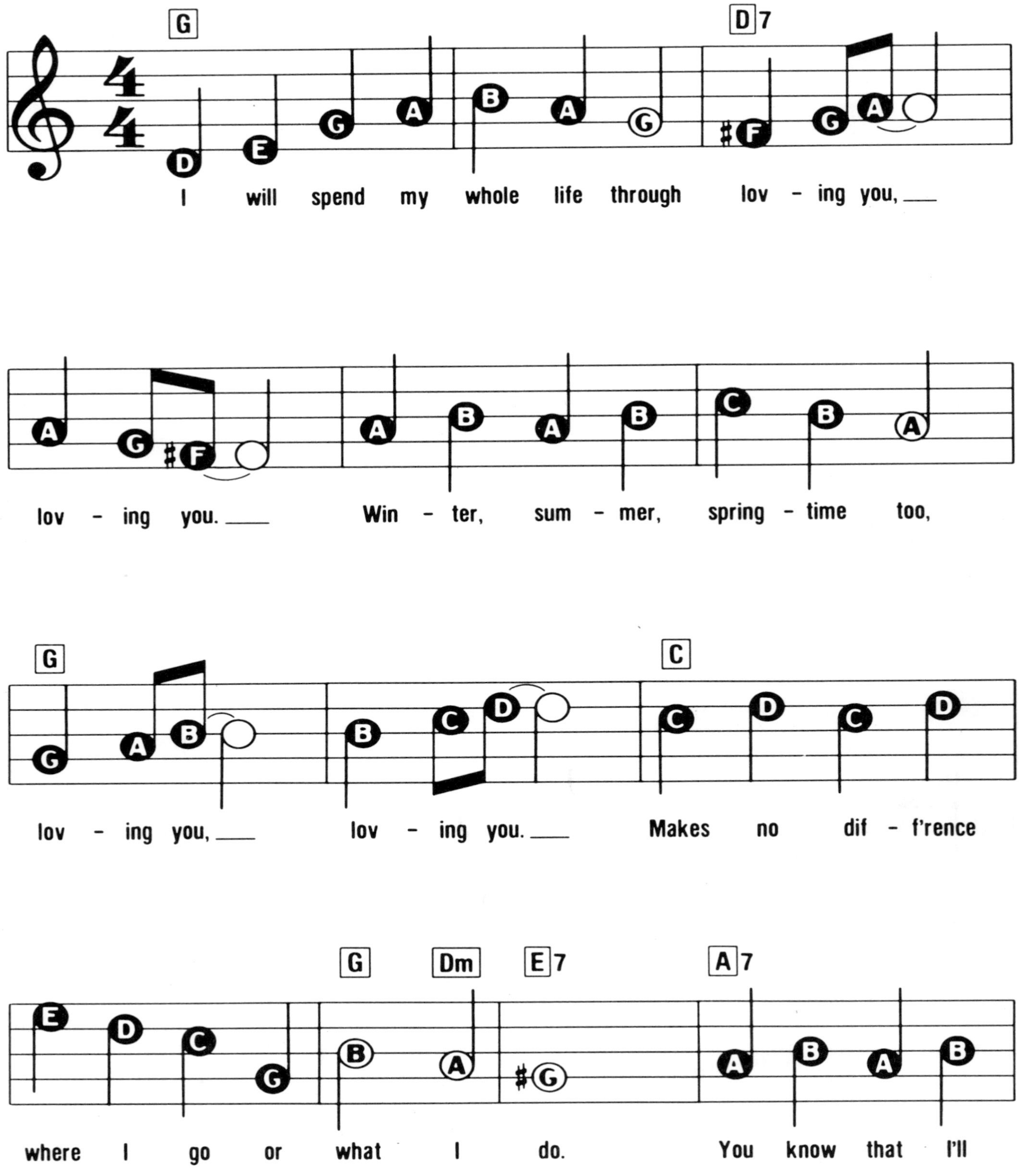
G
D7
I will spend my whole life through lov - ing you,
lov - ing you.
Win - ter, sum - mer, spring - time too,
G
C
lov - ing you,
lov - ing you.
Makes no dif - f'rence
G
Dm
E7
A7
where I go or what I do.
You know that I'll

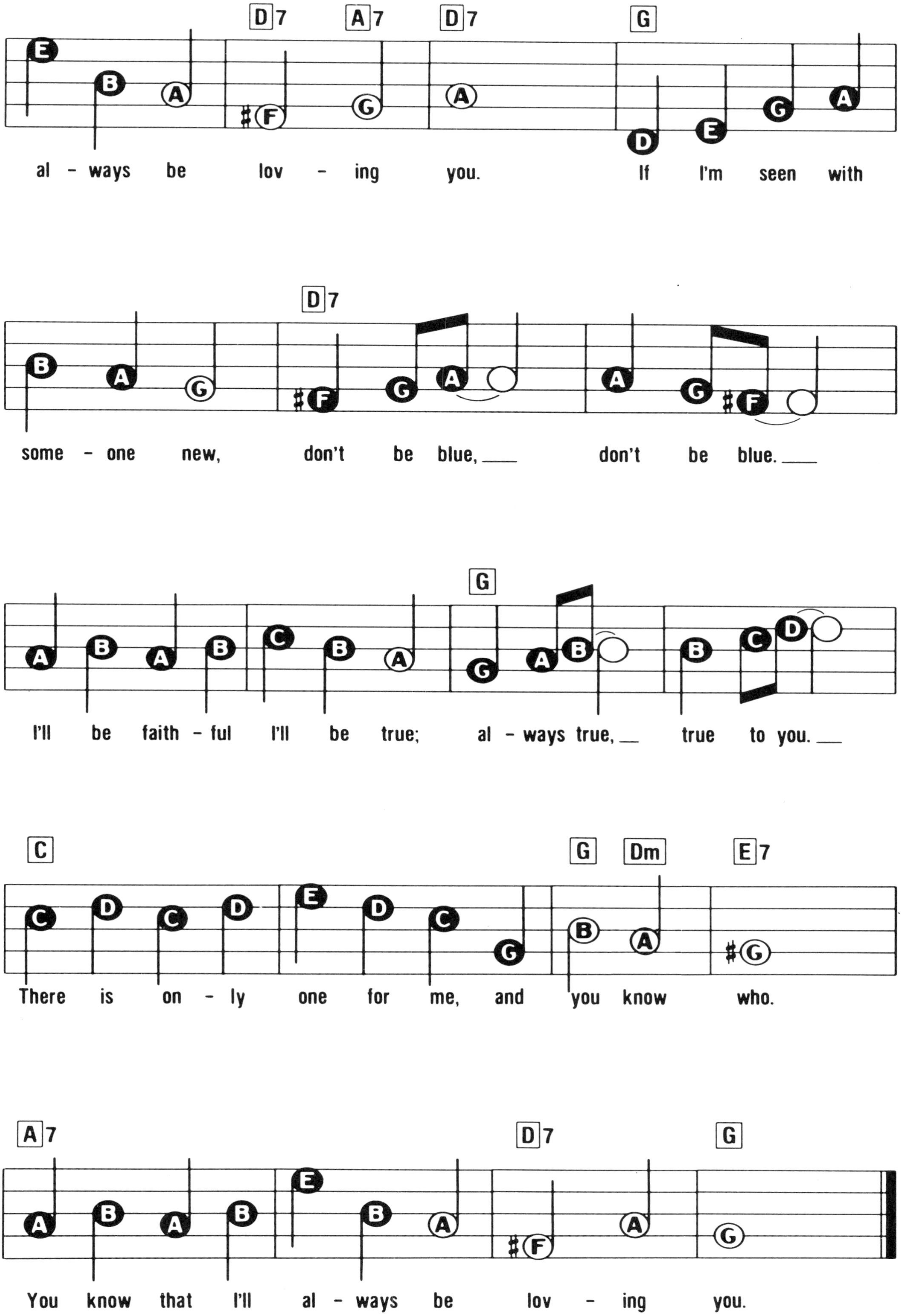
D7 A7 D7 G
al - ways be lov - ing you. If I'm seen with
D7
some - one new, don't be blue, ___ don't be blue. ___
G
I'll be faith - ful I'll be true; al - ways true, __ true to you. __
C G Dm E7
There is on - ly one for me, and you know who.
A7 D7 G
You know that I'll al - ways be lov - ing you.

May You Always

Regi-Sound Program: 10
Rhythm: Slow Rock or Ballad

Words and Music by
Larry Markes and Dick Charles

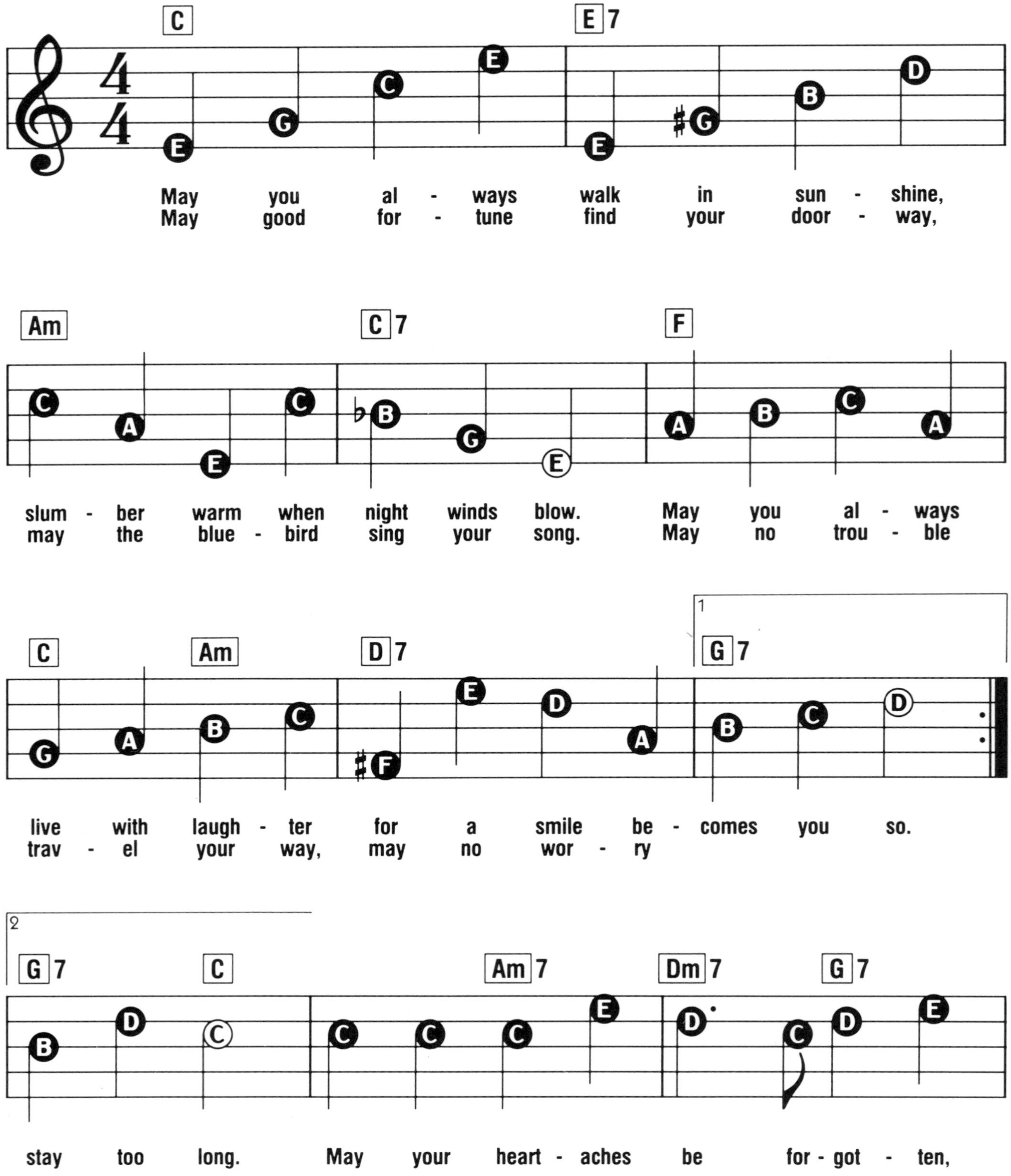

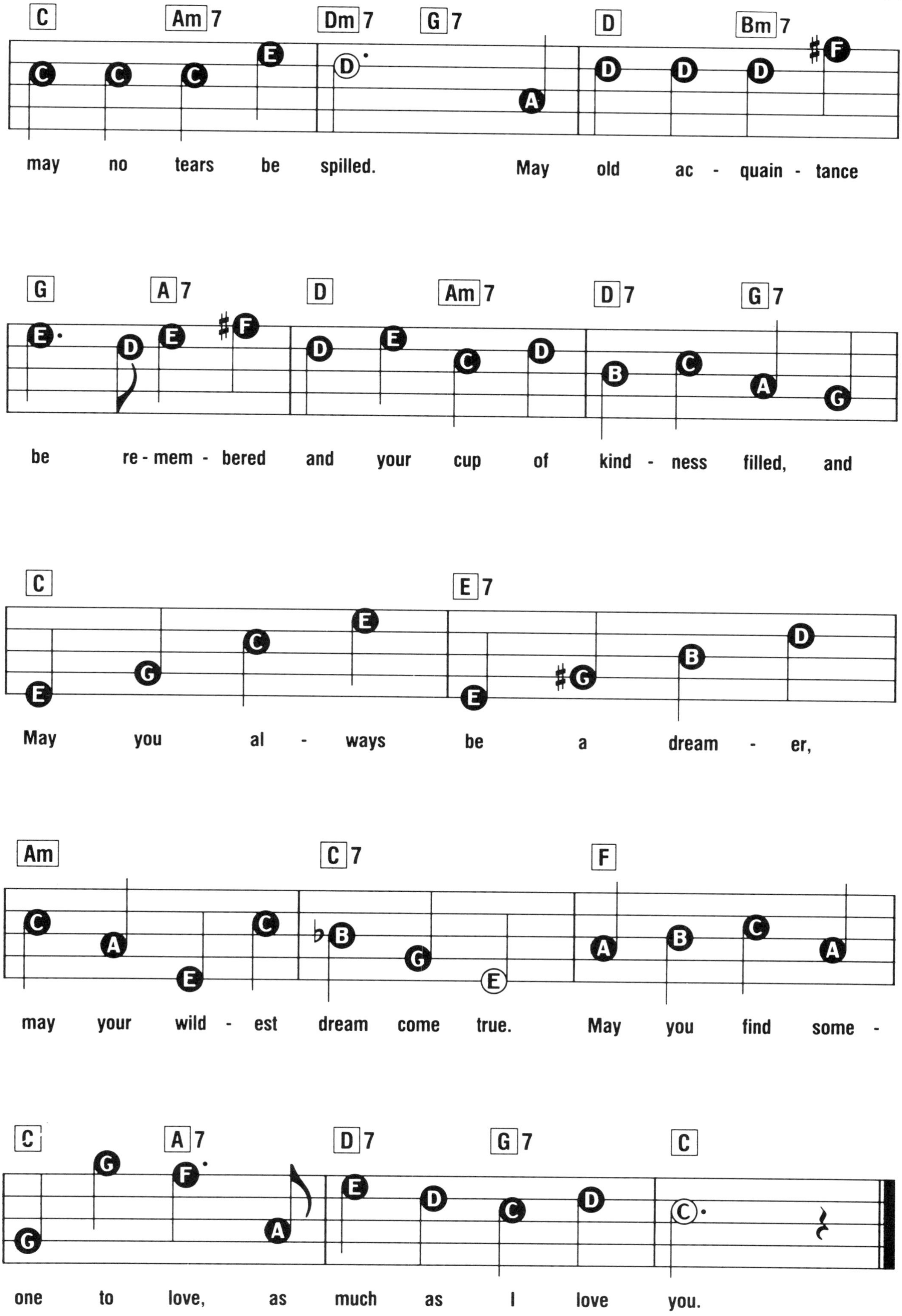
C Am7 Dm7 G7 D Bm7
may no tears be spilled. May old ac - quain - tance
G A7 D Am7 D7 G7
be re - mem - bered and your cup of kind - ness filled, and
C E7
May you al - ways be a dream - er,
Am C7 F
may your wild - est dream come true. May you find some -
C A7 D7 G7 C
one to love, as much as I love you.

My Love And Devotion

Regi-Sound Program: 5
Rhythm: Ballad or Fox Trot

Words and Music by
Milton Carson

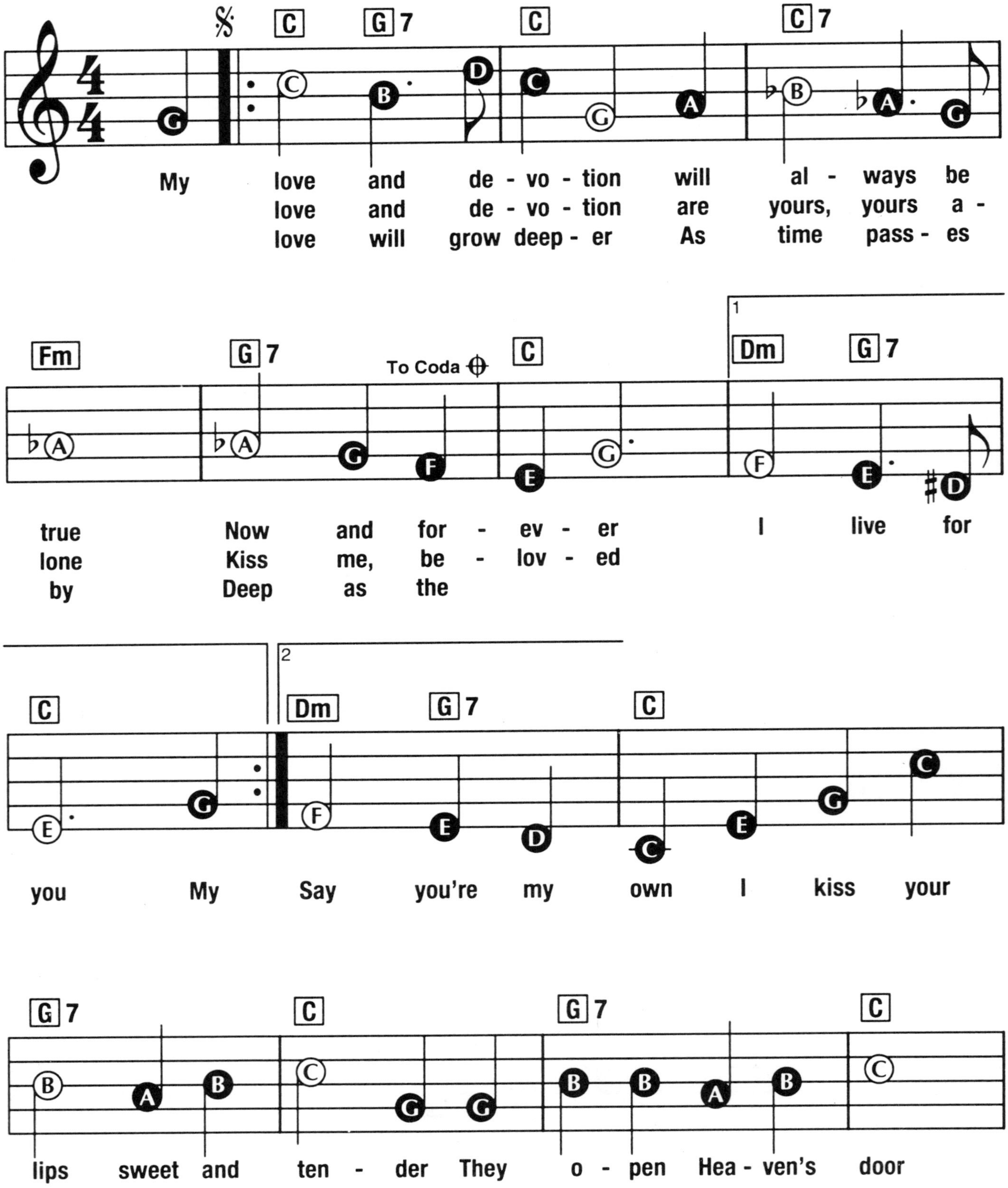

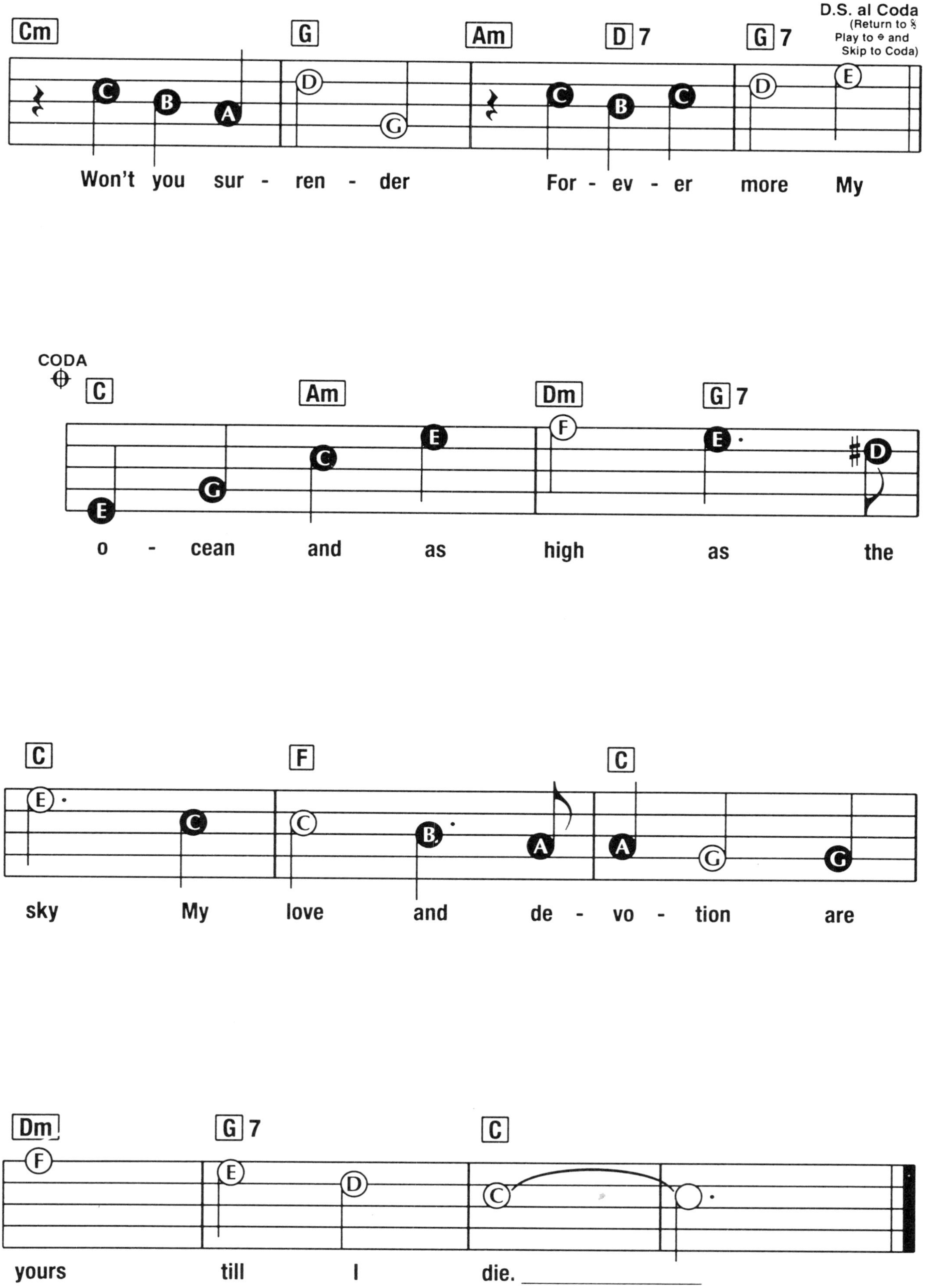
D.S. al Coda
(Return to 𝄋
Play to ⊕ and
Skip to Coda)
Cm G Am D7 G7
Won't you sur - ren - der For - ev - er more My
CODA
C Am Dm G7
o - cean and as high as the
C F C
sky My love and de - vo - tion are
Dm G7 C
yours till I die.

My One And Only Love

Regi-Sound Program: 2
Rhythm: Ballad or Fox Trot

Words by Robert Mellin
Music by Guy Wood

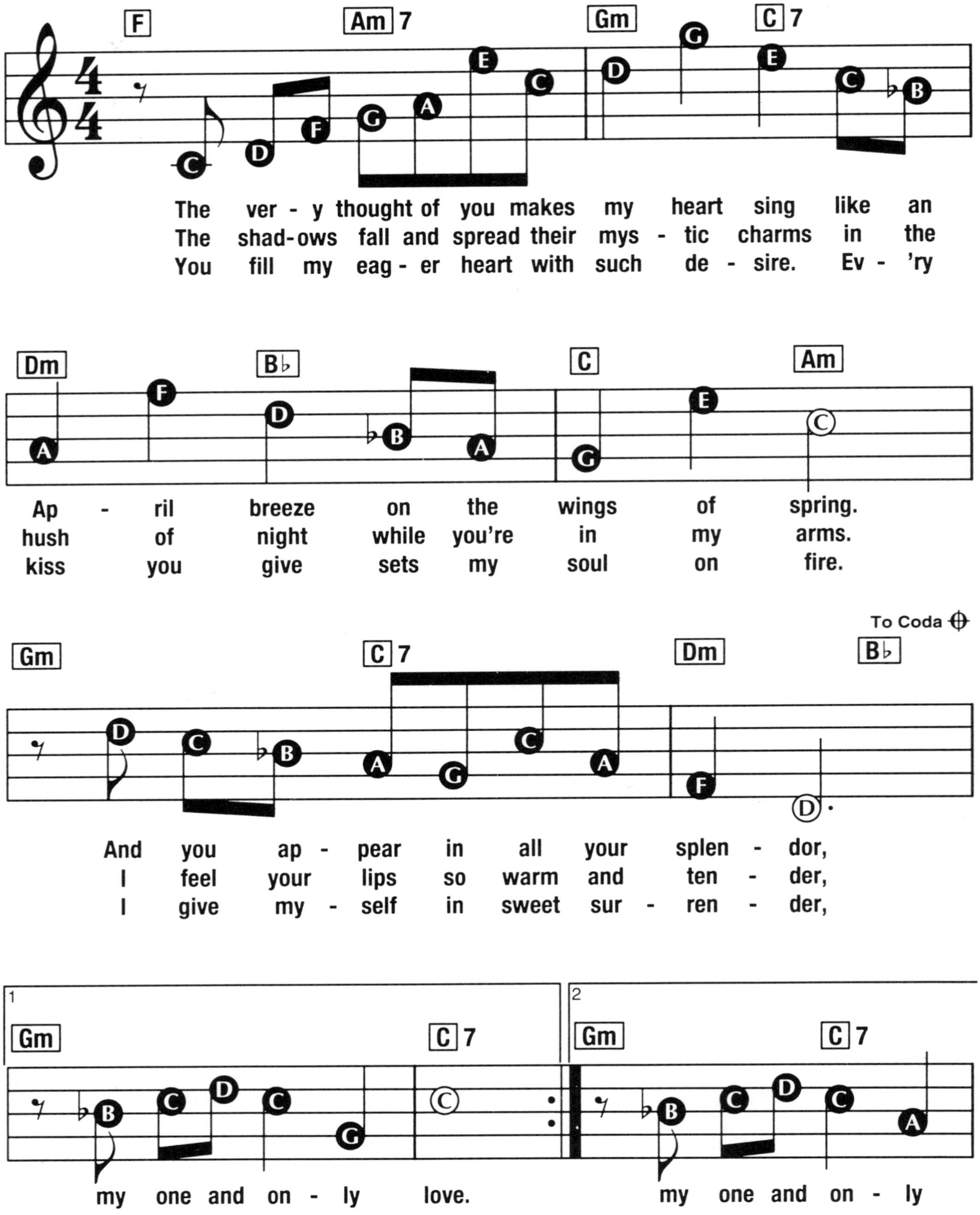
F Am7 Gm C7
The very - y thought of you makes my heart sing like an
The shad-ows fall and spread their mys - tic charms in the
You fill my eag - er heart with such de - sire. Ev - 'ry
Dm B♭ C Am
Ap - ril breeze on the wings of spring.
hush of night while you're in my arms.
kiss you give sets my soul on fire.
To Coda
Gm C7 Dm B♭
And you ap - pear in all your splen - dor,
I feel your lips so warm and ten - der,
I give my - self in sweet sur - ren - der,
1
Gm C7
my one and on - ly love.
2
Gm C7
my one and on - ly

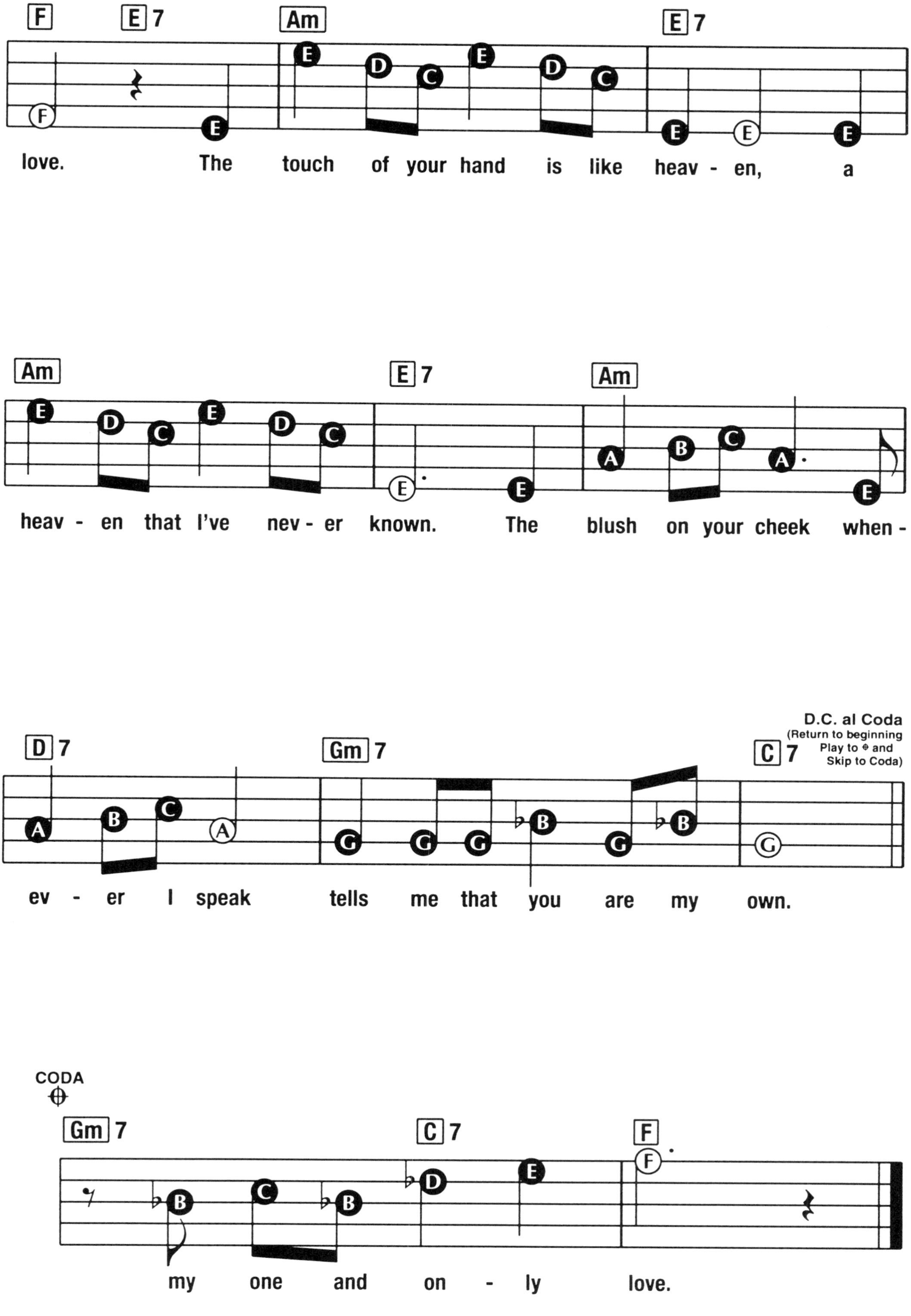
F E7 Am E7
love. The touch of your hand is like heav - en, a
Am E7 Am
heav - en that I've nev - er known. The blush on your cheek when -
D7 Gm7 C7
D.C. al Coda
(Return to beginning
Play to ⊕ and
Skip to Coda)
ev - er I speak tells me that you are my own.
CODA
Gm7 C7 F
my one and on - ly love.

Only Sixteen

Regi-Sound Program: 1
Rhythm: Fox Trot or Ballad

Words and Music by
Barbara Campbell

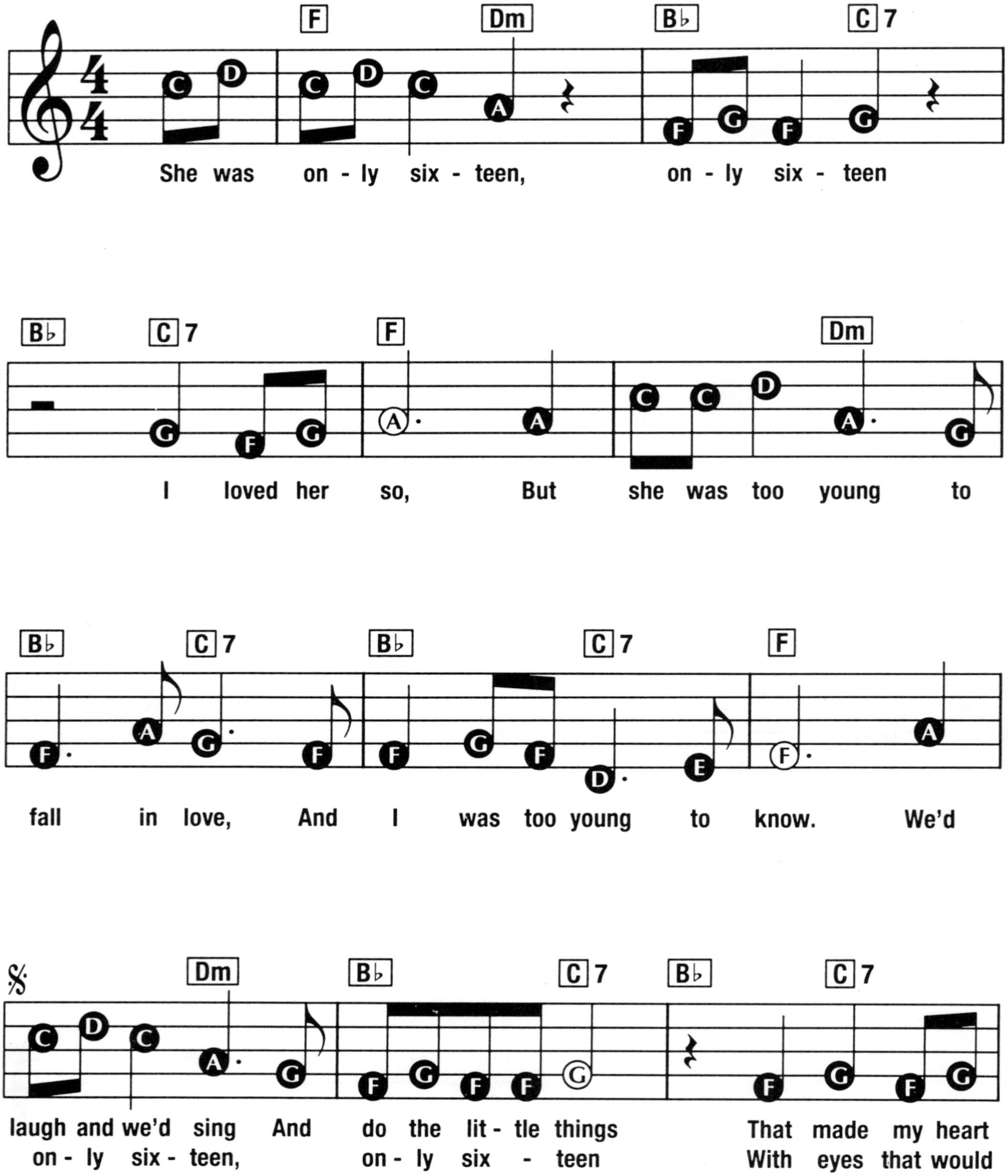
F Dm B♭ C7
She was on - ly six - teen, on - ly six - teen
B♭ C7 F Dm
I loved her so, But she was too young to
B♭ C7 B♭ C7 F
fall in love, And I was too young to know. We'd
Dm B♭ C7 B♭ C7
laugh and we'd sing And do the lit - tle things That made my heart
on - ly six - teen, on - ly six - teen With eyes that would

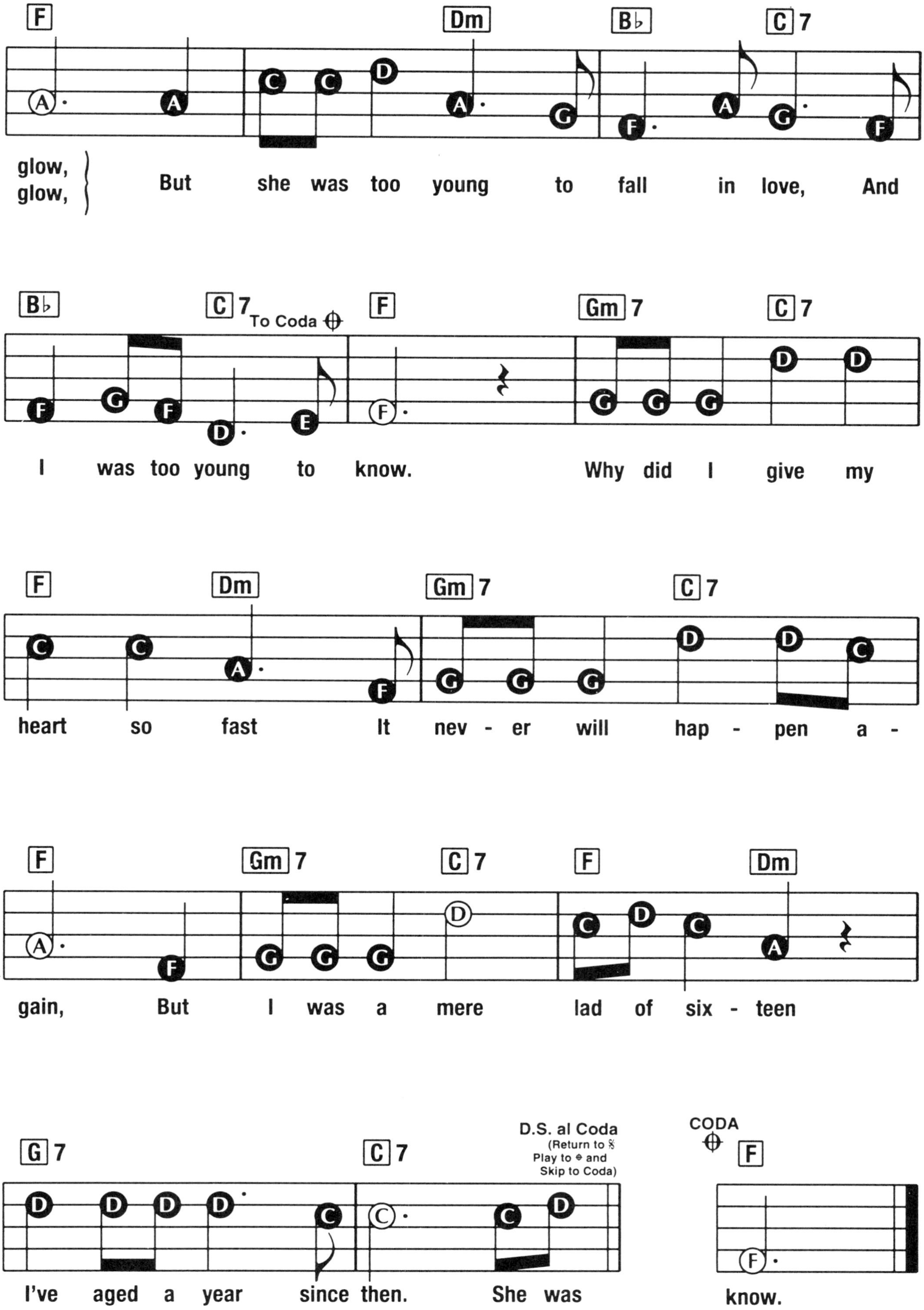
F Dm B♭ C7
glow, glow, But she was too young to fall in love, And
B♭ C7 To Coda F Gm7 C7
I was too young to know. Why did I give my
F Dm Gm7 C7
heart so fast It nev - er will hap - pen a -
F Gm7 C7 F Dm
gain, But I was a mere lad of six - teen
G7 C7
I've aged a year since then. She was
D.S. al Coda
(Return to 𝄋 Play to ⊕ and Skip to Coda)
CODA
F
know.

Out Of Town

Regi-Sound Program: 4
Rhythm: Swing or Fox Trot

Words and Music by Leslie Bricusse
& Robin Beaumont

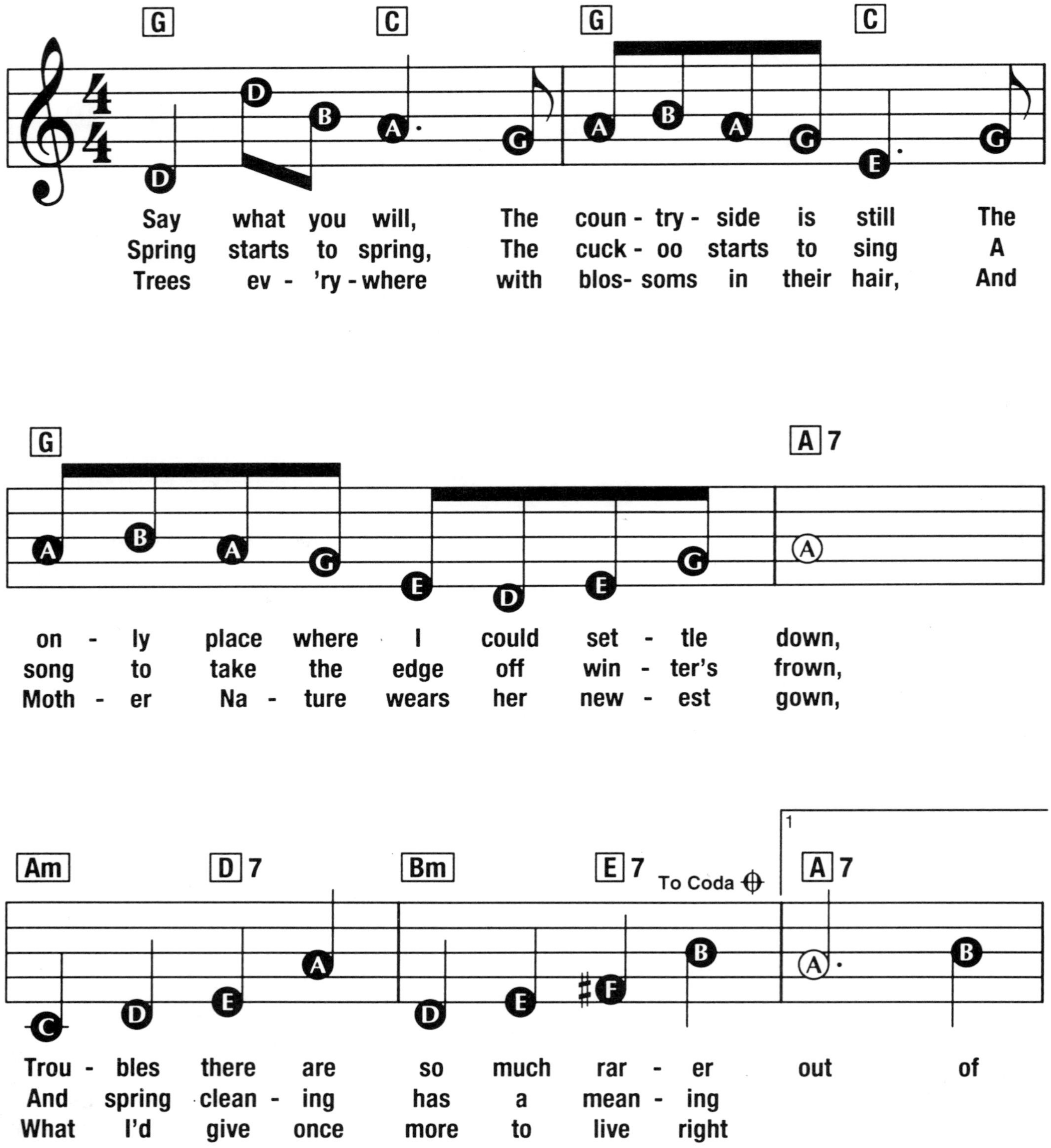
G C G C
Say what you will, The coun - try - side is still The
Spring starts to spring, The cuck - oo starts to sing A
Trees ev - 'ry - where with blos- soms in their hair, And
G A7
on - ly place where I could set - tle down,
song to take the edge off win - ter's frown,
Moth - er Na - ture wears her new - est gown,
Am D7 Bm E7 To Coda 1 A7
Trou - bles there are so much rar - er out of
And spring clean - ing has a mean - ing
What I'd give once more to live right

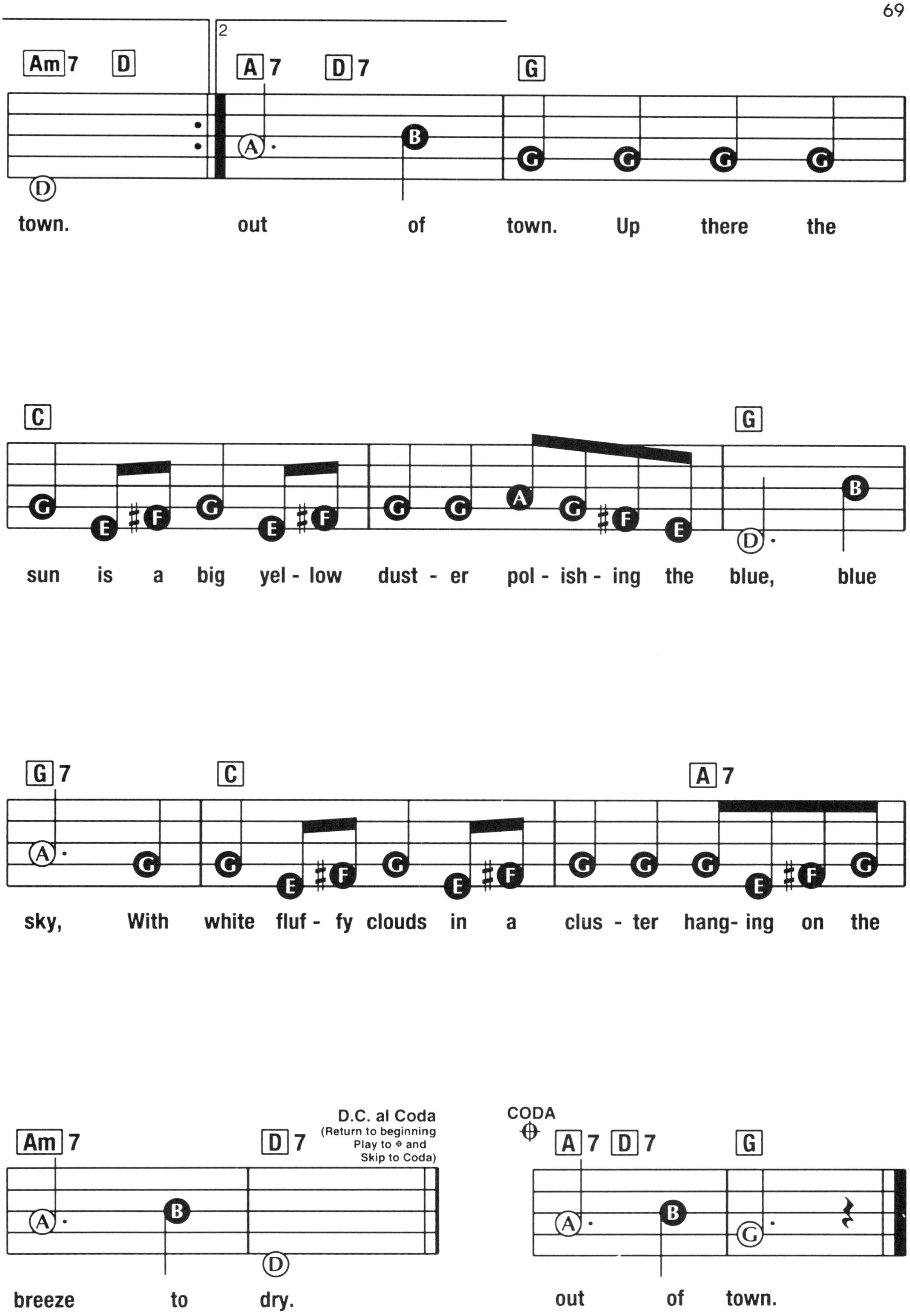
Am7 D
2
A7 D7 G
town. out of town. Up there the
C G
sun is a big yel - low dust - er pol - ish - ing the blue, blue
G7 C A7
sky, With white fluf - fy clouds in a clus - ter hang- ing on the
Am7 D7
D.C. al Coda
(Return to beginning
Play to ⊕ and
Skip to Coda)
breeze to dry.
CODA
A7 D7 G
out of town.

Remember You're Mine

Regi-Sound Program: 3
Rhythm: Ballad or Fox Trot

Words and Music by Kall Mann
& Barnie Lowe

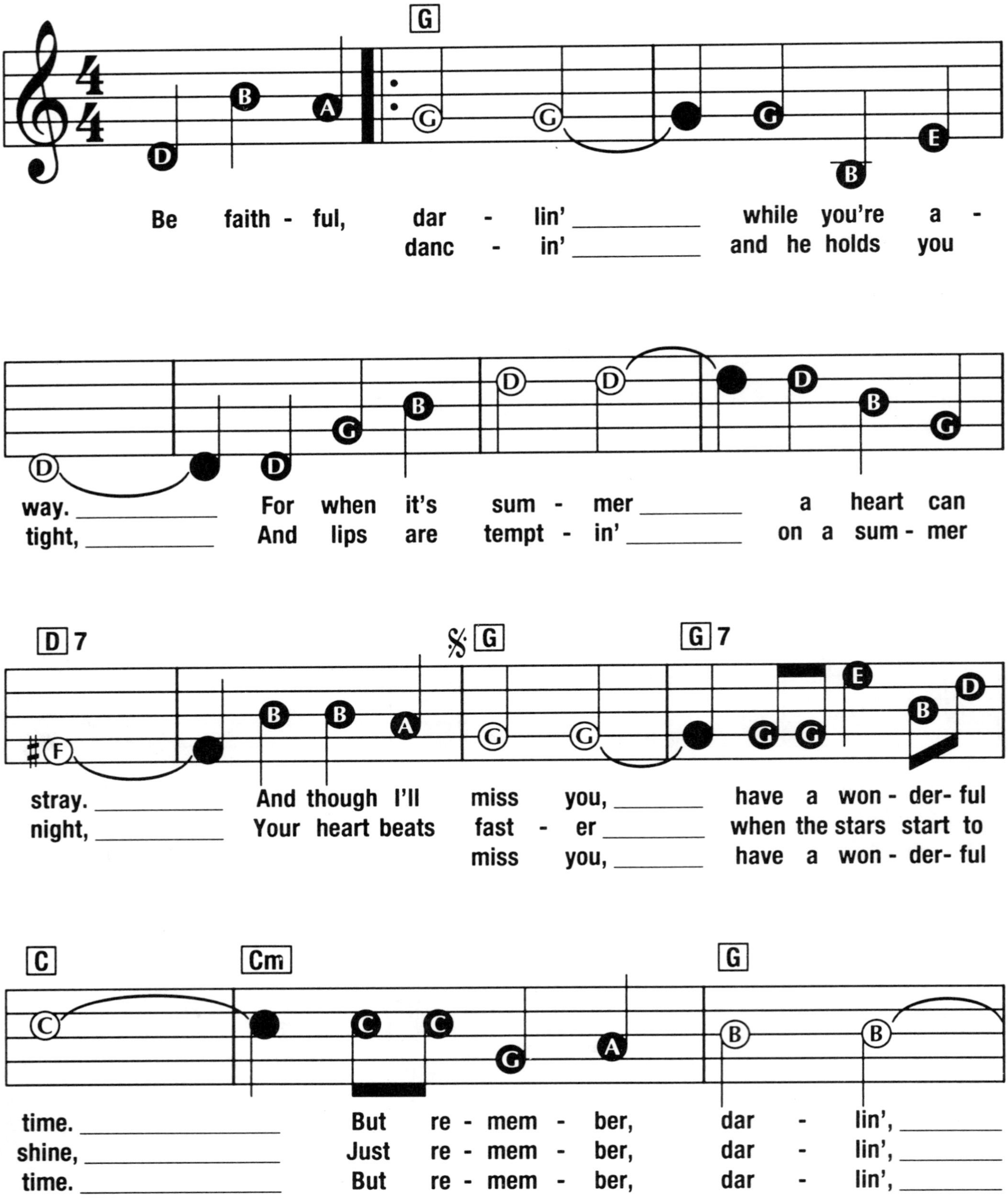
G
D B A G G B E
Be faith - ful, dar - lin' while you're a -
danc - in' and he holds you
D G B D D D B G
way. For when it's sum - mer a heart can
tight, And lips are tempt - in' on a sum - mer
D 7
G
G 7
F B B A G G G G E B D
stray. And though I'll miss you, have a won - der - ful
night, Your heart beats fast - er when the stars start to
miss you, have a won - der - ful
C
Cm
G
C C C G A B B
time. But re - mem - ber, dar - lin',
shine, Just re - mem - ber, dar - lin',
time. But re - mem - ber, dar - lin',

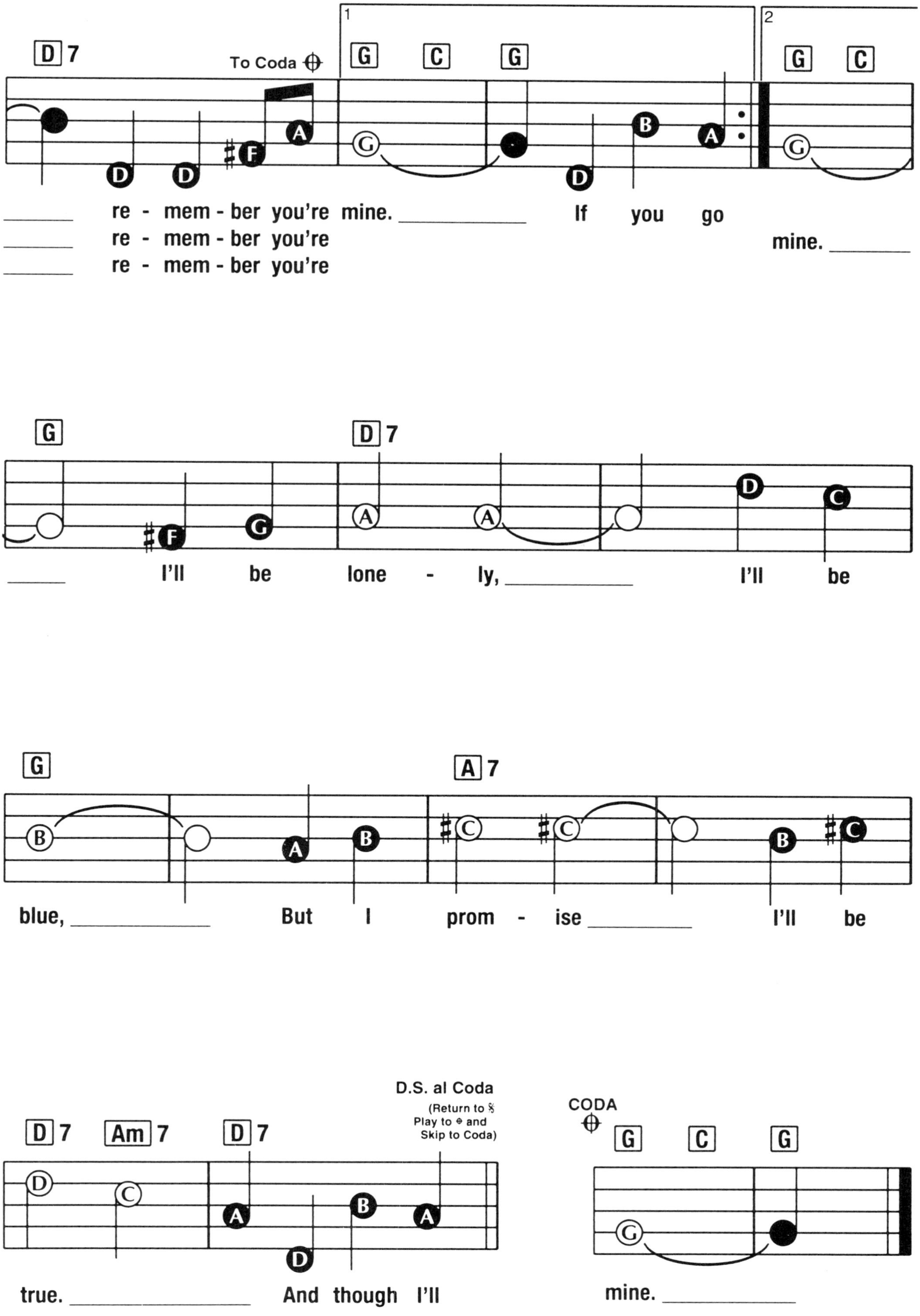
D7
To Coda
1
G C G
2
G C
re - mem - ber you're mine.
If you go
re - mem - ber you're
mine.
re - mem - ber you're
G
D7
I'll be lone - ly,
I'll be
G
A7
blue,
But I prom - ise
I'll be
D.S. al Coda
(Return to 𝄋 Play to ⊕ and Skip to Coda)
D7 Am7 D7
true.
And though I'll
CODA
G C G
mine.

Return To Me

Regi-Sound Program: 3
Rhythm: Latin

Words by Danny Di Minno
Music by Carmen Lombardo

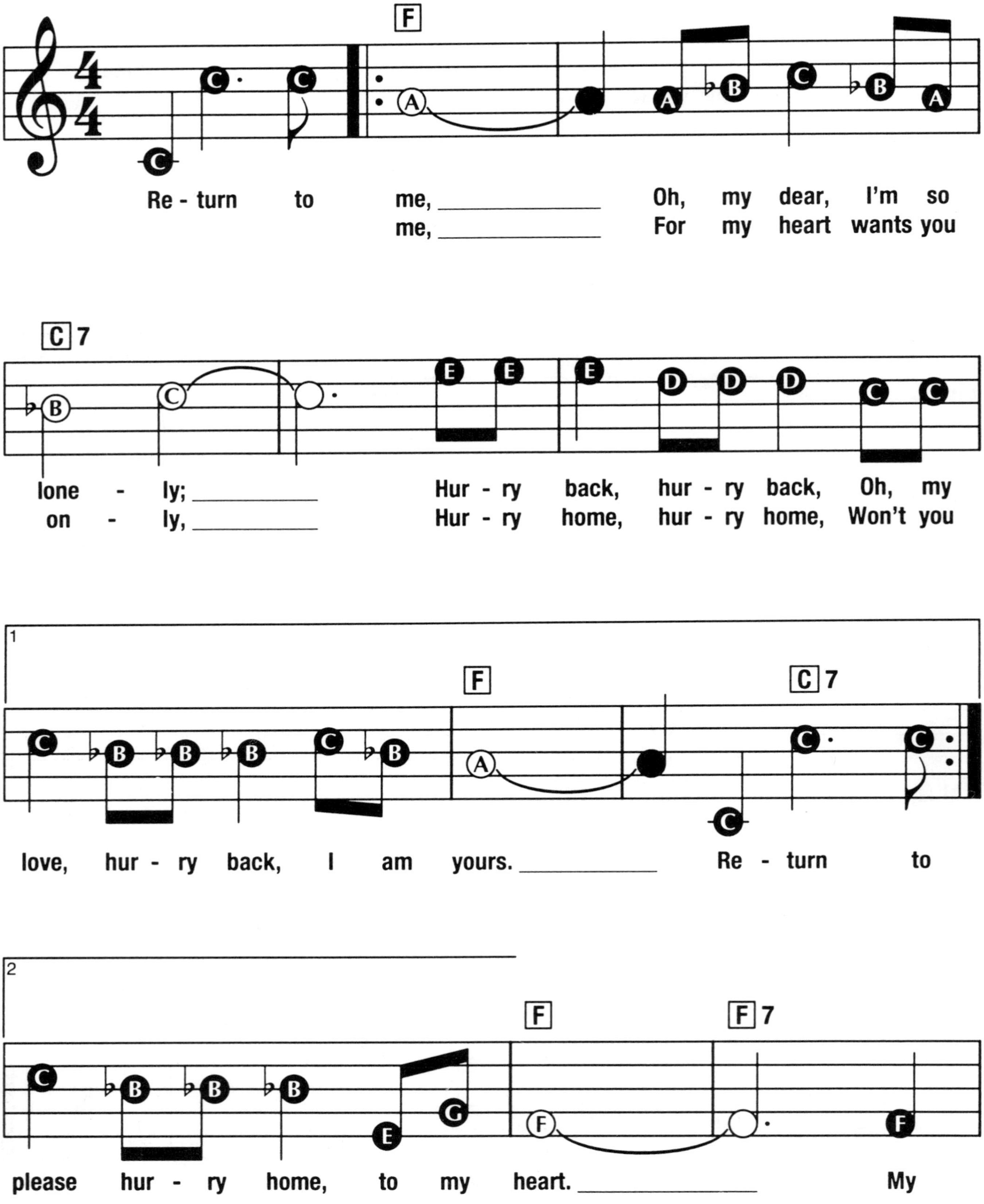
F
Re - turn to me, Oh, my dear, I'm so
me, For my heart wants you
C7
lone - ly; Hur - ry back, hur - ry back, Oh, my
on - ly, Hur - ry home, hur - ry home, Won't you
1
F
C7
love, hur - ry back, I am yours. Re - turn to
2
F
F7
please hur - ry home, to my heart. My

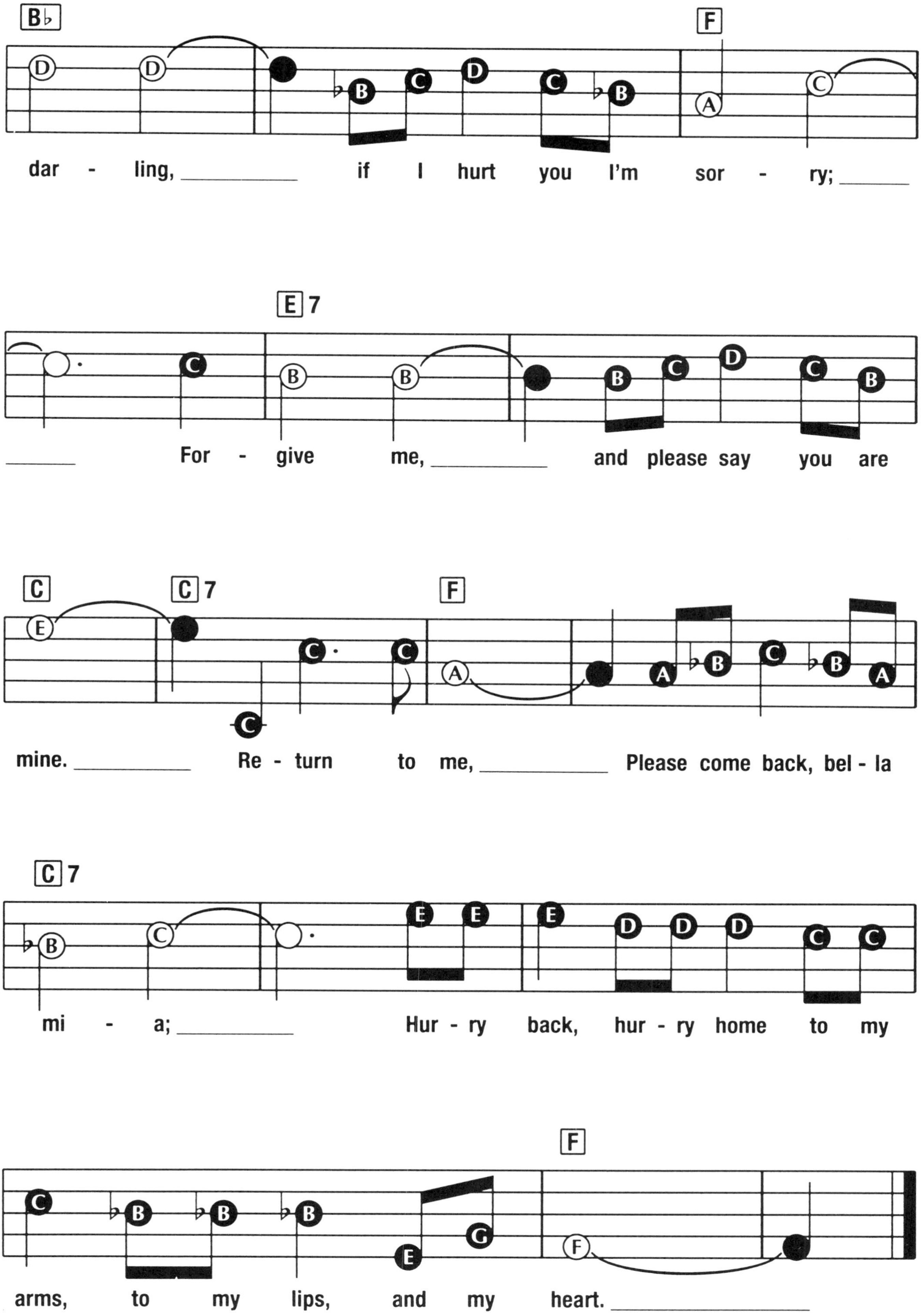
B♭
F
darling, if I hurt you I'm sorry;
E7
Forgive me, and please say you are
C
C7
F
mine. Return to me, Please come back, bella
C7
mia; Hurry back, hurry home to my
F
arms, to my lips, and my heart.

Secret Love

Regi-Sound Program: 9
Rhythm: Swing

Words by Paul Francis Webster
Music by Sammy Fain

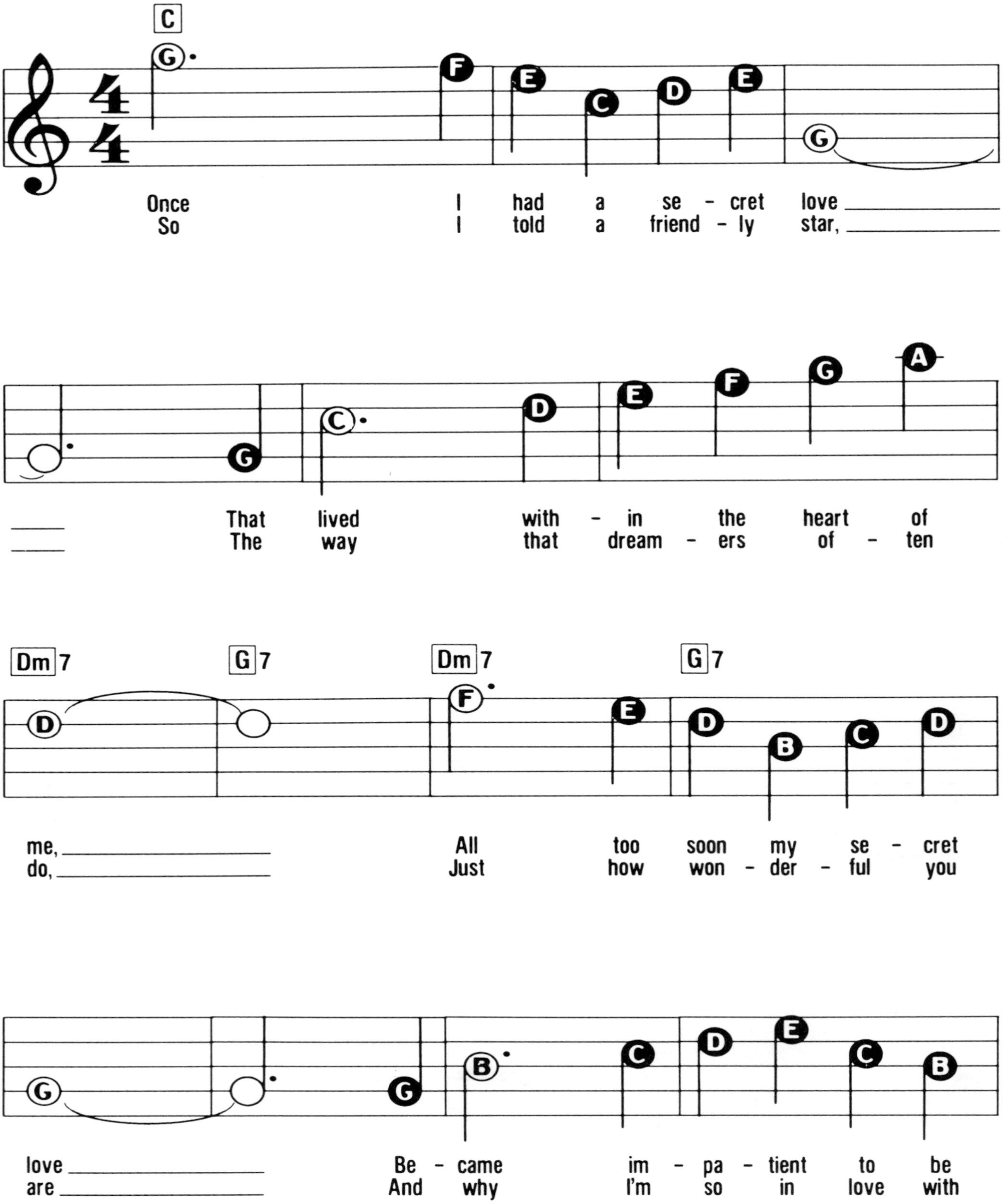
C
G F E C D E G G C D E F G A
Once I had a se - cret love
So I told a friend - ly star,
That lived with - in the heart of
The way that dream - ers of - ten
Dm7 G7 Dm7 G7
D F E D B C D
me, All too soon my se - cret
do, Just how won - der - ful you
G G B C D E C B
love Be - came im - pa - tient to be
are And why I'm so in love with

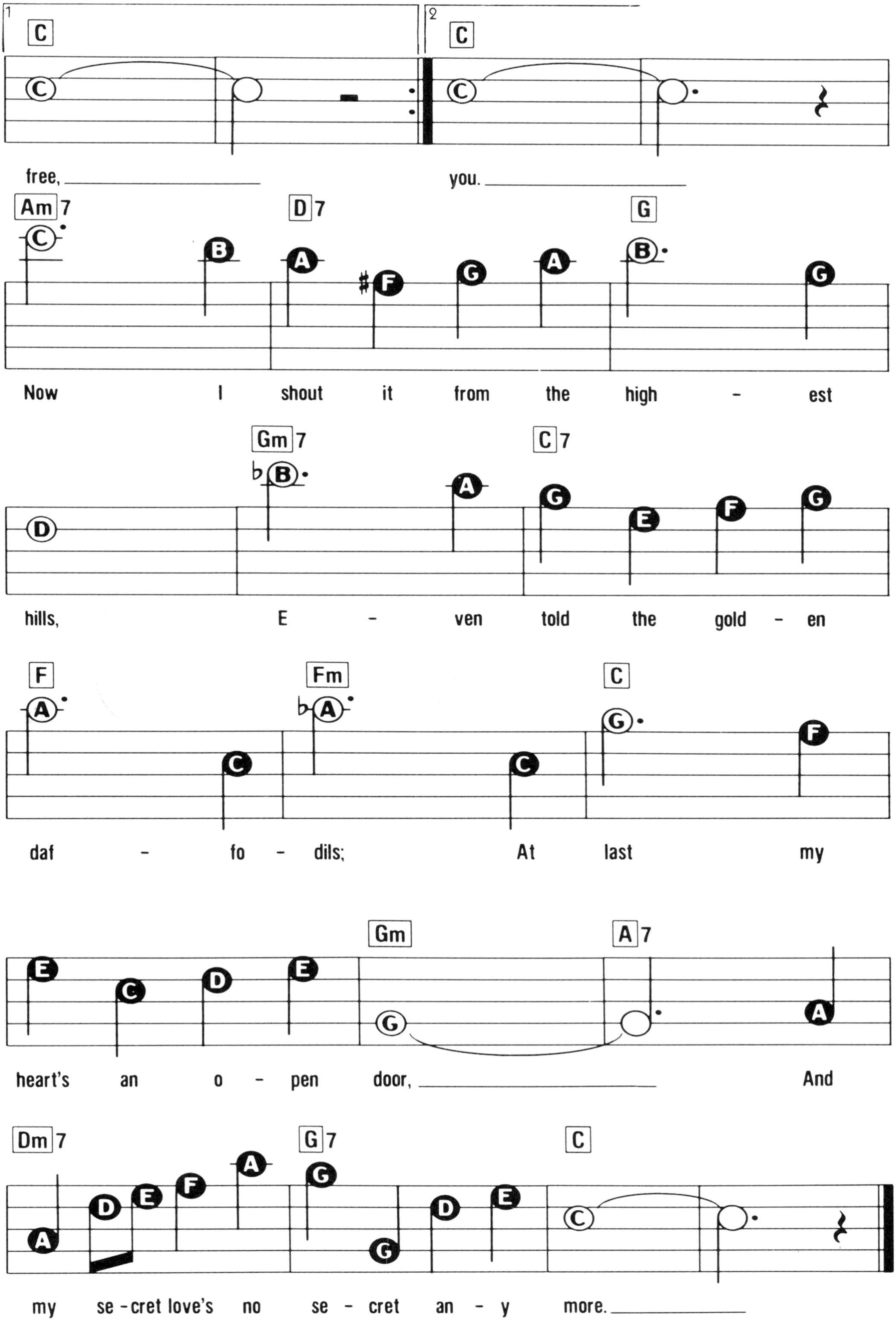
1 C
2 C
free, you.
Am7 D7 G
Now I shout it from the high - est
Gm7 C7
hills, E - ven told the gold - en
F Fm C
daf - fo - dils; At last my
Gm A7
heart's an o - pen door, And
Dm7 G7 C
my se - cret love's no se - cret an - y more.

The Story Of Tina

Regi-Sound Program: 1
Rhythm: Waltz

Words by Christopher Hassell
Music by D Katrivanou

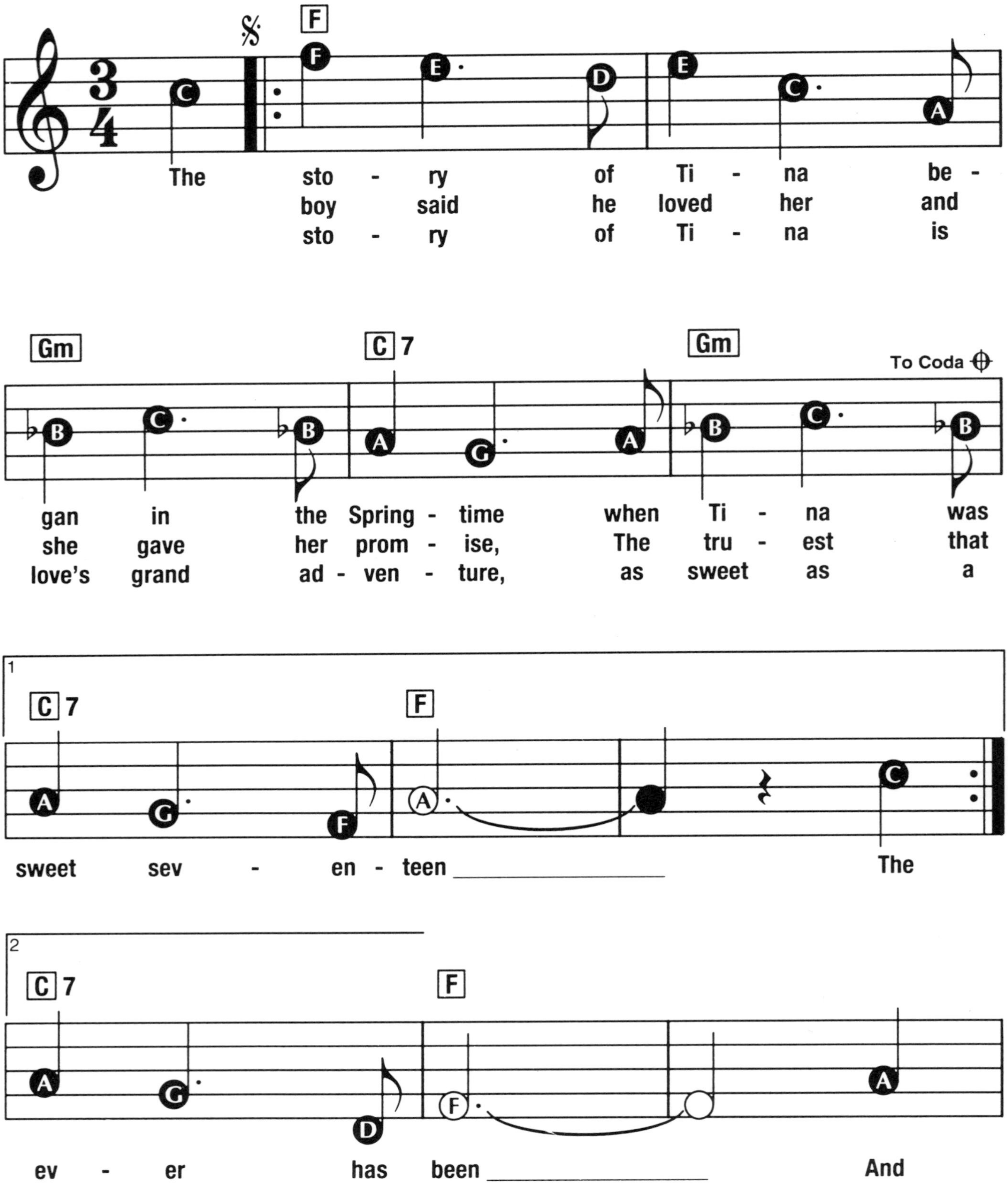

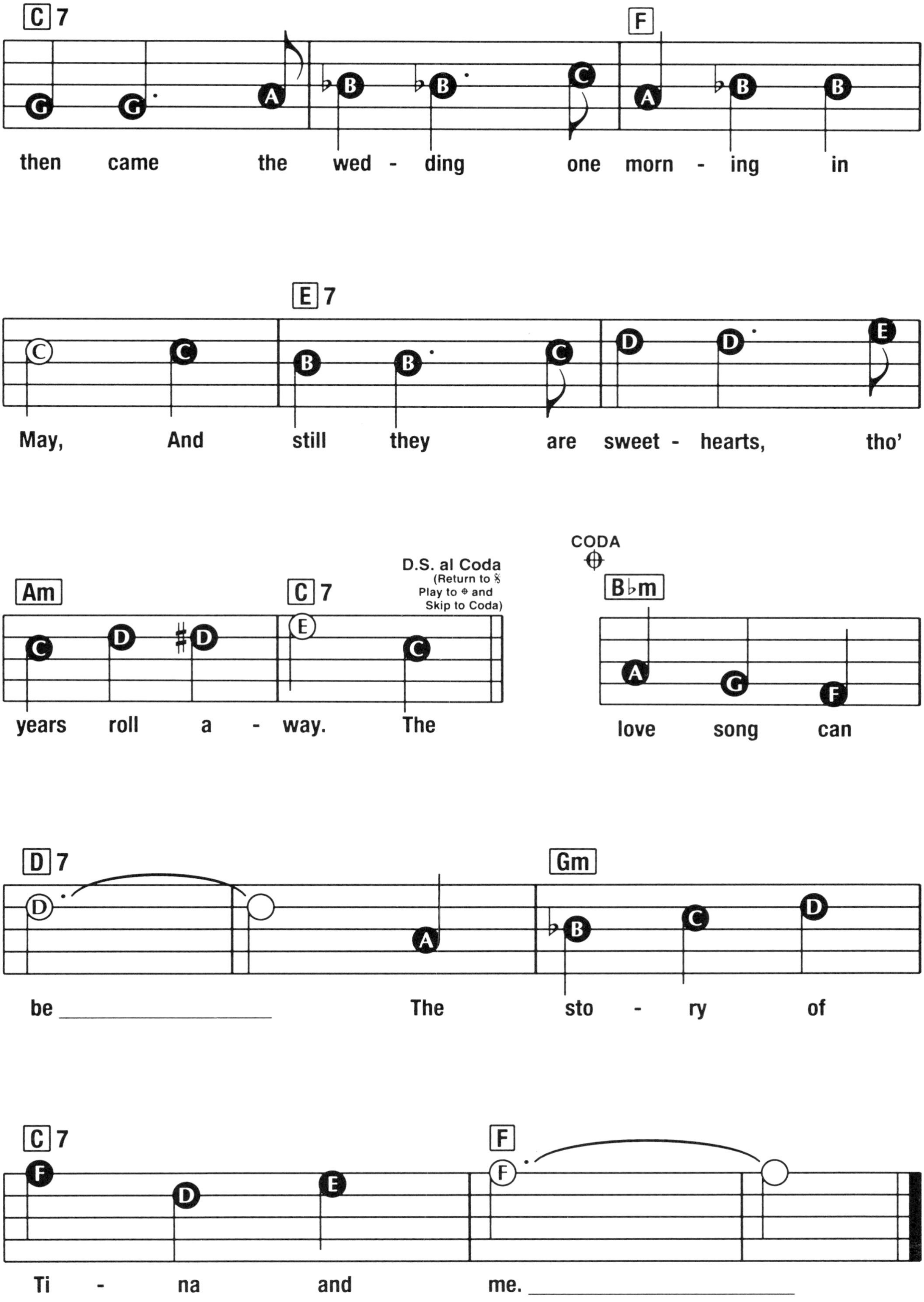
C7
then came the wed - ding one
F
morn - ing in
May, And
E7
still they are
sweet - hearts, tho'
Am
years roll a -
C7
way. The
D.S. al Coda
(Return to 𝄋
Play to ⊕ and
Skip to Coda)
CODA
B♭m
love song can
D7
be ______ The
Gm
sto - ry of
C7
Ti - na and
F
me. ______

Sugartime

Regi-Sound Program: 8
Rhythm: Country Western or Fox Trot

Words and Music by Charlie Phillips
& Odis Echols

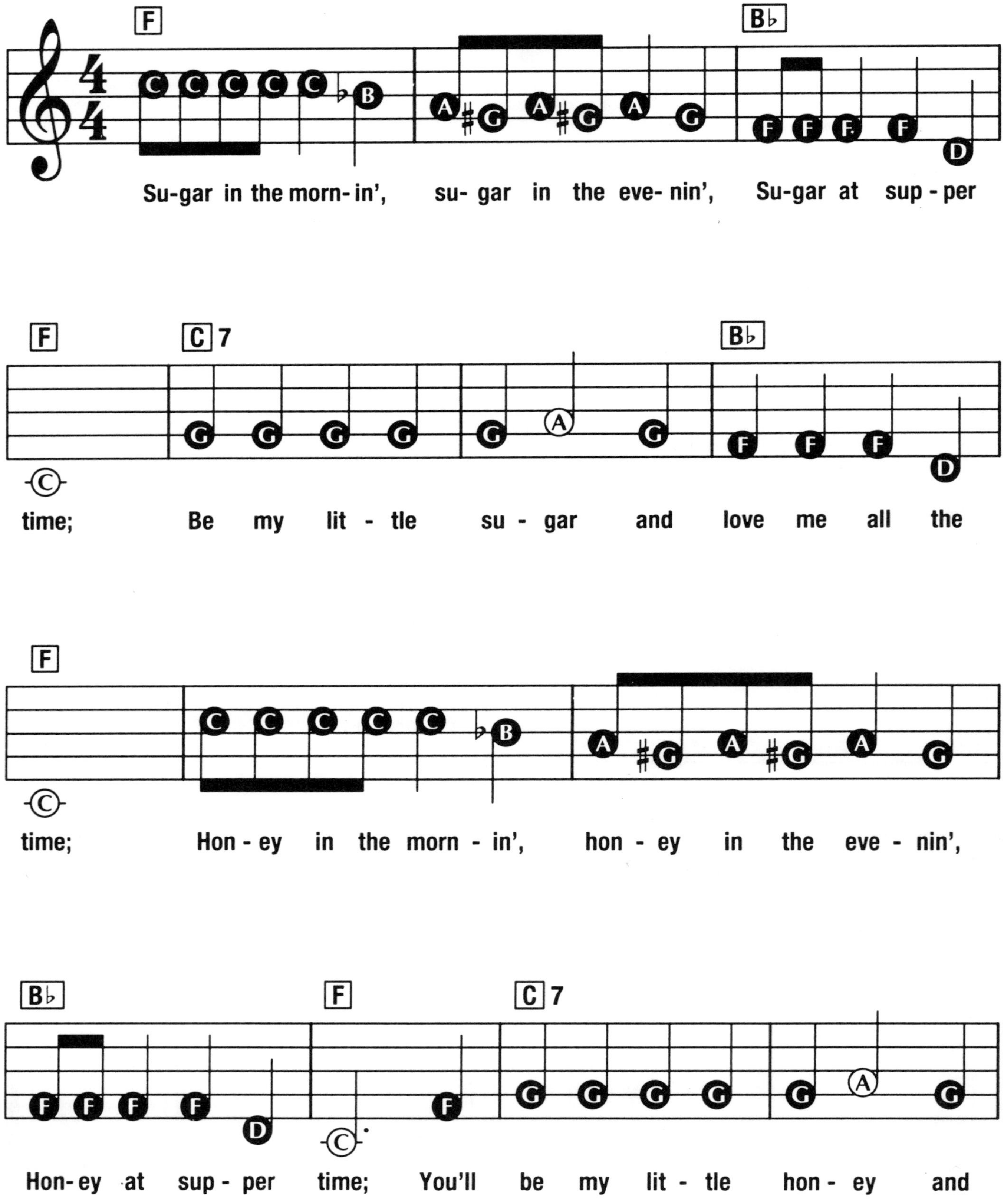

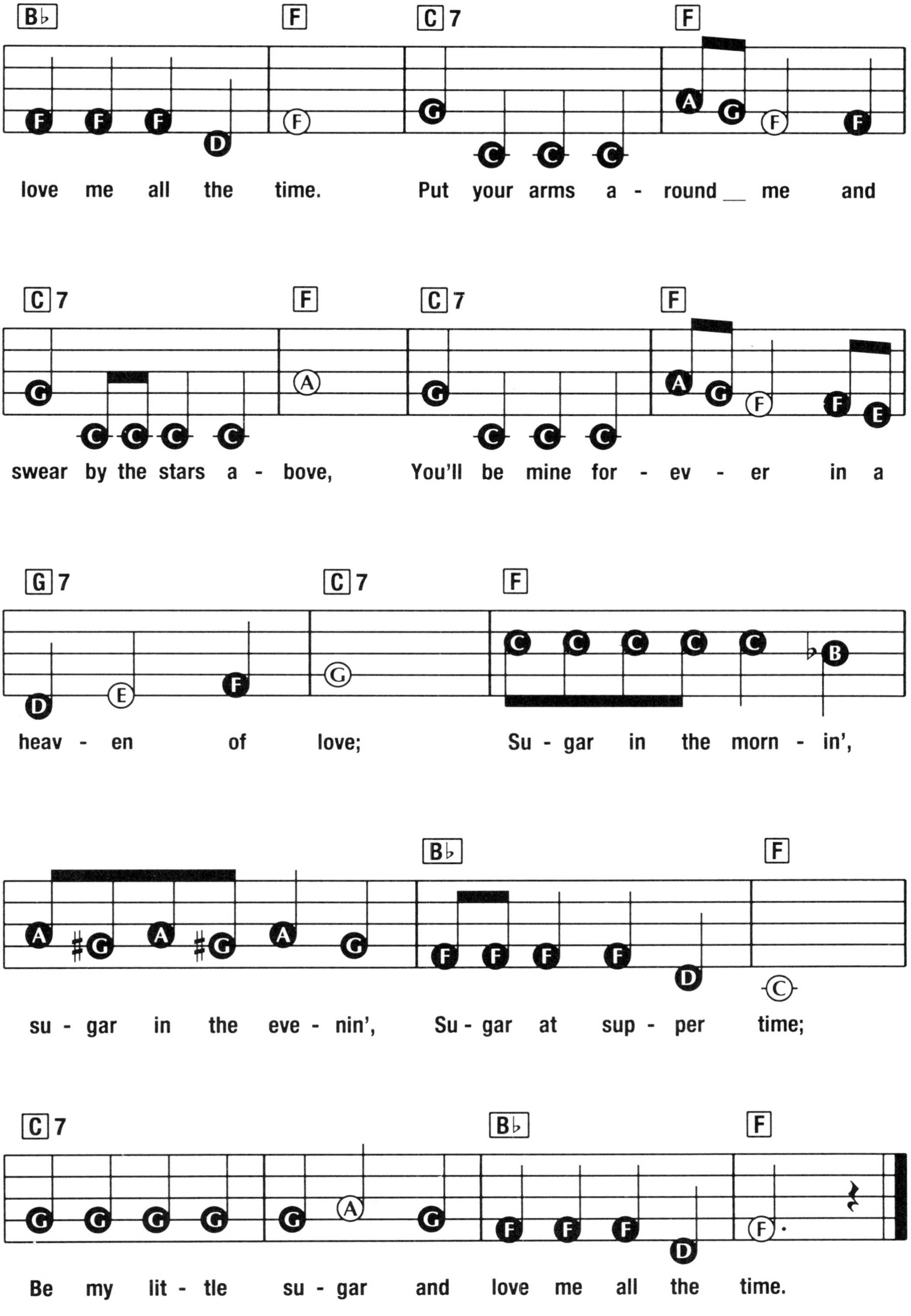
B♭ F C7 F
love me all the time. Put your arms a - round __ me and
C7 F C7 F
swear by the stars a - bove, You'll be mine for - ev - er in a
G7 C7 F
heav - en of love; Su - gar in the morn - in',
B♭ F
su - gar in the eve - nin', Su - gar at sup - per time;
C7 B♭ F
Be my lit - tle su - gar and love me all the time.

A Teenager In Love

Regi-Sound Program: 2
Rhythm: Slow Rock

Words and Music by
Doc Pomus and Mort Shuman

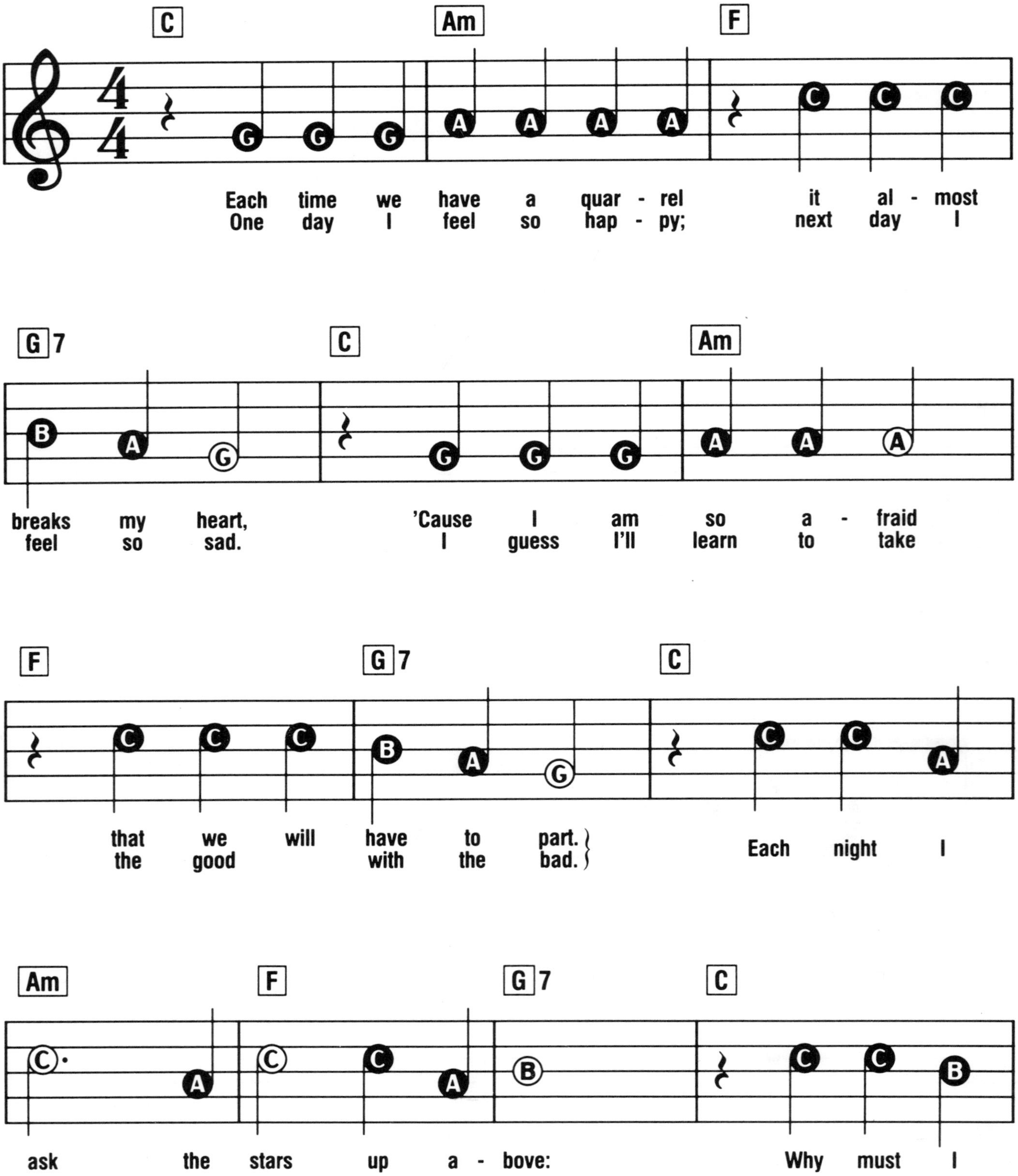
C
Am
F
4/4
Each time we have a quar - rel it al - most
One day I feel so hap - py; next day I
G7
C
Am
breaks my heart, 'Cause I am so a - fraid
feel so sad. I guess I'll learn to take
F
G7
C
that we will have to part. Each night I
the good with the bad.
Am
F
G7
C
ask the stars up a - bove: Why must I

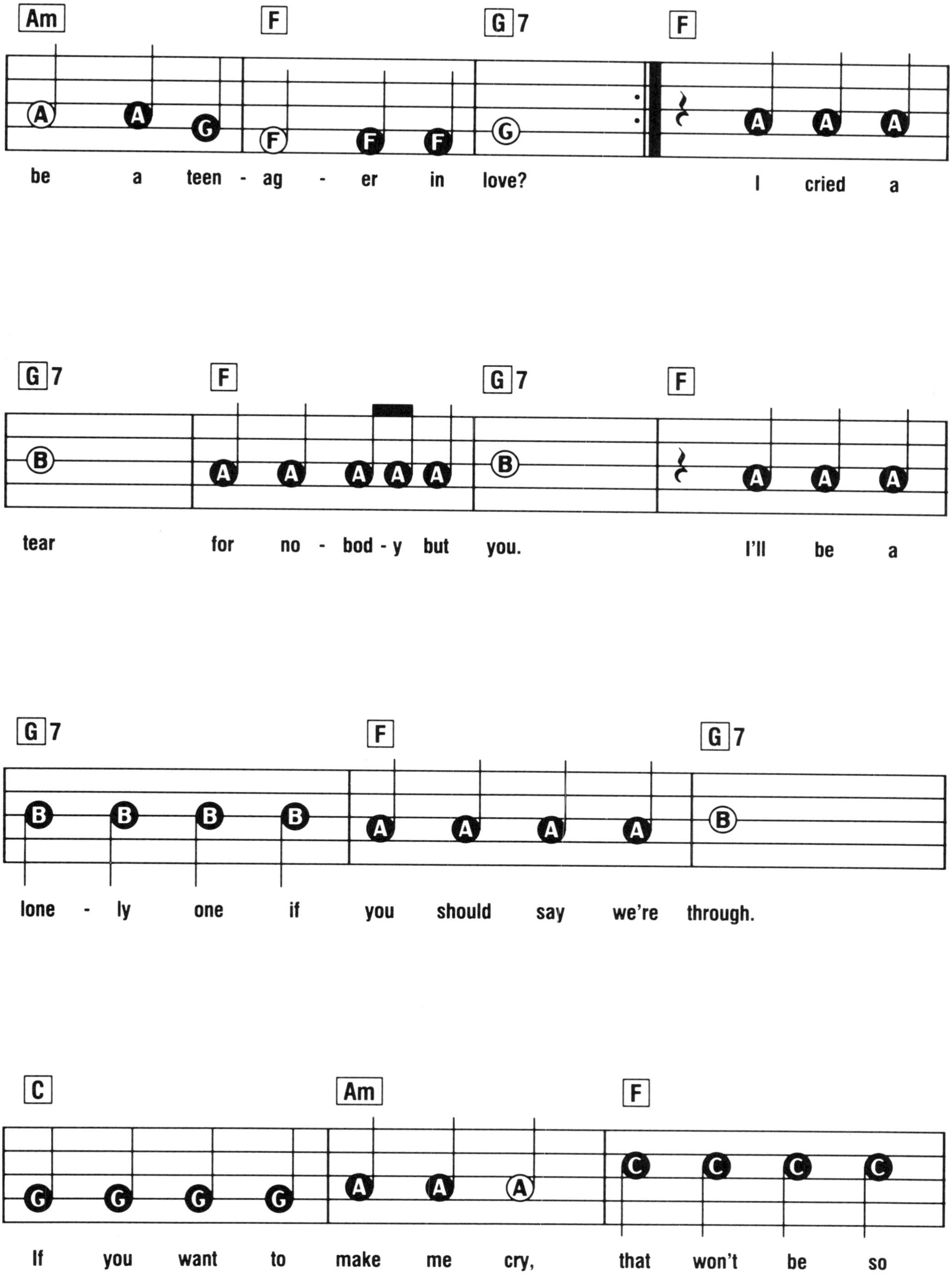
Am F G7 F
A A G F F F G A A A
be a teen - ag - er in love? I cried a
G7 F G7 F
B A A A A A B A A A
tear for no - bod - y but you. I'll be a
G7 F G7
B B B B A A A A B
lone - ly one if you should say we're through.
C Am F
G G G G A A A C C C C
If you want to make me cry, that won't be so

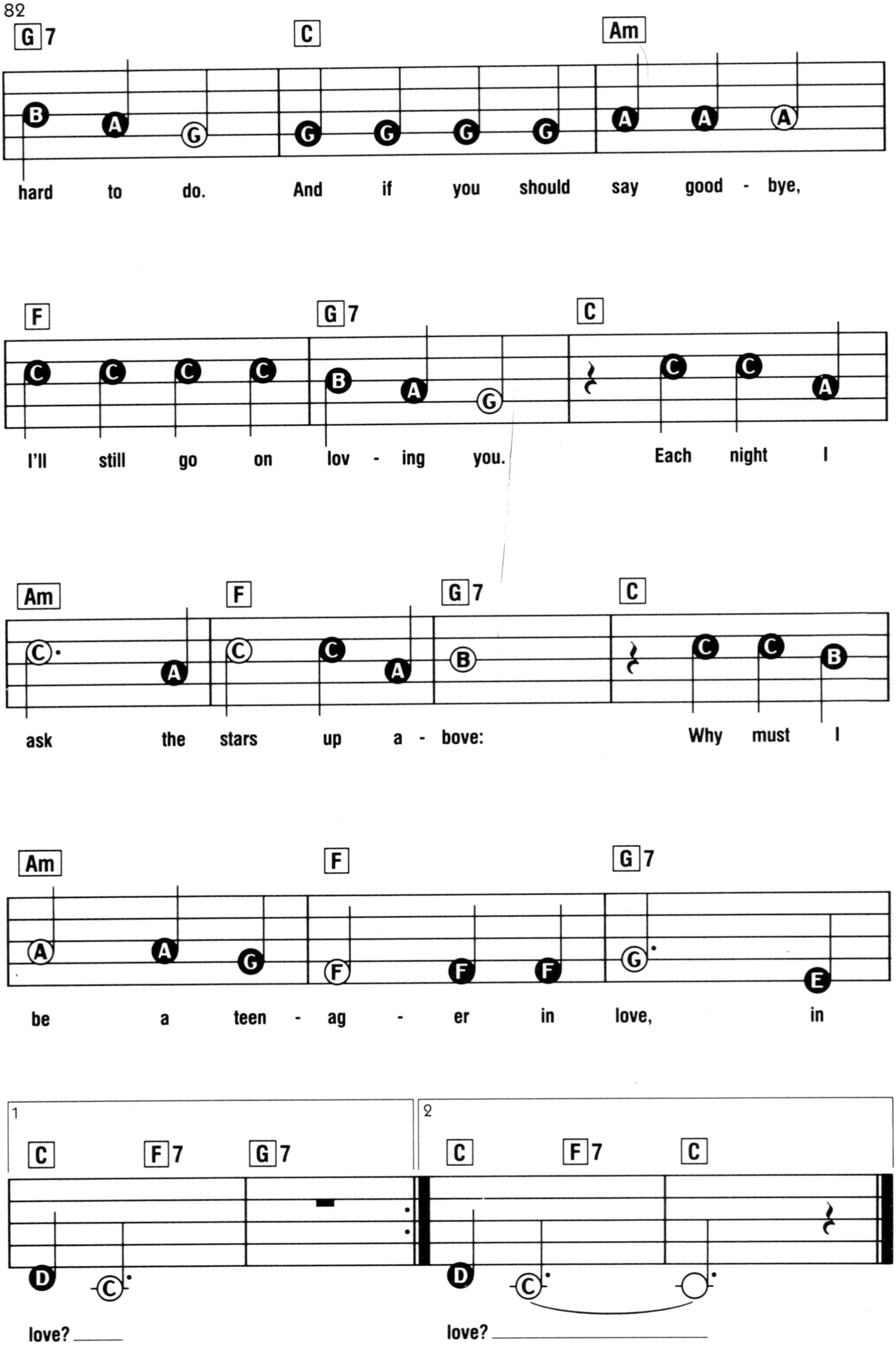
G7 C Am
hard to do. And if you should say good - bye,
F G7 C
I'll still go on lov - ing you. Each night I
Am F G7 C
ask the stars up a - bove: Why must I
Am F G7
be a teen - ag - er in love, in
1 C F7 G7
love?
2 C F7 C
love?

Travelin' Light

Regi-Sound Program: 6
Rhythm: Country or March/Polka

Words and Music by
Sid Tepper and Roy C. Bennett

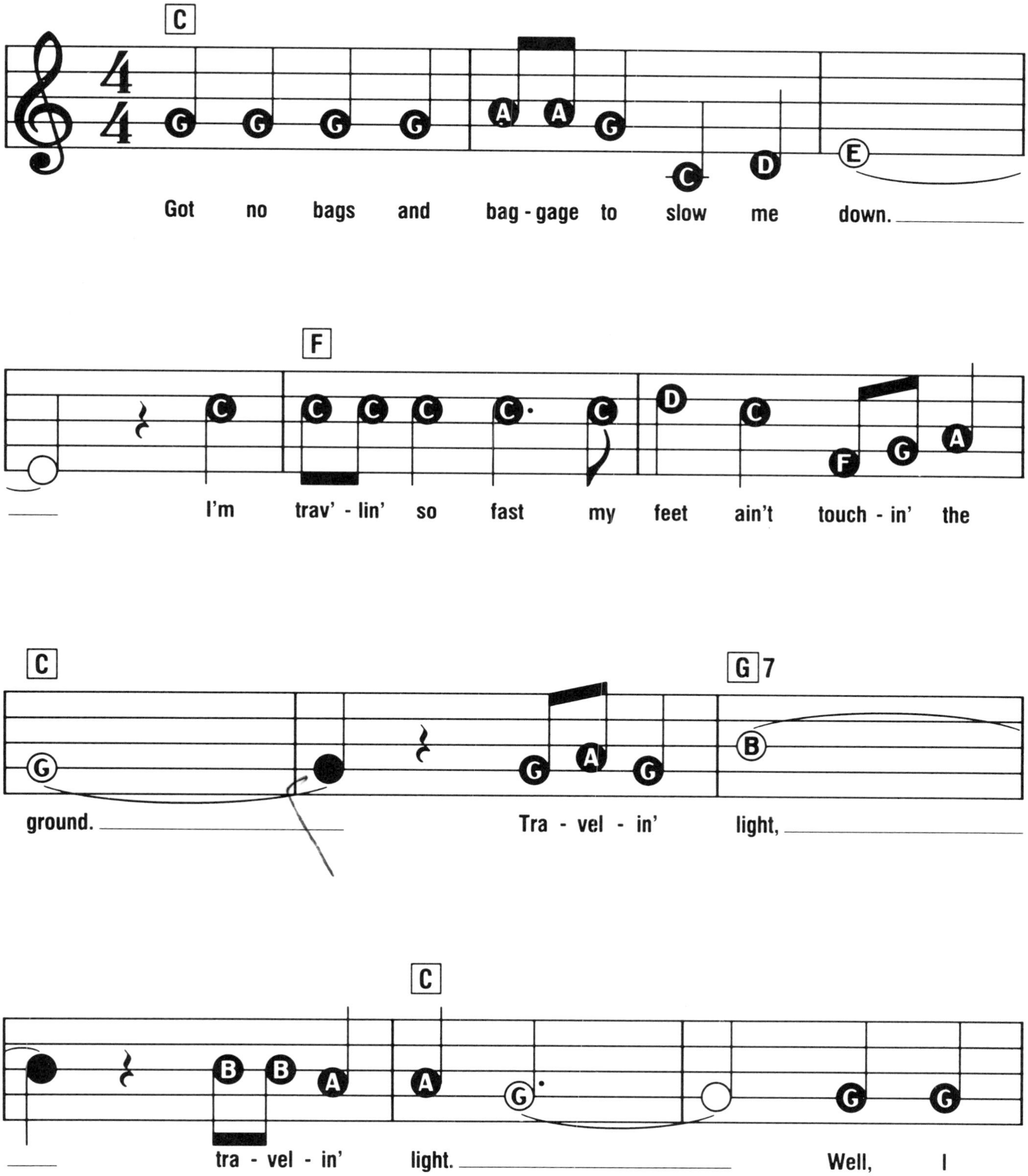
C
Got no bags and bag - gage to slow me down.
F
I'm trav' - lin' so fast my feet ain't touch - in' the
C
ground.
G7
Tra - vel - in' light,
C
tra - vel - in' light.
Well, I

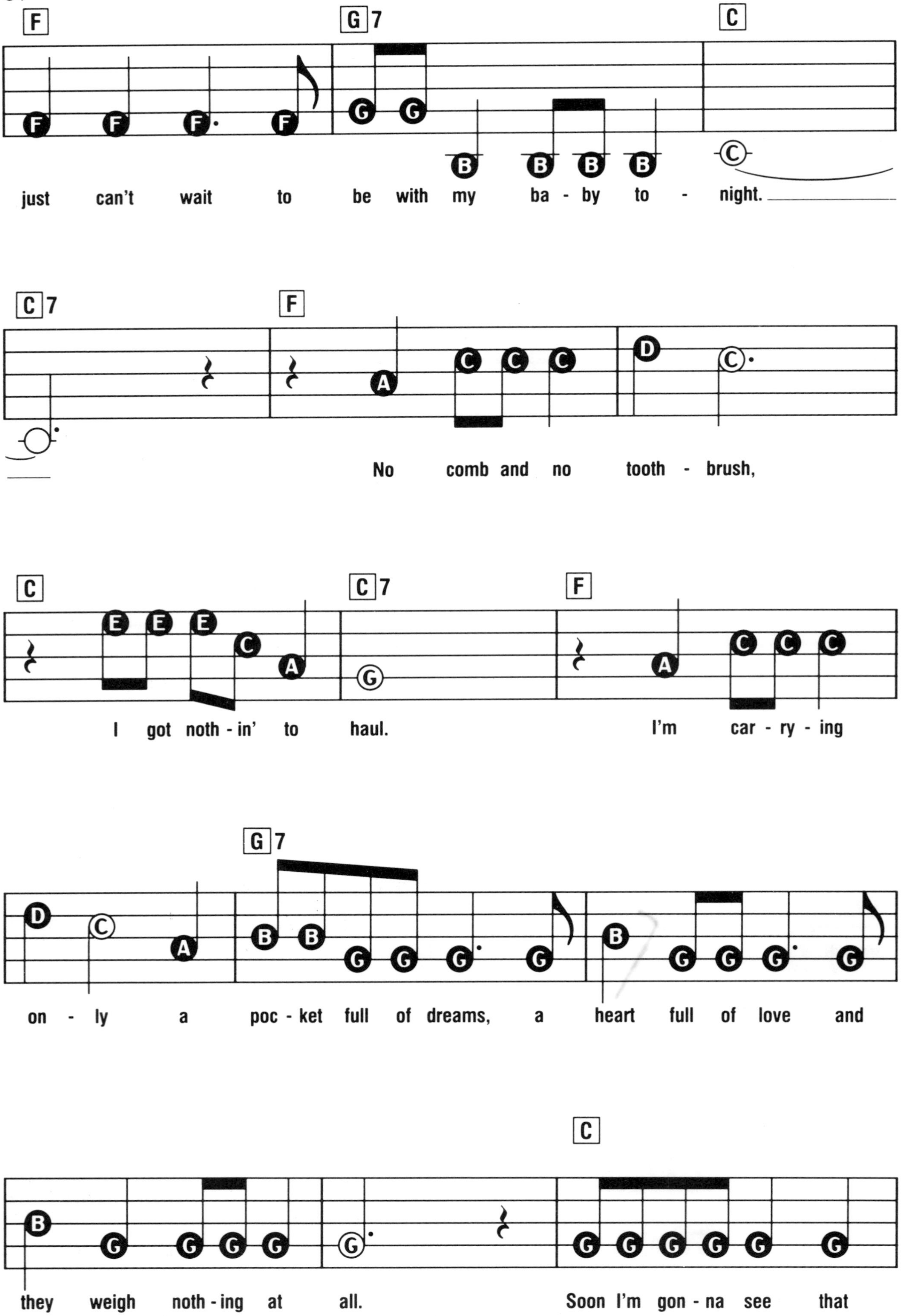
F
G7
C
just can't wait to be with my ba - by to - night.
C7
F
No comb and no tooth - brush,
C
C7
F
I got noth - in' to haul.
I'm car - ry - ing
G7
on - ly a poc - ket full of dreams, a heart full of love and
C
they weigh noth - ing at all.
Soon I'm gon - na see that

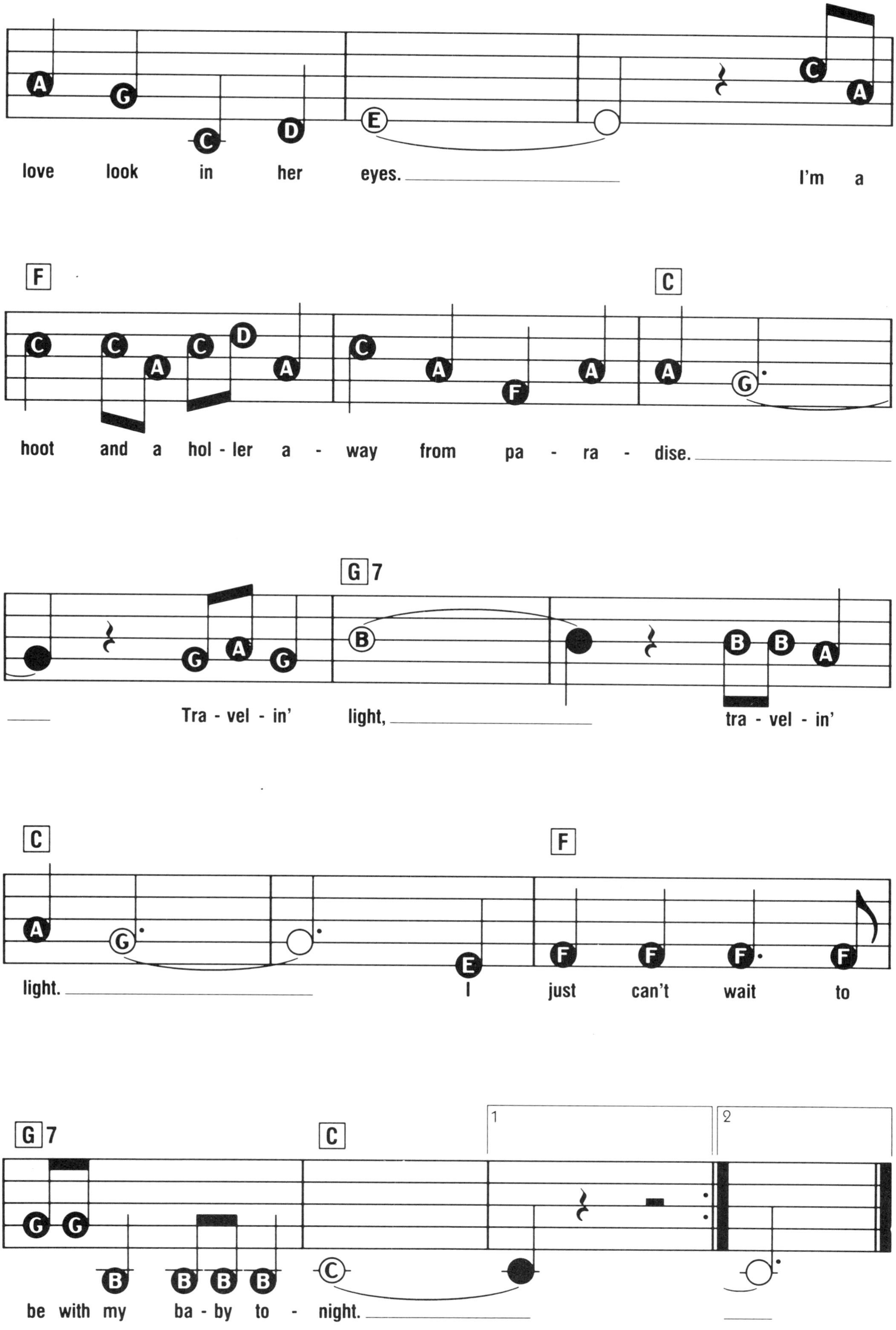
A G C D E C A
love look in her eyes. I'm a
F C
C C A C D A C A F A A G
hoot and a hol - ler a - way from pa - ra - dise.
G7
G A G B B B A
Tra - vel - in' light, tra - vel - in'
C F
A G E F F F F
light. I just can't wait to
G7 C
1 2
G G B B B B C
be with my ba - by to - night.

True Love Ways

Regi-Sound Program: 4
Rhythm: Ballad or Swing

Words and Music by
Norman Petty and Buddy Holly

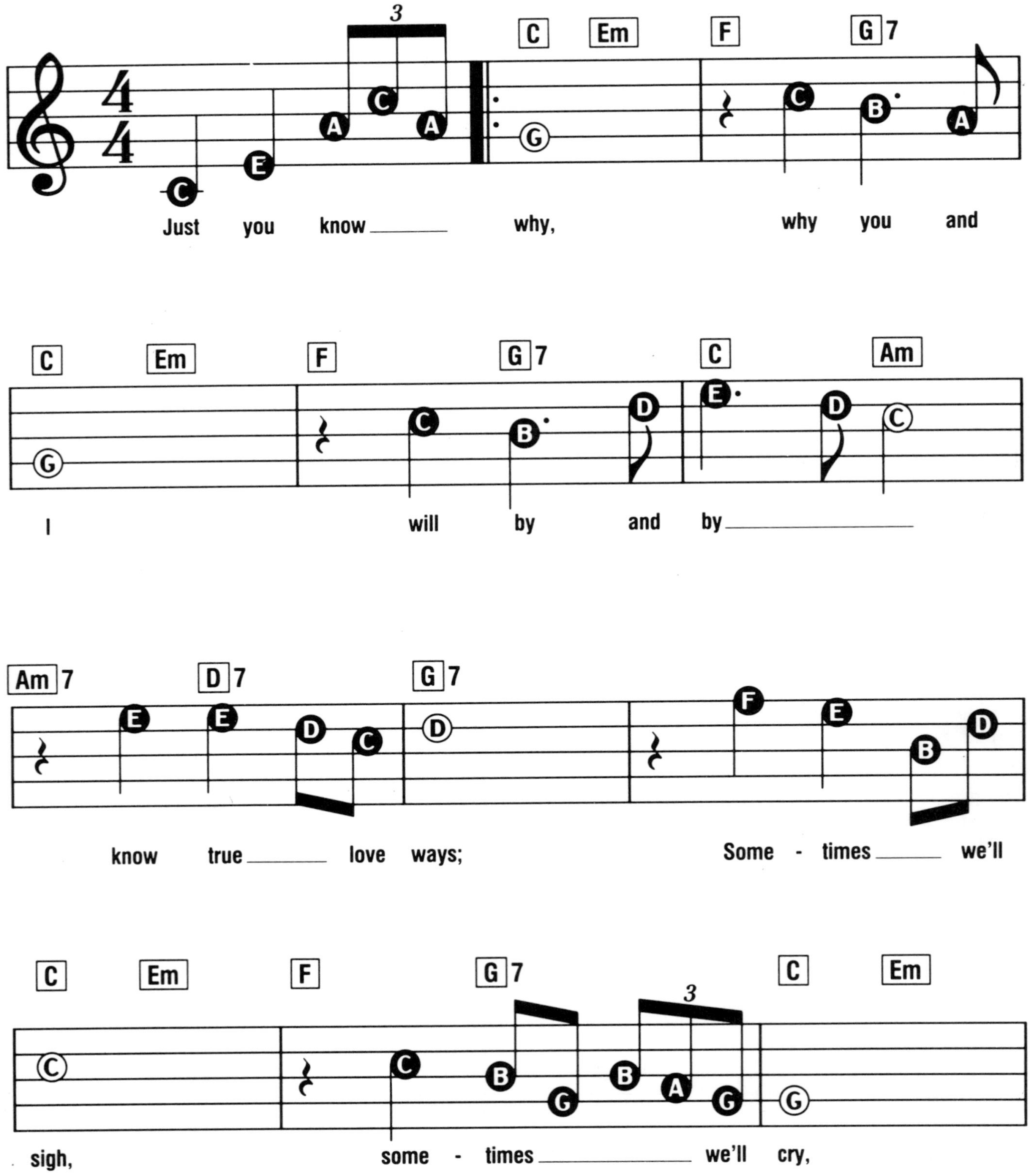
C Em F G7
Just you know why, why you and
C Em F G7 C Am
I will by and by
Am7 D7 G7
know true love ways; Some - times we'll
C Em F G7 C Em
sigh, some - times we'll cry,

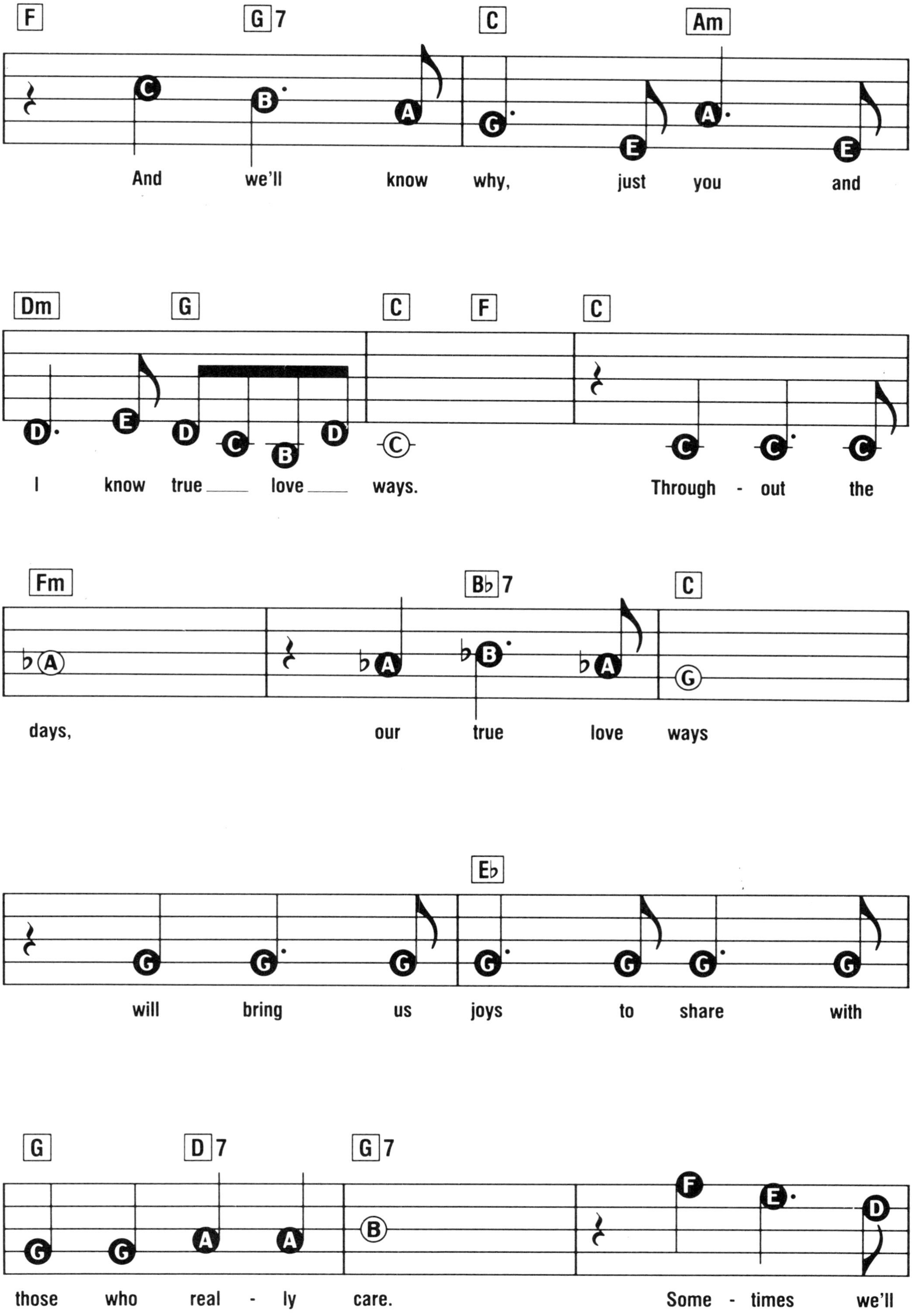
F G7 C Am
And we'll know why, just you and
Dm G C F C
I know true love ways. Through - out the
Fm B♭7 C
days, our true love ways
E♭
will bring us joys to share with
G D7 G7
those who real - ly care. Some - times we'll

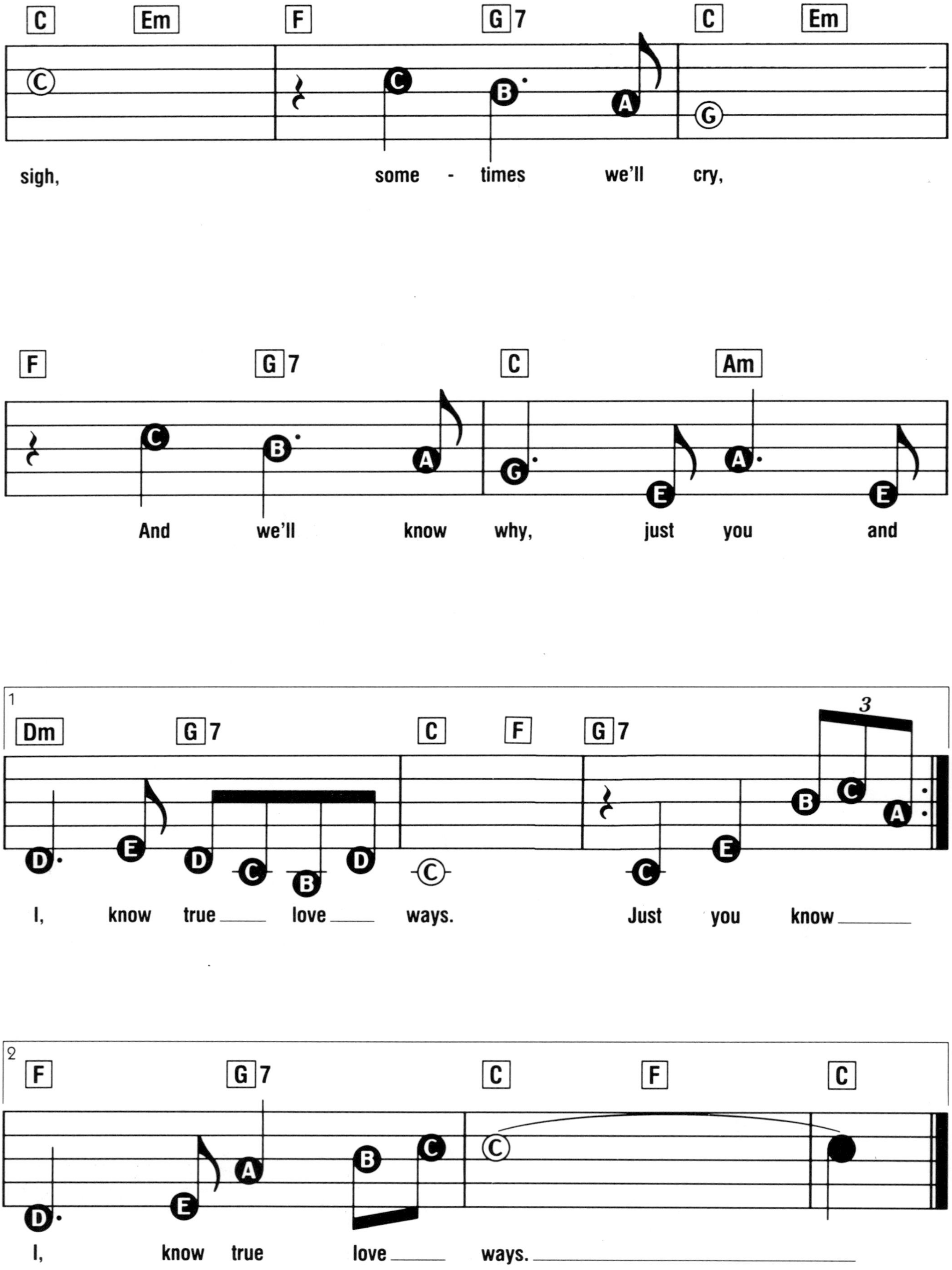
C Em F G7 C Em
sigh, some - times we'll cry,
F G7 C Am
And we'll know why, just you and
1
Dm G7 C F G7
I, know true love ways. Just you know
3
2
F G7 C F C
I, know true love ways.

Volare

Regi-Sound Program: 1
Rhythm: Swing

English Words by Mitchel Parish
Music by Domenico Modugno

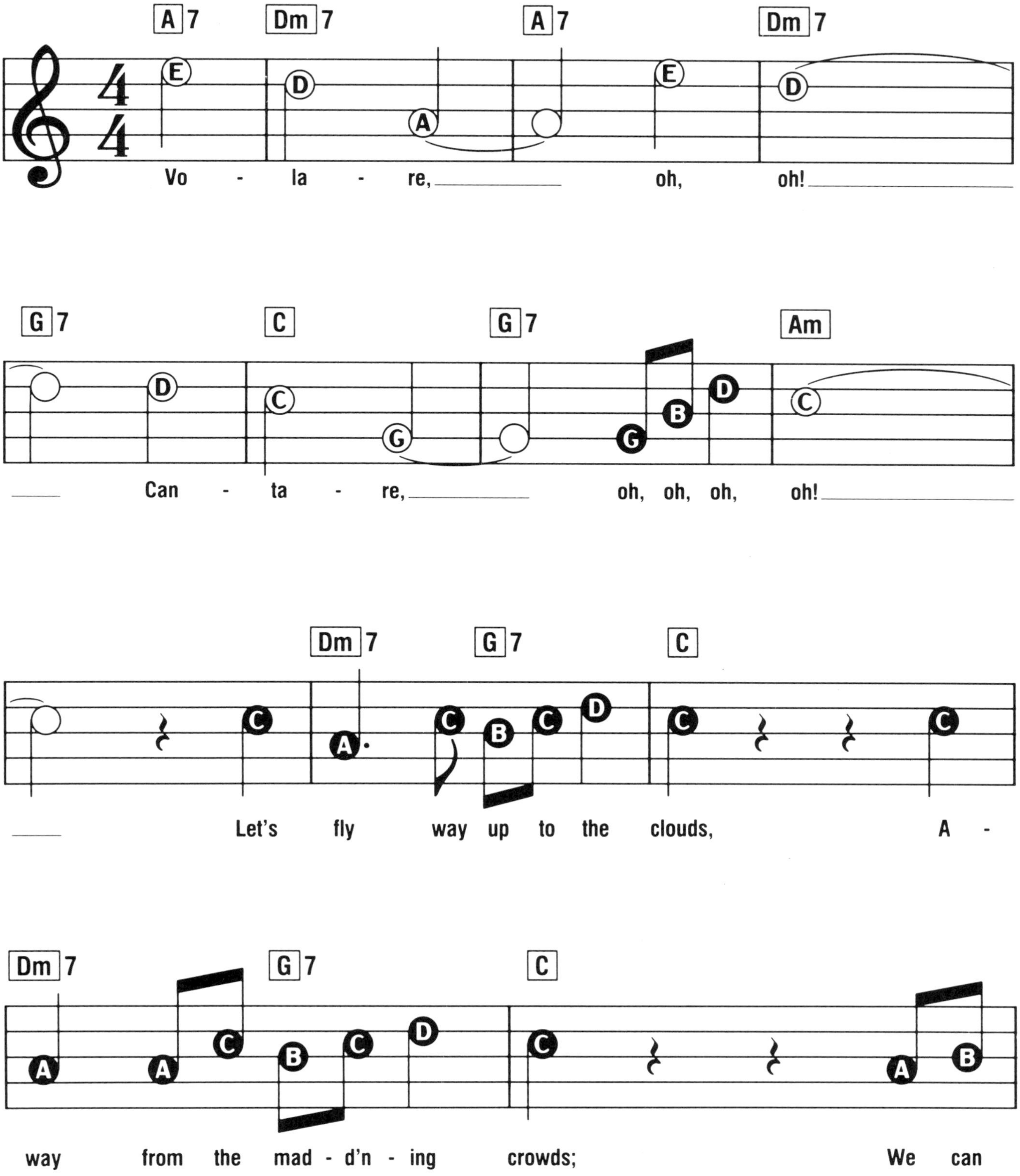
A7 Dm7 A7 Dm7
Vo - la - re, oh, oh!
G7 C G7 Am
Can - ta - re, oh, oh, oh, oh!
Dm7 G7 C
Let's fly way up to the clouds, A -
Dm7 G7 C
way from the mad - d'n - ing crowds; We can

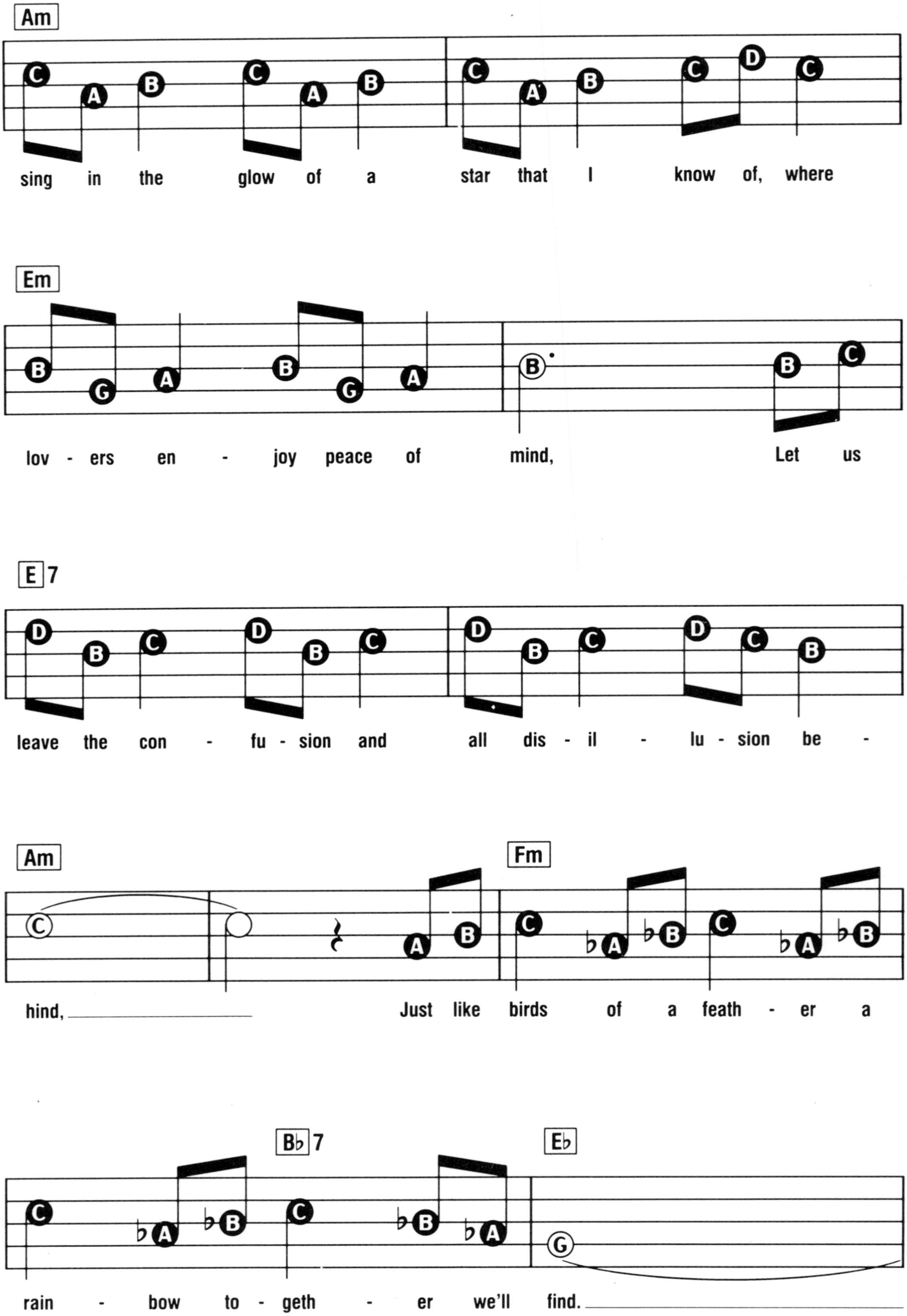
Am
sing in the glow of a star that I know of, where
Em
lov - ers en - joy peace of mind, Let us
E7
leave the con - fu - sion and all dis - il - lu - sion be -
Am
Fm
hind, Just like birds of a feath - er a
B♭7
E♭
rain - bow to - geth - er we'll find.

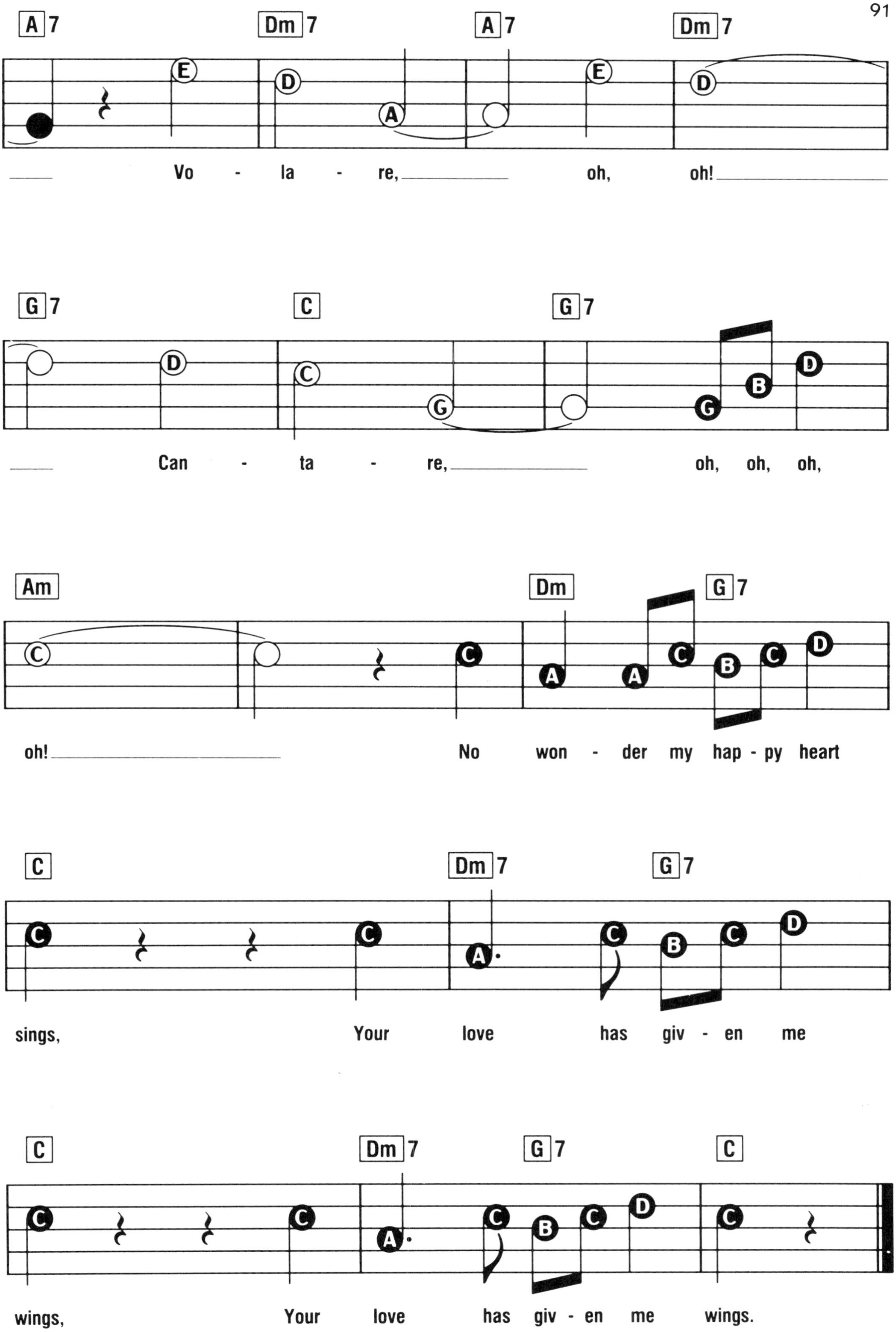
A7 Dm7 A7 Dm7
Vo - la - re, oh, oh!
G7 C G7
Can - ta - re, oh, oh, oh,
Am Dm G7
oh! No won - der my hap - py heart
C Dm7 G7
sings, Your love has giv - en me
C Dm7 G7 C
wings, Your love has giv - en me wings.

With These Hands

Regi-Sound Program: 3
Rhythm: Ballad or Fox Trot

Words by Benny Davis
Music by Abner Silver

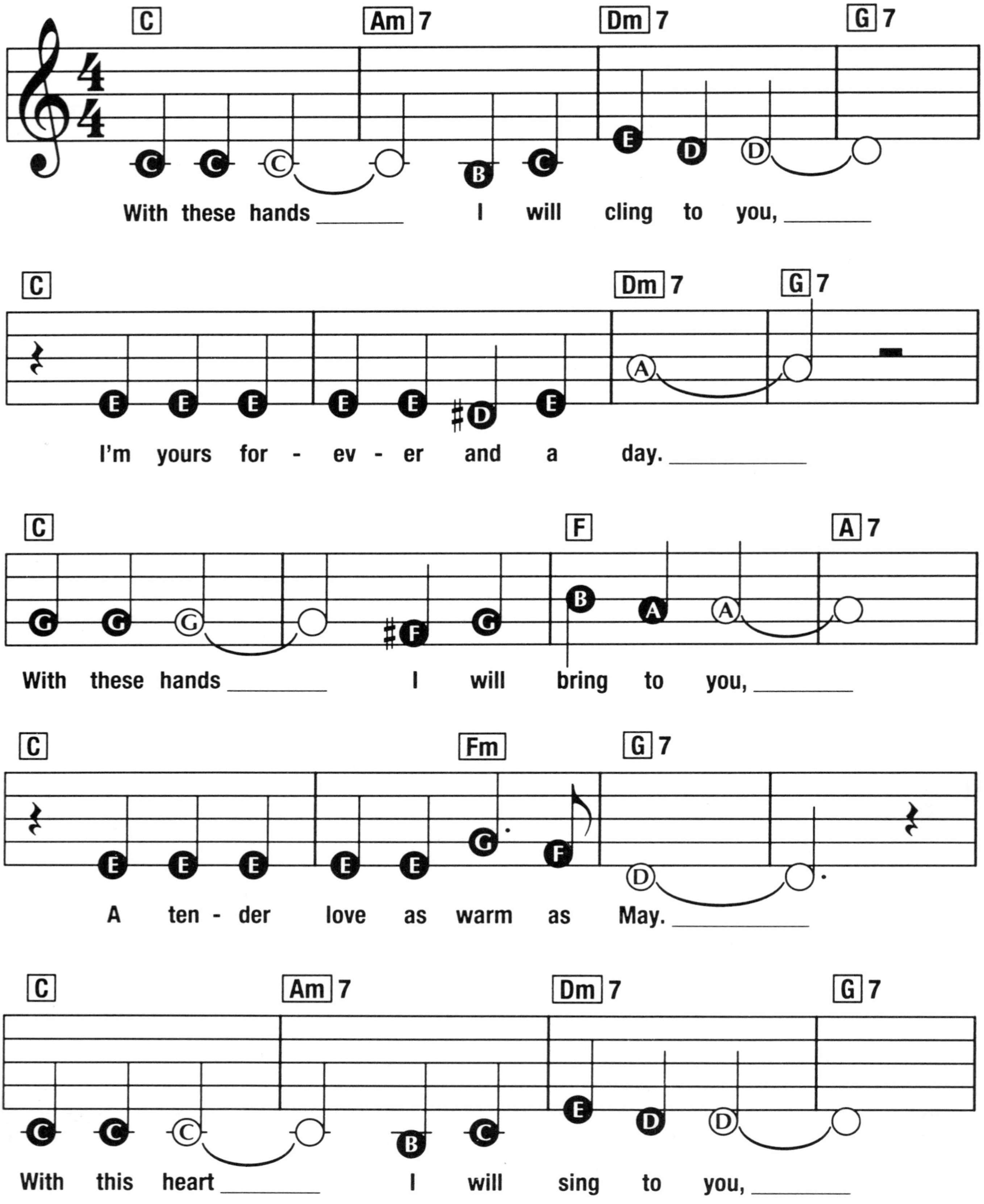

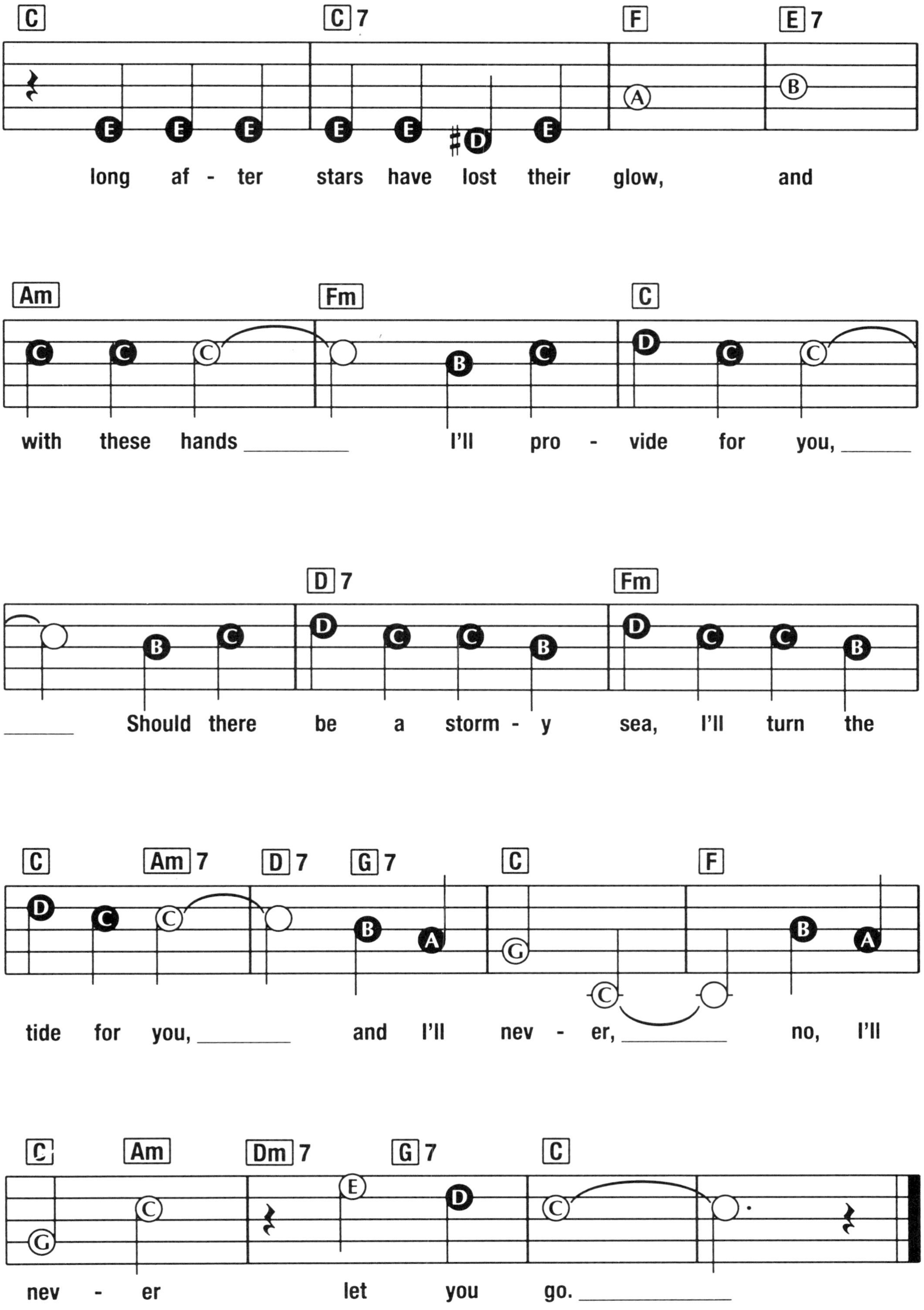
C C7 F E7
long af - ter stars have lost their glow, and
Am Fm C
with these hands I'll pro - vide for you,
D7 Fm
Should there be a storm - y sea, I'll turn the
C Am7 D7 G7 C F
tide for you, and I'll nev - er, no, I'll
C Am Dm7 G7 C
nev - er let you go.

Mr. Wonderful

Regi-Sound Program: 9
Rhythm: Fox Trot

Words and Music by Jerry Bock,
Larry Holofcener and George Weiss

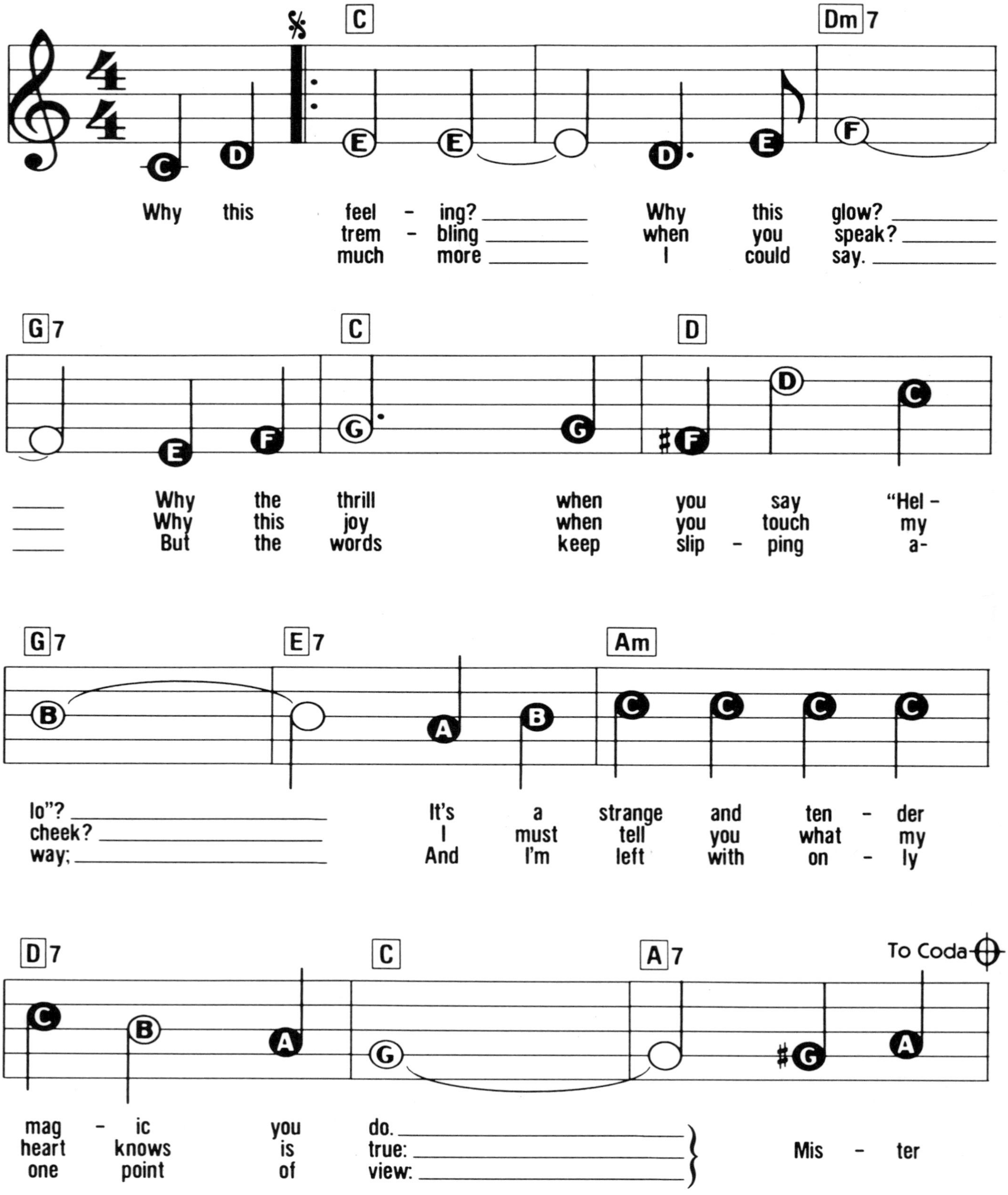

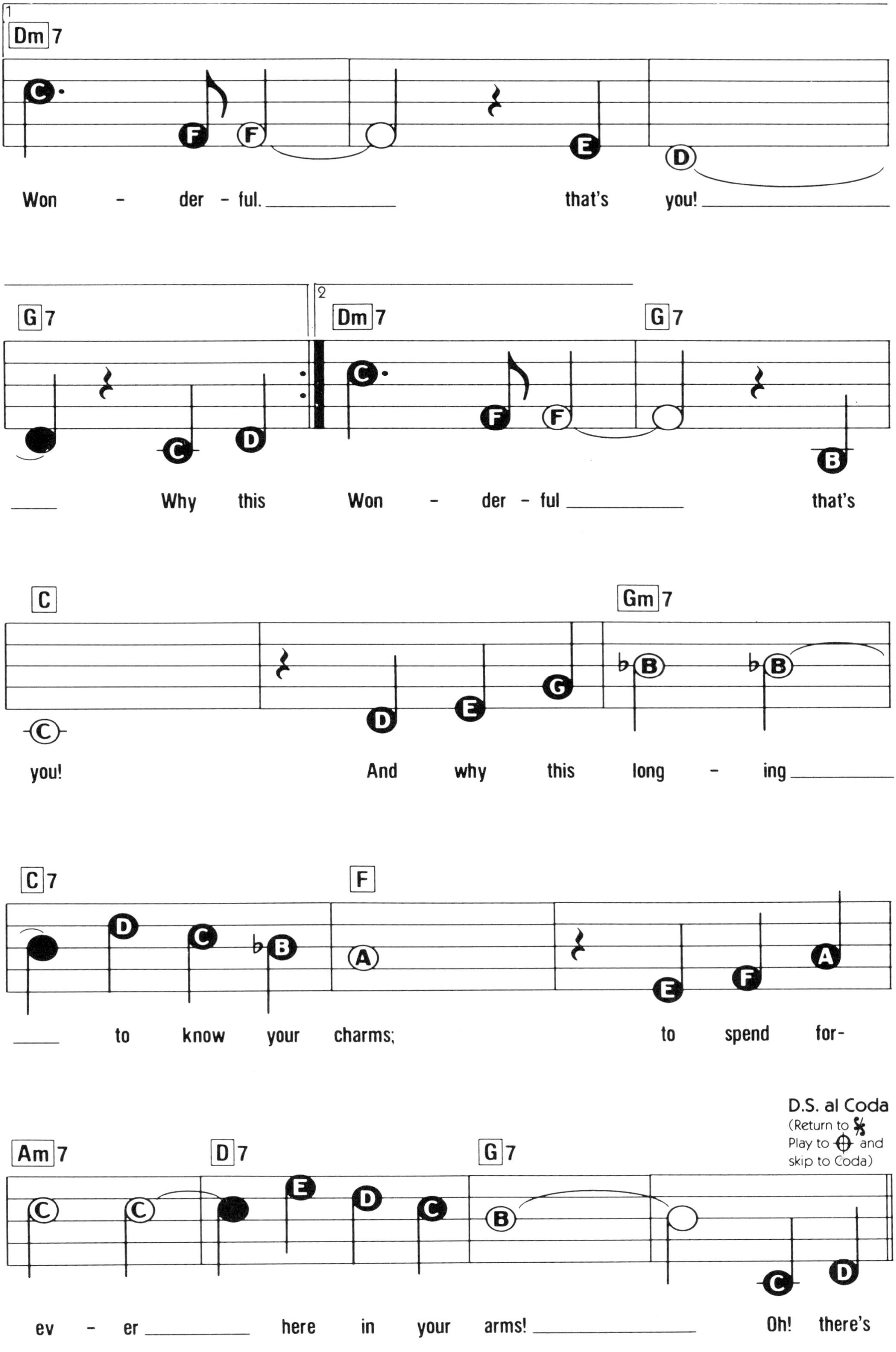
1
Dm7
Won - der - ful. that's you!
G7
Why this
2
Dm7
Won - der - ful
G7
that's
C
you!
Gm7
And why this long - ing
C7
to know your charms;
F
to spend for-
D.S. al Coda
(Return to 𝄋
Play to ⊕ and
skip to Coda)
Am7
ev - er
D7
here in your
G7
arms!
Oh! there's

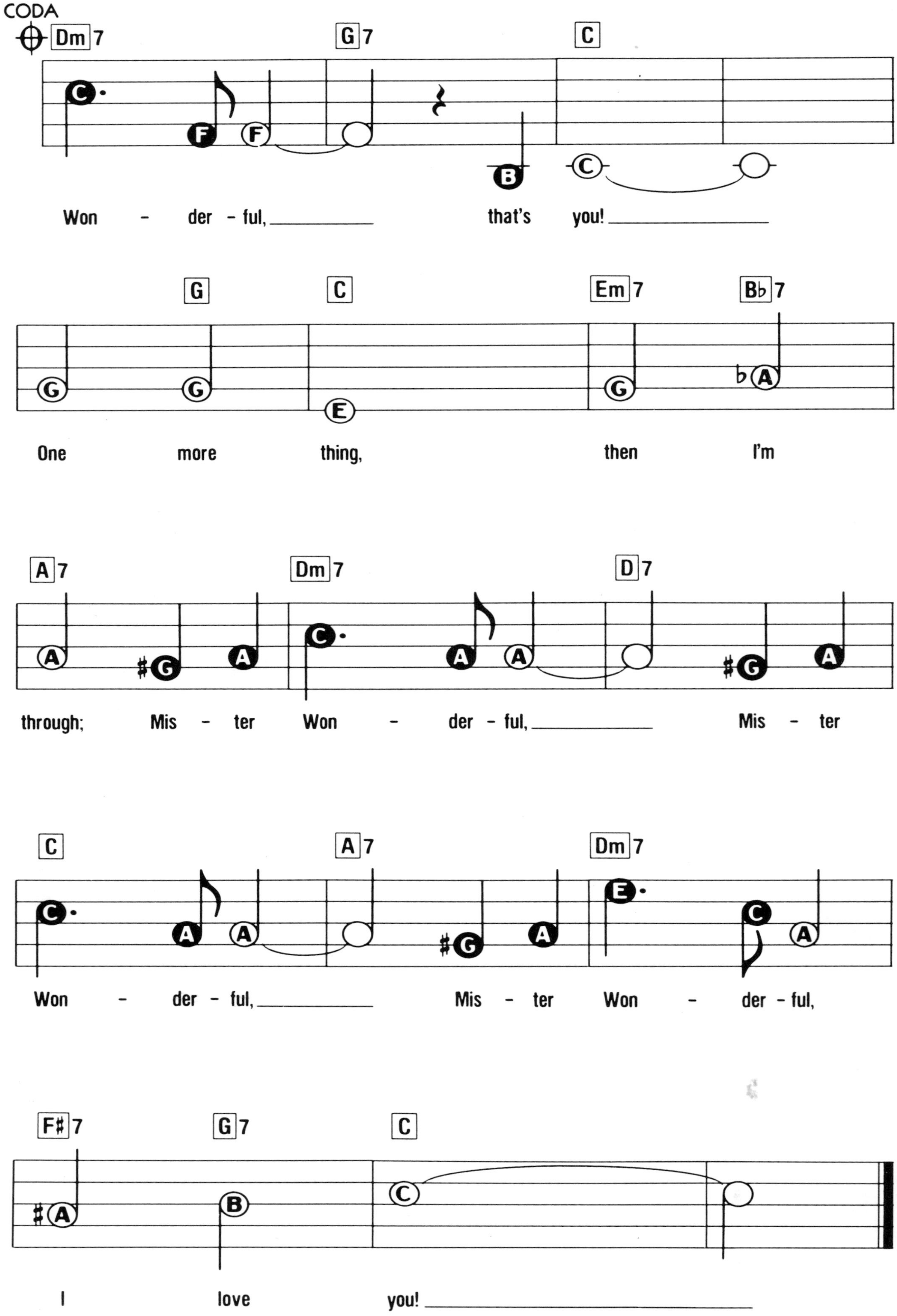
CODA
Dm7 G7 C
Won - der - ful, that's you!
G C Em7 Bb7
One more thing, then I'm
A7 Dm7 D7
through; Mis - ter Won - der - ful, Mis - ter
C A7 Dm7
Won - der - ful, Mis - ter Won - der - ful,
F#7 G7 C
I love you!